Beauty and the Beast

Arnold Arluke and Robert Bogdan

Beauty
AND THE
BEAST

Human-Animal Relations
as Revealed in Real Photo Postcards,
1905–1935

Syracuse University Press

For a listing of books published and distributed by Syracuse University Press,
visit our Web site at SyracuseUniversityPress.syr.edu.

ISBN: 978-0-8156-0981-0

LIBRARY OF CONGRESS CATALOGING-IN-PUBLICATION DATA

Arluke, Arnold.
Beauty and the beast : human-animal relations as revealed in real photo postcards, 1905–1935 /
Arnold Arluke and Robert Bogdan. — 1st ed.
p. cm.
Includes bibliographical references and index.
ISBN 978-0-8156-0981-0 (cloth : alk. paper)
1. Photography of animals. 2. Photography, Artistic. 3. Human-animal relationships—
Pictorial works. I. Bogdan, Robert. II. Title.
TR727.A75 2010
779'.32—dc22   2010028188

Manufactured in the United States of America

Contents

Illustrations

Preface

*W*e started this book as an experiment. The question that drove us was what would happen if we took a large number of old photographs from a particular historical period that contained information about a specific topic and treated them as data? Our idea was to apply some of the same logic and techniques we had used as qualitative sociologists to analyze interview transcripts and field notes (Glaser and Strauss 1967). Given Arluke's background in the study of human-animal relations (Arluke and Sanders 1996, 2008), that subject became our topic. Bogdan's knowledge of the history of photography led us to choose real photo postcards as our database (Bogdan and Weseloh 2006).

We set out to study as many examples of real photo postcards whose content related to human-animal relations as we could find. We used contacts from past projects and referrals to get started. This took us to many private collections as well as to a few institutional archives. People also sent us copies of images through the mail and over the Internet. In addition, we collected and bought images ourselves by going to post-card shows where postcards are sold, and we regularly visited eBay.

We studied thousands of images and obtained copies of many. In thinking about the book we would write, we wanted to have high-quality illustrations that were rich in documentary detail, revealing, interesting, and technically well executed. When we found such images, we did high-quality scans or asked our collaborators to scan them for us. We collected and copied many more images than we could possibly use because we wanted a wide range of choices to compose the book. In discussing the book with our publisher, we agreed that approximately 350 illustrations should be the limit. Although some would have been redundant, we could have easily included twice as many without compromising quality or documentary relevance. We also learned from images that were not of the highest quality, and we sometimes refer to them in the text.

Our way of studying these images was unconventional. Most researchers begin with a broad idea that narrows and becomes more focused. As we studied the postcards and discerned patterns and themes, our subject expanded. The organization of the book as well as the individual chapters evolved, resulting in eleven chapters examining a wide range of roles animals play in human lives.

For whom did we write the book? The answer to that question also evolved. At first we targeted scholars and the educated public interested in human-animal relations and the history of photography or both. As we embraced the idea of producing a broad visual survey of human-animal relations during the early twentieth century, a time when these relationships were undergoing significant change, we realized that our book would have wide appeal. It could also be used as a text for courses that were geared toward exploring the history, anthropology, or sociology of human-animal relations and related topics. Postcard collectors and dealers will also find it useful as they study their own collections.

Although we devote some sections of the book to specific topics, given the breadth of what we cover, nothing is explored in great depth. When we committed ourselves to doing a survey, we hoped that our work would still appeal to graduate students and advanced scholars. As you will see, we introduce many topics that have never been addressed in the literature. We provide many beginnings for research projects that could easily lead to articles, papers, dissertations, and other monographs.

The number and scope of the illustrations we use are unusual, as are our detailed examination of each photograph and our national survey of the topic. To the extent that our methods are successful, as well as stimulating, the book should be of value to social scientists and other scholars who are interested in using visual data and other alternative ways of approaching research. Finally, the book should appeal to certain members of the general public, people who love animals and are concerned about their welfare as well as those individuals who embrace postcards as a hobby.

This book has been a huge endeavor. It would not have been possible without the enthusiastic and generous contributions of many people. Thank you to those who bigheartedly allowed us to examine their collections and use their images as illustrations. They include all the people in the list of abbreviations that immediately follows this preface. Some of the people included are amateur scholars and historians who supplied information and insights that helped us put the images in context. A few even had firsthand knowledge of the practices captured in the pictures, such as wolf hunts on the Great Plains and mascots on the high seas.

We would be remiss not to mention the special contribution made to the project by three specialty collectors. The chapter on mascots relied almost exclusively on the collection of Brian Buckberry. The rodeo postcards in chapter 11 came primarily from the collection of Susan Nichols. Trenton Boyd's contribution to the project has been extensive, especially in supplying real photo postcards and information for the chapters dealing with veterinarians, produce, and working animals.

Special thanks to Joel Wayne, Bruce Nelson, and Leonard A. Lauder, longtime collectors of exceptional real photo postcards who generously encouraged the project by giving us access to their extensive collections and by guiding us in our quest. We also thank Mr. and Mrs. Leonard A. Lauder; the Dean's Office, School of Education at Syracuse University; and Bruce Ronkin of the Dean's Office, College of Arts and Sciences, Northeastern University, for their financial support.

Many others helped us as well. Our thanks go to collectors, scholars, dealers, and others: Jack Beiderbecke, Meg Bogdan, Anthony d'Offay, Nancy Foutz, Dennis Goreham, Carl Griffin, Lynda Klich, Larry Meyer, Bunny Moses, Jose Rodriguez, Robert Rydell, Sharon Schmitz, George Sinclair, Hans Tanner, Jim Taylor, Mahlon Wagner, and Barbara Mathe, museum archivist and head of the Library Special Collections, American Museum of Natural History, New York City.

In addition, colleagues provided an important service by reading early drafts of chapters as well as the entire manuscript, offering corrections and suggestions and in other ways engaging us about our writing and ideas. They include Janet Bogdan, Glenn Gritzer, Peg Hanousek, Hal Herzog, Alan Klein, Jack Levin, Clay McShane, Patricia Morris, Bruce Nelson, Lauren Rolfe, Clint Sanders, and Joel Wayne. We are grateful to them, but we alone assume the responsibility for inaccuracies and other imperfections in our work.

All illustrations included here were scanned from real photo postcards whose actual dimensions are approximately three and a half by five and a half inches. We did crop a few of the original images, and we eliminated the white borders on many cards. You can assume that if a caption does not identify the photographer who took the image or the place it was taken, then we do not have that information.

Abbreviations

Aikenhead Coll.	Douglas Aikenhead Collection, Ann Arbor, Michigan
Anton van Dalen Coll.	Anton van Dalen Pigeon Image History Collection, New York City
Arluke Coll.	Arnie Arluke Collection, West Roxbury, Massachusetts
B. Nelson Coll.	Bruce Nelson Collection, Portland, Maine
Bogdan Coll.	Robert Bogdan Collection, Orwell, Vermont
Brian Buckberry Coll.	Brian Buckberry Collection, Knoxville, Tennessee
Bryan Hartig Coll.	Bryan Hartig Collection, Worthington, Ohio
C. Trenton Boyd Coll.	C. Trenton Boyd Postcard Collection, Columbia, Missouri
Coll. of Leonard A. Lauder	Collection of Leonard A. Lauder, New York City
Cynthia Elyce Rubin Coll.	Cynthia Elyce Rubin Collection, Orlando, Florida
Daniel Elvrum Sr. Family Coll.	Daniel Elvrum Sr. Family Collection, Neah Bay, Washington
Dan Kerlee Coll.	Daniel Kerlee Collection, Seattle, Washington
Dingman Coll.	Don Dingman, Kearney, Nebraska
Don and Newly Preziosi Coll.	Don and Newly Preziosi Collection, Medham, New Jersey
George C. Gibbs Coll.	George C. Gibbs Collection, Latham, New York
Jim and Kayce Dimond Coll.	Jim and Kayce Dimond Collection, Pittsford, Vermont
Jim Matthews Coll.	Jim Matthews Collection, Los Angeles, California
Joel Wayne, Pop's Postcards Coll.	Joel Wayne, Pop's Postcards Collection, Los Angeles, California
Kobel Coll.	Craig Kobel Collection, El Dorado, Kansas
Lew Baer Coll.	Lew Baer Collection, Penngrove, California
M. Maslan	Michael Maslan Collection, Seattle, Washington
Marder Coll.	Stephen Marder Collection, Shillington, Pennsylvania
Michael J. Semas Coll.	Michael J. Semas Collection, Hanford, California
MSPCA Archives	Massachusetts Society for the Prevention of Cruelty to Animals, Boston, Massachusetts
Ottaway Coll.	Hal Ottaway Collection, Wichita, Kansas
Pierce Coll.	Edward Pierce Collection, Central Square, New York

Private Coll.	Private collections whose owners do not want to be credited in the book
Ralph DeLuca Coll.	Ralph DeLuca Collection, Madison, New Jersey
Rodrigues Archives, LLC	Jose L. Rodrigues Archives, LLC, Cheshire, Connecticut
Ruth Hanchett Coll.	Ruth Hanchett Collection, Owasso, Oklahoma
Sarah Duzynski Coll.	Sarah Duzynski Collection, St. Paul, Minnesota
Semel Coll.	Gene Semel Collection, Maitland, Florida
Steven S. Cohen Coll.	Steven S. Cohen Collection, Lumberville, Pennsylvania
Susan Nichols Coll.	Susan Nichols Collection, Huntsville, Texas
Terry Brykczynski and Andrea Miller Coll.	Terry Brykczynski and Andrea Miller Collection, New York City
Todd Weseloh Coll.	Todd Weseloh Collection, Syracuse, New York
Tom Gates Coll.	Thomas A. Gates Collection, Ava, New York
Vaule Coll.	Rosamond B. Vaule Collection, Brookline, Massachusetts
Ziegler Coll.	Ben Ziegler Collection, Los Angeles, California

Beauty and the Beast

1

Animals, Humans, and Postcards

1.1. "Beauty and the Beast," 1907. Bogdan Coll.

𝒯his book uses photo postcards to tell the story of human-animal relations in the United States from approximately 1905 to 1935.[1] Photo postcards,

postcards printed directly from negatives on commercially produced postcard stock, bring us back to a time when human-animal relations were pervasive and diverse. During these thirty years, as postcards will show, Americans experienced profound changes that altered our connection with animals and influenced our perception and treatment of them today. In 1905 photo postcards surged in popularity; by the mid-1930s the demand for this genre of photography was all but over.

The scope of our coverage is broad. We discuss pets, the most common role animals play in the lives of most Americans today, but pets will not dominate. Other animal roles will be of equal concern, with each chapter covering one of these roles.[2] Thus, you can insert the phrase "Animals as . . ." before the title of each chapter to capture the approach we are taking (for example, animals as workers).

A HUMAN-ANIMAL TALE

From fairy tales to photography, nowhere is the complexity of human-animal relations more apparent than in the creative arts. Art illuminates the nature and significance of animals in modern Western thought. Encounters with animals—whether fictionalized in fables or visualized in paintings and photographs—compel us to question what it means to be human and how we differ from and are similar to them (Bettelheim 1977).

---

1. Some scholars and animal advocates prefer the term *nonhuman animals* over *animals* because the longer phrase is zoologically accurate and reminds readers of our kinship. We share this sentiment but favor the less wordy referent *animal*.

2. We use the word *role* with some trepidation, knowing that it is typically reserved for humans and may imply conscious participation on the part of animals. Our use of *role* is not meant to assert a position about animal consciousness.

We borrow the title *Beauty and the Beast* because, like the story, our work is about people's relationships with animals and the story contains themes relevant to our concerns.

Beauty and the Beast is an ancient fairy tale that has been told in different versions, published in many languages, and adapted for stage, screen, and television (V. Hearne and Hollander 1991). One example is the postcard in illustration 1.1, produced in 1907 to publicize a play based on the tale. The story, in whatever version, is part of our culture, read to and seen by millions of children each year. Most of us know the basic plot. An evil fairy transforms a handsome prince into a ferocious-appearing animal who lives in a castle deep in the forest. In some versions he is lionlike; in others he resembles a wolf. Humans fear and shun him. Beauty's father, after being imprisoned by the Beast for stealing the creature's flowers, gives the attractive and young Beauty to the Beast in exchange for his freedom. The captive, lovely, and sensitive Beauty penetrates the Beast's facade, discovers his admirable inner qualities, and learns to love him.

A captivating story, but, at a deeper level, *Beauty and the Beast* captures the complicated union that has long existed between the animal kingdom and us. This union is so knotted with ambivalence that the only consistency in human-animal relations is inconsistency (Herzog 1993). One common contradiction, expressed in modern Western cultures and mirrored in *Beauty and the Beast,* is the view of animals as both objects and pets—just an animal in one situation and practically human in the next. In the fairy tale, the Beast is half-animal, half-human. The Beast is just a beast and has to undergo transformation through the magical power of human love in order to be seen as just like us rather than as the "other"—to please us rather than threaten us, to be appealing and attractive to us rather than repellent and ugly.

We do not have to search far and wide to see evidence of our contemporary confusion of animals as objects and pets. Although pet keeping and positive perceptions of some animals grew in the decades following the postcard era, the expansion of industrial capitalism provided great incentive for humans to treat animals as machines, material resources, and produce (Mullen and Marvin 1987). From one moment to the next, they are objects then lovable pets, distant then humanlike. Animals are objects to be hunted, fattened, harvested, slaughtered, and transformed into meat and clothing. Simultaneously, we pamper our adorable pets, call them by name, include them in our families, gratify them with abundant food and lavish accommodations, and grieve them when they die.

The tale of *Beauty and the Beast* captures other paradoxical ways that humans interact with animals. We can experience wild animals in their natural habitat where their behaviors are authentic and not significantly altered by human culture or experience them removed from their own world, tamed by humans. Although the Beast in the fairy tale appears at first to be wild and fierce, over time he is revealed to be human with all the emotions and needs that being human implies. Our heroine loves him and accepts his wildness. But when she looks into the Beast's eyes, she sees his human heart and soul. They both become more human. In the closing scene, the Beast is dying from a heart broken by his belief that the young woman he loves has deserted him. When Beauty returns to his side, her tears strike his face and the animal turns back into a handsome prince. He shares with her the secret of how his animal body was a punishment for spurning the evil fairy. Thus, the monstrous creature, both human and animal, is freed from his duality by a person's compassion.

This split has been exacerbated by the onset and dominance of our contemporary way of life. Urban growth and human encroachment upon the wilderness have reduced our encounters with untamed animals and increased contact with house pets. In addition to becoming estranged from animals in their natural environments, most of us have lost touch with a range of domesticated creatures, those animals like cows and pigs that have been shaped by humans to live in our environment and be of tangible use to us. Over the past century, the increasing physical gap between humans and animals used for food and clothing has made them, with the exception of media depictions, all but invisible to most Americans.

Many have mourned the loss of real animals and their gradual disappearance from human lives (for example, Berger 1980). Modernization has worked to limit common human contact with living animals to interaction with family pets. As we shall see, many pet owners develop an intimacy with their animal companions that strains the human-animal boundary and brings dogs, cats, and other animals into the family fold. Contacts with "wildlife" are infrequent and limited to trips to zoos where animals are unnaturally confined to parks and preserves to be observed from car windows or elevated trams. Movies, television, and photography have replaced the physical animal with media-produced substitutes—cartoons, animations and wild-kingdom documentaries. Shaped by culture, civilized and tame, they become our friends. The result is a fantasy relationship.

Another human-animal duality echoed in *Beauty and the Beast* is the view that some animals are good because they contribute to our general happiness and welfare, while others are bad because we see them as threats to our well-being. Indeed, the very use of the word *beast*, with its worst negative connotations, suggests an inferior nonhuman partner that is brutal and contemptible. At the beginning of the tale, the Beast is a bad animal, viewed as a predator that instills fear and hatred in humans. Some versions of *Beauty and the Beast* refer to the Beast as a monster—ugly, mean-spirited, and terrible. He has been cast out, exiled from the human community; he is a creature to be hunted. In most of the Beast's early contacts with humans, he lives up to his reputation, although he gradually softens.

Humankind has benefited psychologically and in other ways from setting humans against animals, whether they are perceived as good or bad. We derive comfort about who we are by thinking about who we are not—we are not animals. This mentality also allows us to use certain animals for pleasure and companionship, to perform labor, to entertain us, and to slaughter for our consumption. We may love our pets, and like the fact that we can use other animals for power or produce, but we still label other animals vermin and hate them. We have only to think of the phrase "humans and other animals" to realize that we pay lip service to our biological place in the animal kingdom. We opportunistically separate ourselves from other living creatures (Shepard

1997), and do so by ranking ourselves at the top of the chain of life, followed by those animals that we like and depend on, with others we fear and hate at the bottom.

Beauty and the Beast also shows the dual functions that animals can play in human society by either bringing people together or keeping them apart. Animals' capacity to build relations as well as destroy them is evident in *Beauty and the Beast*. The Beast separates humans by confining Beauty to his world away from her family and community. Eventually, she begs the Beast to let her visit her kin, and he agrees. By the end of the tale, the Beast unites the family and community in a happy, fairy-tale ending. The Beast, transformed into a prince, marries Beauty, and the two live happily ever after.

This duality is a familiar part of modern life. Animals can connect people in different ways. The simplest is in everyday life when people are drawn to a pet being walked by a stranger and find it safe and easy to strike up a conversation because of the animal's presence. In a more complex way, animals create human communities by becoming the object of common concern and interest. Bird watchers form clubs around their interest in spotting birds (Donnelly 1994), people who own and train horses develop an identity and culture around that interest (Brandt 2004), and every breed of dog has a following that manifests itself in networks, meetings, shows, and other gatherings. Huge networks and working relations have developed between people in animal-related industries such as farming and meat processing. Hunting and fishing clubs and more informal sporting groups are the basis of many friendships. The circus, the rodeo, and other animal-centered entertainment bring both participants and observers together.

But animals can also be used to separate people from each other and become instruments of conflict. Sometimes this separation is achieved physically, when the sheer size and strength of an animal are used to strike terror in the opposition and keep them at bay. The psychological impact of Hannibal's elephants on terrified Roman troops at the battle of Cannae in 216 BC is legend. The United States in the 1950s and 1960s saw police dogs used to strike fear into civil rights demonstrators and saw mounted police used to intimidate and manipulate antiwar crowds and other protesters.

Animals can also separate humans at a symbolic level. Linking members of particular racial and religious groups to specific animals, calling them vermin or using animal imagery to describe them, is a common way to drum up hatred, divide the enemy, and build solidarity among the name callers. At the beginning of the twentieth century, African Americans were often portrayed in cartoons and other literature as apelike, women as chicks or foxes, and Jews as ferrets or rats (Arluke and Sanders 1996). During wars, animals such as the American eagle are used to build solidarity among the troops, while animals symbolizing the enemy are used to evoke hatred (Baker 1993).

Although animals have their own physical and psychological being, once in contact with humans they are given a cultural identity. They are brought into civilization and transformed in the minds of humans. Thus, we have to look beyond what is perceived as innate appearance, behavior, and cognitive abilities in order to understand them (Arluke and Sanders 1996). Being an animal during the postcard era, as well as in modern times, may be less a matter of biology than it is an issue of human culture and perspective. It is not whether they are inherently like us or not; it is what we make of them.

EARLY-TWENTIETH-CENTURY AMERICA

Photo postcards were immensely popular in the United States from approximately 1905 until 1935, the people's photography (Bogdan and Weseloh 2006). Millions were produced. Fundamental social changes occurred during this postcard craze that profoundly altered the situation of animals and their connection to people. This nodal point in the modern history of human-animal relations is documented in the photography examined in this book.

The era spans the terms of seven presidents, from Theodore Roosevelt (1901–9) to Franklin Delano Roosevelt (1933–45). Theodore was known for both his dedication to the preservation of animal habitat and his prowess as a hunter, but he also loved his pets. He had at least five dogs while president, including a pit bull terrier, Pete, who made news when he ripped the pants of the French ambassador at the White House (Kehl 1980). Franklin was a conservationist but not the outdoorsman that Theodore was. Nevertheless, he had a strong connection to animals. Franklin's Scottish terrier, Fala, enhanced his gentlemanly demeanor. Fala charmed Americans and came to be associated with the president's compassion.[3]

During the time of photo postcards, the country moved from being predominately rural and small town—locations where humans and other animals lived in close proximity and in mutually dependent relationships—to being predominately urban, where animals were relegated to the roles of pet, pest, or zoo creature. As part of this movement, a society dominated by local economies and face-to-face trading transitioned into a society dominated by commercial production of manufactured goods. Before the late 1930s farmers and local butchers produced and processed meat and other animal products for consumption by locals. In the new urban order, large retail corporations came to dominate the production of animal products for the table and for dress. Slaughterhouses with assembly lines processed tons of pork, chicken, and beef each day along with an endless supply of animal skins.

Changes in transportation and sources of energy during this time had profound implications for human-animal relations. Horse-drawn transportation and machinery dominated early-twentieth-century America, but in a few decades these methods were replaced by vehicles and equipment powered by internal combustion engines. The transition from the ubiquitous horse to automobiles, trucks, and other machinery required radical changes not only in the economy but also in the way people lived.

With the rise of mass consumerism, large companies began manufacturing animal-related goods. Pet products, such as cat and dog food, birdcages, and animal toys, appeared as pet shops became a standard retailing venue in cities. In rural areas manufactured feed supplanted free-range grazing.

Animals also became part of advertising campaigns as symbols of national brand-named products. Pictures

3. Franklin had at least six other dogs. Fala starred in a Hollywood movie about the dog's life in the White House. He is depicted in the Franklin Delano Roosevelt Memorial in Washington, D.C.

of animals appeared on packaging and in advertisements not only for products geared toward animal owners but also for goods that had nothing to do with pets. Companies were not the only organizations to incorporate animals as symbols; most schools and sports teams adopted animals as their mascots.

The early twentieth century also saw the rapid professionalization of animal-related occupations. Most notably, veterinary medicine followed in the footsteps of human medical care. Animal doctors, like physicians, developed specialized organizations, training standards, licensing, and codes of ethics. In addition, animal doctors switched from primarily attending large animals, mainly horses and cattle, to serving house pets. Even taxidermy, once a folk art handed down generation to generation, became a trade with professional pretensions accompanied by specialized schools and credentials.

Selective breeding of animals for characteristics useful to humans started long before the postcard era. During this period, *pedigreed* took on new meaning as champion stock, animal shows, and the production of the biggest and the best became a goal of animal keepers and animal scientists alike.

Although widespread hunting and trapping of game continued through the postcard era, the decline of the wilderness and wildlife led to the growth of the sports hunter and efforts at conservation. As people attempted to curtail the widespread slaughter of certain species, hunting and fishing became regulated and other conservation methods came into being.

During the Progressive movement, reformers demanded improvements in the welfare of children and the poor, but they also raised questions about the status and treatment of animals. The mid-1860s saw the founding of New York City's American Society for the Prevention of Cruelty to Animals (ASPCA) and Boston's Massachusetts Society for the Prevention of Cruelty to Animals (MSPCA). With horse abuse as their primary concern, these humane societies, and soon others like them, became a prominent force in protecting and regulating the care of companion animals during the postcard era. Both societies worked to pass anticruelty laws and developed humane law enforcement departments to enforce these regulations. At the same time, the first

humane shelter appeared in Philadelphia and became a model for other organizations that sought to find homes for unwanted animals or to humanely euthanize their charges.

Other changes occurred in the lives of working animals and their relationships to humans. Beginning with the Spanish-American War and continuing in World War I, animals went into combat both as mascots and as workers. Although animals had always fought alongside humans, the twentieth century saw them being trained for more specialized tasks such as carrying messages and medical supplies. Dogs began to play a prominent role in guiding the blind. They also joined the police and other law enforcement agents to control mobs and sniff out missing persons and runaway convicts.

During the period of real photo postcard popularity, movies replaced vaudeville and animals became stars of the big screen. It was a time when large tented circuses with menageries and performing animals toured the country, and rodeos became not just local affairs but also played Madison Square Garden. Also, by the start of the twentieth century, most major cities opened large zoological parks, modeling themselves after America's first zoo in Philadelphia and trying to set themselves apart from menageries and traveling animal shows.

PHOTO POSTCARDS

Why did we choose photo postcards to chronicle human-animal relations and the changes that occurred during this period? Photo postcards were the most popular format for both commercial and amateur photographers at the time. People were wild about them—they were a craze, a fad that lasted longer than most. Their appeal was that they were cheap, they cost less than alternative photo formats, they were a convenient size for collecting, and they were practical for mailing to friends and family. People of every socioeconomic level, ethnic group, and geographic location produced, bought, sent, and collected them. Because of postcard collectors, the hobby started early in the century and continues today. Ordinary people kept their postcards in family albums to document their lives, so a huge number of them are available for study.

The large number of photo postcards produced was the result of a significant transition in the history of photography. Before the period we are discussing, commercial photographers took most photographs. In 1900 the Brownie and other inexpensive cameras were introduced, and more people took their own family pictures rather than having local studio portrait photographers do so. As the postcard format became the rage, studio photographers attempted to interrupt the decline in their customer base by printing their studio portraits on postcard stock.

With the increase in amateur photographers, many commercial photographers moved from being predominately picture takers to merchants selling photo equipment and frames as well as providing developing, printing, and other services. Some were able to remain photographers, if only part-time, by producing town views and other images on postcard stock. They sold these items in their own stores as well as wholesaling them to local stores, hotels, and tourist establishments. When postcards were at the height of their popularity, they were a significant source of income for some photographers. Because customers wanted variety, the number of views proliferated. This demand, combined with snapshot amateur photo postcard production, accounts for the huge quantity that were produced. Because of real photo postcards, the first third of the twentieth century was likely the most photographed period of American history.

The importance of real photo postcards goes beyond their abundance, however. They are special because of who took them and how they were used. Local commercial photographers or amateur picture takers produced the great majority of real photo postcards. The images they produced both document the times and are documents of their time. For the most part, the photographers were part of the communities they photographed, insiders to their subject matter, folk documentarians. Some of the photographers were common people with an uncommon talent. Their intimacy with the people and places they captured resulted in a vernacular record of the life and times of the period unavailable in other kinds of photography (Bogdan 1999, 2003; Bogdan and Weseloh 2006).

We had other reasons for choosing photo postcards. They provide an enormous and relatively untapped visual archive to document and investigate our topic. Yet social scientists often dismiss photos as a source of data because they are difficult to interpret. Scholars believe they cannot understand what place these images had in the cultures that produced them, what photographers thought they were depicting, and what those individuals who were pictured or viewed images made of them—that is, the postcard's social context.[4] We have spent a great deal of time studying not only the images in this book but also the people who produced and used this genre of photography. We believe we have a deep understanding of the place photo postcards held in American culture and in people's lives.

In addition to our understanding of the social context of photo postcards, the cards themselves provide more information about their meaning than do other forms of photography. Many cards have captions or notations on the image side that describe the photos, offer commentaries about their importance, and help decipher where and when the images were produced. Also, photo postcards were produced with a space to send a message. They are the only form of photography that invites commentary. Many postcard senders and owners made use of the space to write notes describing the image and how it related to their own lives. Other senders commented on themselves and their own lives. Some senders included remarks about the pictured animals, personalizing and articulating the meaning of the animals to them. For example, one image of a dog includes a notation of the dog's name and that it is the sender's "eldest son," indicating its importance and role in that family. We include the messages written on the cards we refer to throughout the book.

We will also discuss the photographers who took the illustrations. As you will see, although most were the local town photographers or amateurs we referred to earlier, a few do not fit those labels. They include itinerants who traveled from town to town freelancing or attached to

---

4. Howard S. Becker (1986) and Douglas Harper (1994) are two sociologists who have been at the forefront of discussing these issues.

circuses and rodeos and other traveling amusement organizations, or they were the designated photographers on ships. When photo postcards became popular, large commercial firms began producing them to augment their line of printed cards. The ones that we use here are images of silent-movie stars and other celebrities. In addition, museums and zoos produced their own photo postcards to sell to visitors. Both the large-run commercial cards and the cards produced by public organizations were made for the mass market and are more uniform and professional looking than the postcards by local and itinerant photographers. The few we use of the former illustrate the mass marketing of animals and their use by organizations for public relations more than the other cards we use. Rather than vernacular, they are corporate.

Animals appear in many photo postcards. Horses, cattle, pigs, sheep, rabbits, dogs, cats, and other species were so ubiquitous in early-twentieth-century American life that it was difficult to take a town or farm view without including them. They appear as natural parts of ordinary life. Animals also played an important part in a town's special events—fairs, circuses, holidays, celebrations, community hunts. Local photographers as well as amateur photographers covered these events. People were often fond and proud of the animals they owned, whether they were their favorite horse, prize-winning cow, or just the family pet. They wanted photos of them. They either took the pictures themselves or called upon local commercial photographers to capture their living possessions.

Although animal and animal-owner portraits were most often taken on location, it was also common for animals, especially house pets, to be posed in photo studios. Individual photographers often used animals, especially dogs and cats, to boost their own business prospects. The large number of photo postcards taken as studio portraits of dogs and other small animals are testimony to the importance of animals in the lives of early-twentieth-century Americans. One of the many ironies we shall encounter is that photographers did not just point their lenses on live loved animals. Portraits of hunters with their dead trophies abound, too.

An untold number of real photo postcards of animals were produced between 1905 and 1935. In addition to people's interest in pets, game, and other roles animals played, other factors account for the profusion of animal images. The major manufacturers of photo postcard stock (the paper used to print photo postcards) and other photography equipment capitalized on the human-animal connection by encouraging the idea that photographers' portfolios and family albums should include images of animals. They marketed this idea by including pictures of animals in their advertising. Doing so added impetus to the public's inclination to photograph animals. Kodak led the way in promoting animal photography. It provided its retailers with personalized versions of animal-illustrated advertising that, for example, featured a litter of adorable pups.

OUR APPROACH

We approached this book with broad ideas about what we might cover, derived from our own previous research and what others have written. At first we looked for illustrations that fitted our notions of what was important and what needed to be shown. As we immersed ourselves in thousands of images housed in the archives of private collections, we realized that our preconceived ideas and categories did not adequately account for what we were seeing. We had to rethink our assumptions. Thus, the pictures included here are not just illustrations that embellish what we say; they have also helped generate the insights we present.

In choosing what images to include in the book we considered two aspects of the pictures: their documentary value and their aesthetic character. Ideally, each illustration is an image that teaches something about human-animal relations, while at the same time being a well-composed and -exposed photograph that moves the viewer. Although most of the images obtain this standard, we include some because of their documentary value, even though they might fall short in the realm of aesthetics.

Most people think that to understand social life it is better to know the facts than to experience it emotionally or aesthetically. But these dimensions of understanding can be complementary. A truly compelling photograph possesses the dual function of instruction and affective impact (Asma 2001, 244–45). This project brings these aspects of knowing together to bear on the subject of human-animal relations. Real photo postcards contain facts as well as provoke feeling and aesthetic appreciation. A good photograph can make social science issues clearer, while good social science analysis can make good photographs more compelling.

Although there are more than 350 illustrations in this book, it is not a "picture book." Each chapter of *Beauty and the Beast* is a photo essay of sorts. In a photo essay the words and pictures are interdependent. Our book needs to be read with this idea in mind. People often look at photo books by thumbing through them, stopping at the images that catch their eye. The text is ignored or read only when an image raises questions they want clarified. On the other hand, people read text-based books by concentrating on the words and only occasionally paying casual attention to the photographs and the relationship between the sentences and the images. To read this book effectively you need to change your reading habits. When we refer to an illustration in the text, stop and examine it. We say examine rather than look at because we want you to pay careful attention to the image as a whole as well as to its detail. Study it section by section. Look at its overall composition. We encourage you to go back and forth between what we say and your own scrutinizing.

Pets

2.1. Man with pet dog, ca. 1908. Private Coll.

tried to contain a smile provoked by his pet's show of affection—the dog might have just licked him. After a series of pictures were taken and the proofs were ready, the man chose this one to be printed in multiple copies on postcard stock. He kept one for himself and sent others to relatives and friends. The picture and the circumstances surrounding it personify the dog as "best friend." As sentimental and clichéd as the phrase is, real photo postcards verify its relevance.

Like the dog in the illustration, a pet is an animal that has a special affectionate relationship with a human, is usually kept at home, and provides companionship for the owner.[1] Children grow up with pets, newly married couples get them to rehearse child rearing, people rely on them for company, and nursing home residents look forward to their visits.[2] They are such a part of the American social fabric that census forms include dogs, insurance companies offer coverage for veterinary bills, grocery stores stock gourmet pet foods, and cities provide dog runs for off-leash recreation. For most Americans, beginning in the postcard era and continuing today, pet keeping became the only regular and direct contact people have with animals.

Well-treated pets are lucky animals: they are named, played with, spoken to, fed regularly, groomed, treated for diseases, allowed to sleep indoors, caressed, and pampered. Labeled by the cat's owner as "Upper

*T*he contented fellow in the illustration above put on his best clothes and took his dog to a local photographer to have this picture taken. He placed the dog on the chair and tried to get him to look at the camera, but the dog preferred his master's face. The owner

1. This chapter draws heavily on Katherine Grier's important book, *Pets in America: A History* (2006).

2. Some scholars and animal advocates prefer the terms *companion animal* over *pet* and *guardian* over *owner* because they assert that animals are not merely property. As with the term *animal*, we share the sentiment but favor the briefer referents.

Upper and Lower Berths, Harry

2.2. Upper and lower berths, ca. 1909. Tom Gates Coll.

and Lower Berths," illustration 2.2 shows the easy life some pets experienced.

Americans have long had a love affair with their special animals. They kept pets in the early years of the country (M. Schwartz 1998). The practice significantly increased and changed after the Civil War. During the postcard era, companion animals continued to become more common and the relationship between humans and their pets more intimate. Urbanization accounts for some of the change. The companionship that went along with the extended family that characterized rural life dwindled as people adapted to urban living. As citizens left rural areas and immigrants settled in cities, they faced an impersonal environment bereft of the farm creatures and wildlife that once were a regular

part of their lives (Kete 1995). With the dissemination of urban lifestyles into rural areas through personal contact as well as mass-circulation magazines, companion animals became more a part of town and rural living. Many contemporary aspects of pet keeping appeared as Americans enthusiastically embraced pets as valued companions.

Prior to the advent of photo postcards, most people did not record images of their pets and their affection for them. Owners could hire a portrait painter, an option available only to the wealthy. Early photographic images were much less expensive than paintings, but were still pricey enough so that people of lesser means were reluctant to have their pictures taken regularly. These pre-twentieth-century photos of people and their pets are not as abundant as photo postcards. Photo postcards put image making within the reach of almost all pet owners by making this process cheaper and easier. Faster film was an innovation that allowed photo postcard photographers to take subjects, such as animals, that had trouble holding a pose. In addition, multiple copies of images could easily be produced and mailed to friends and family as well as kept in family albums.

Some postcards were accomplished by people taking their pets to the photographer's studio for formally posed portrait sittings, just as they did with other family members. The fact that a person would go through the trouble of taking their pet to a photo studio signifies the importance of these animals to their owners. So, too, do the thousands upon thousands of real photo postcard snapshots taken and kept by owners, friends, and relatives showing people and their pets.

KINDS OF OWNERS

Pets rapidly became an important feature of human life in early-twentieth-century America. We came across hundreds of photo postcards where pets appear with children and adults (tots to the elderly) of every class, gender, race, and ethnic background and in every location, whether in the city or countryside, at home or at work.

Although pets were commonplace, everyone did not keep the same kinds of animals, nor did they treat them the same way. Wealthy Americans could afford

2.3. Jack Pickford with collies, Hollywood, California, 1924. B. Nelson Coll.

2.4. Man with mixed-breed dog, ca. 1908. Steven S. Cohen Coll.

rare and expensive animals. With dogs, for example, the well-to-do could pay for what we now call pedigreed or purebred dogs. In illustration 2.3, Jack Pickford, playboy film and stage star and the brother of Mary Pickford, poses in a Hollywood photographer's studio with his pet collies.

Formalizing the distinction between pedigreed and other dogs began in the last decades of the nineteenth century but became popular and a standard distinction for buyers during the first half of the twentieth.[3] Breeders and dog fanciers developed specific definitions for

3. The most influential such organization in the United States was the American Kennel Club, founded in 1884.

different kinds of dogs and documented ancestry in dog registries. Pedigreed dogs had "papers," certification that they came from purebred stock, such as the dogs in illustration 2.3.

Dogs that did not have "papers" were grouped into general dog types, such as hounds and terriers, or lumped into the category of mongrel, of mixed or unknown parents. Middle-class and poorer Americans acquired dogs belonging to either of these groups. Dogs of various types were rare compared to mongrels and were often bought and sold, while mixed breeds, such as the dog in illustration 2.4, were given away or picked up as strays.

By comparison, everyday types of working dogs, like a coonhound, cost rural people ten to fifty dollars

2.5. Family with purebred dog, ca. 1910. Bogdan Coll.

mild manner made it a perfect companion and playmate for privileged children. The beautifully saddled and groomed pet pinto pony in illustration 2.6 is affectionately nuzzled by her young well-dressed owner as she holds a teddy bear.

Social class intersected with gender when it came to selecting specific types of animals, especially dogs. The purebred became a fashion accessory and status symbol for wealthy men and women. The divide between women's pets and gentlemen's dogs ironically grew as interest surged in women's suffrage (Derr 2004). Well-heeled women often chose small purebred dogs, or "toy dogs." Posing in a photographer's studio, the fur-clad woman in illustration 2.7 sits for a portrait with her pedigreed pet dog at her side.

A larger and tougher-looking purebred dog was considered to be the right choice for the prosperous man of the day. Following this expectation, illustration 2.8 shows a boy from an affluent family with his Staffordshire bull terrier.

Middle- and working-class people also embraced pet keeping, but animals were not kept as status accoutrements or solely for pleasure. Many served the dual role of pet and worker. Domestic pets for the rural and urban lower classes served practical roles in addition to being companions, too. Cats were "mousers," a term used to describe their duties of controlling the rodent population. Guard dogs protected property. We will discuss farm animals and their ambiguous pet status later in the chapter.

Class differences between owners resulted in different methods of pet care and maintenance. What pets ate and where they slept varied. Although canned dog food did not become widely available until after the postcard era, dry food, dog biscuits, and other manufactured eatables were available, and people who had disposable income bought them.

Working-class dog owners let their dogs roam and scavenge for food or eat table or cooking scraps (Grier 2006). Wealthy individuals tended to confine their pets to their homes or property and cooked special food for them. A missing pedigreed pet was cause for alarm, and the well-to-do took direct action. Owners would have local photographers produce a "reward for lost

in contemporary money, while a prestigious purebred dog, like a collie or Saint Bernard, such as the one in illustration 2.5, could cost as much as thousands of dollars (Derr 2004). When adjusted for inflation in today's dollars, the cost of a purebred dog from prize stock could be as much as twenty thousand dollars.

Upper-class families also could afford to pamper and keep pets for their pure delight rather than use them as working animals. Thanks to indulgent parents, children in wealthy families delighted in having their own Shetland ponies.[4] A Shetland's small size and

4. Shetland ponies originated in the Shetland Isles, Scotland, and were brought in the 1880s to the United States, where they were bred with other ponies, creating the American Shetland.

2.6. Girl with pony, ca. 1909. Joel Wayne, Pop's Postcards Coll.

2.7. Upper-class woman and dog, ca. 1911. Private Coll.

2.8. Boy with Staffordshire bull terrier, ca. 1912. Private Coll.

dog" photo postcard to have the city marshal distribute throughout town. People of lesser means were more nonchalant about missing pets.

The relationship between race and pet keeping was even more complex than the connection created by social class. Income certainly influenced the kinds of animals available to African Americans and their ability to have pets solely for enjoyment. African Americans of means kept pets in much the same mode as did whites of their own income bracket. The urban African Americans in illustration 2.9 smoked cigars and dressed in hip suits for the special occasion of having their picture taken with their pet poodles. All four subjects stare directly at the camera, looking quite fashionable.[5]

2.9. African American men with poodles, ca. 1924. Don and Newly Preziosi Coll.

Prior to emancipation it was illegal, in many areas, for slaves to own dogs, but afterward there was growing demand among African Americans for domestic pets (Derr 2004). Their experience during slavery may have influenced their attraction, or lack thereof, to dogs (Katherine Grier, personal communication, June 27, 2008).[6] Because of the long-standing use of dogs to track escaped slaves or to otherwise terrorize African Americans, a phobia about dogs lingers for some people today, especially among rural southern African Americans.[7] In the North pet dogs were probably kept as often among poor and middle-class African Americans as they were among whites of similar class standing.

Native Americans also had complex relations with animals. Long before European settlers arrived with their imported animals, Native Americans kept what might be considered pets. Young tamed wild animals lived in villages as companions and playthings (Grier 2006). Domesticated canines also lived with Native Americans. Native Americans valued dogs for their ability to herd, hunt, pull, and play.[8]

As Native Americans absorbed Western values and norms, they came to develop pet relationships that resembled the attachment of other Americans. In illustration 2.10 the ninety-nine-year-old Native American mother, Kil-So-Quah, and son Anthony Revarre from northern Wisconsin made sure to include their pet dogs when making this postcard. (A second dog stands immediately behind the one that is plainly visible.) While they loved their dogs, the dogs probably also served to guard their other animals and valuable possessions.

6. There are also issues with the collecting of photographs by public institutions. Photography of African Americans was neglected until recently.

7. "Nigger dogs" or "Negro dogs" were specially trained to hunt and capture runaway slaves.

8. How dogs were treated varied greatly from tribe to tribe. A few tribes ate dogs. Although Europeans often presented dog feasts as a standard Native American practice, it was rare. Most tribes never ate dogs, whereas other tribes did so only on special occasions and as a form of ritual sacrifice (Derr 2004). From a Western perspective, dog eating was an unsavory and disgusting practice that reinforced the belief that Native Americans were uncivilized.

5. This photograph contradicts the pit-bull image associated with African Americans in today's news media.

2.10. Kil-So-Quah, aged ninety-nine, and her son, northern Wisconsin, ca. 1908. Private Coll.

KINDS OF PETS

The variety of animals kept as pets during the post-card era matched the diversity of pet owners and came close to the variety we see today with some differences. Caged birds were much more popular than they are now and were the favorite indoor family pet. The canary was most popular, but native birds were often trapped, caged, and kept, too. The popularity of caged birds was a function of their singing. Prior to the phonograph and the radio and aside from live music, there were no melodious sounds in the home without birds. The two elderly sisters in illustration 2.11 thought enough of their canaries to include them in their portrait that included a hand-painted photograph of one of their deceased husbands.

Parrots were exotic favorites, but less common than small birds because they were expensive to purchase, cage, and feed. They also were more demanding: they chewed their cages, needed wing clipping, tossed their food around, and screamed rather than sang. Then, as now, their owners enjoyed the bird's intelligence and ability to mimic the human voice and other sounds (illustration 2.12).

Dogs were the most commonly kept pets and appeared on more photo postcards than any other kind of animal. As already noted, most families owned mixed breeds. With the definition and evolution of new breeds, fads and fashions influenced which dogs conveyed social status and were most desirable to own.[9] The development of the system of classification and the breeding practices that went along with it created a hierarchy of dogs and a status ladder for ownership of different types of canines. Having such dogs conferred on their owners a cachet of gentility and respectability (Shelton 2001). What dogs were "in" has varied over the years.

Choice of types and breeds of dogs for much of the nineteenth century was limited to spaniels, hounds, setters, pointers, terriers, mastiffs, and bulldogs. By the early twentieth century dog shows to exhibit pedigreed breeds gradually became more common, as did the variety of breeds available to prospective owners. Collies, pugs, Saint Bernards, and German shepherds became almost faddish during the postcard era. Interestingly, pit bulls were one of the most popular breeds at this time (illustration 2.13). Counter to their contemporary reputation as vicious killers associated with dogfighting and city gangs, they were widely beloved and cherished for being faithful and smart. Petey, the dog star of the famous *Our Gang* and *Little Rascals* comedy series, was a pit bull, as was Shirley Temple's pet in her early movies.

Mixed-breed cats were very popular and common, while purebreds, such as the Angora or Maltese, were rare. Most owners acquired their mixed-breed cats by picking up strays or from friends. All but the most expensive purebreds were kept outside, with many serving as

9. There also was some effort to promote purebred dogs as ideal family pets (Grier 2006).

2.11. Elderly women with canaries, 1928. Private Coll.

2.12. Man with parrot, ca. 1906. Don and Newly Preziosi Coll.

predators of the local rodent population around homes, barns, markets, stores, and stables.

Although many cats were treated as marginal pets, or even neglected, there were devoted cat lovers, too (Grier 2006). Because cats were difficult to pose and more taken for granted than dogs, there are relatively few real photo postcards of cats. The photo postcard in illustration 2.14 is unusual in that it was taken at a photographer's studio. The woman in the picture obviously adored her cats.

Dogs and cats had many progeny. Owners purposely mated some pure breeds and specific types of dogs and cats because they were desired and could be sold or given as gifts. This situation was probably the case for the young man in illustration 2.15, who sits behind a litter of sheepdog puppies. Since they resembled purebred dogs, he could sell or give them away.

Mixed breeds were another story. Dogs and cats reproduced too easily. Most litters were the result of unplanned encounters between neighborhood animals. During the postcard era, spaying and neutering were not common (Grier 2006), and many pets reproduced so quickly that there were more animals than people who wanted to care for them. Out of a litter of mutts a single animal might be spared, but the rest were abandoned or killed. Typically, animals would be drowned. The abandoned animals created an overpopulation of

2.13. Boys and pit bull at play, ca. 1911. Private Coll.

2.14. Woman with cats, ca. 1912. B. Nelson Coll.

strays, a condition that continues to burden humane societies throughout the United States today.

Although they were cheap and could be easily kept in small spaces, rodents were a less popular choice for pets than birds, dogs, and cats. Some households raised pet guinea pigs or white mice and rats. In our search for images, we found no photo postcards of these animals, perhaps because rodents were so rare as pets and of low status.

Before 1912 rabbits were officially classified as rodents (Rodenitia), but afterward they were placed in their own category, lagomorphs. Because rabbits reproduce so quickly, children and adults sometimes made a hobby of husbandry, keeping small herds of rabbits, some of which remained as pets while they sold the rest. By the latter part of the nineteenth century and the start of the twentieth, selective breeding had created specific types of rabbits that became desirable as pets. Rabbit fanciers formed organizations and displayed their prize rabbits at shows. One breed in particular, the Belgian hare, was a popular choice as a household pet.[10] Beatrix Potter, an early-twentieth-century British writer who became popular in the United States, kept pet Belgian hares that inspired her Peter Rabbit books. Small family-run rabbit

10. The Belgian hare is actually a rabbit.

2.15. Sheepdog litter, ca. 1916. Ralph DeLuca Coll.

2.16. Jones, "Home of the Belgian Hare," National, California, ca. 1917. M. Maslan Coll.

farms were common during the postcard era. Illustration 2.16 shows a family-run Belgian-hare farm in California.

Exotic animals such as monkeys also became pets. For most of the nineteenth century, these animals were brought home by seamen and given as gifts or sold. By the end of the century pet stores were stocking imported animals that had been caught in the wild (Grier 2006). Upper- and some middle-class families were among the few who could afford these expensive animals. Primates were a popular choice, but were often difficult to

manage and prone to disease. All dressed up for their studio image, the young girl in illustration 2.17 and the family's pet monkey sit still for the photographer.

In rural areas it was common for wild animals to be tamed and made into pets. The most common route to becoming a pet was for baby animals to be captured, fed, tamed, and integrated into human life. Although some animals remained pets into adulthood, most often the baby animals were kept until they grew out of their cuteness and the difficulties involved in raising

2.17. Pet monkey, Stockton, Maine, ca. 1910. Photo by Miller. Private Coll.

them became apparent. The brothers in illustration 2.18 appear enthralled with their large litter of coyote pups, but the odds were strong that the animals would be put to death or abandoned before they matured.

In the early nineteenth century young deer were popular pets among prosperous families (Grier 2006), a practice that lingered into the postcard era. Making a photograph of an undomesticated animal was a considerable challenge to the studio photographer (Palmquist 1981). Illustration 2.19 shows a pet fawn sharing a plate of food with the family dog as they stand on an oriental carpet in front of a dropped canvas in a photographer's studio.

Although some people kept birds of prey for hunting, a more unusual pet was the owl. The boy sitting on the bench with two young owls perched on his lap in illustration 2.20 seems to be unsure of how his pets might behave.

Many animals had an ambiguous status as pets. Dogs were pets, but they were also herders. They hunted with their owners, stalking wildlife and retrieving kills. The hunter in illustration 2.21 no doubt regarded his pet dogs as both friends and coworkers. (For further discussion of this topic, see chapters 4 and 8.)

Particular horses might be viewed with great affection but simultaneously expected to work as draft animals. The girl in illustration 2.22 had a close relationship

2.18. Boys with pet coyotes, ca. 1924. Aikenhead Coll.

2.19. Deer and dog pets, 1913. Private Coll.

2.21. Farmer with hunting dogs, Minnesota, ca. 1917. Photo by Stephenson. Private Coll.

2.20. Boy with owl pets, ca. 1911. Private Coll.

with her colts and probably named them, stroked them, played with them, and continued to be close to them as they grew, but that close tie did not prevent the horses from becoming farm laborers.

In addition to working animals, farms had species that were raised for meat, or were kept because they produced eggs, dairy products, or wool. In the nineteenth century *pet* meant "favorite," and it was applied to farm animals that were singled out as special and treated with more affection and care than the others. These animals were pets of sorts, but that status did not relieve them of making a tangible contribution to the good of the family. They had to be productive. They were treated as pets one moment and as food the next when served for dinner. This apparent contradiction in roles was common during the early part of the twentieth century. The fancily dressed teenager in illustration 2.23, with her arm affectionately wrapped around the calf's neck, apparently had

2.22. Farm girl with horses, ca. 1915. Vaule Coll.

2.23. Teenager with calf, ca. 1910. Private Coll.

2.24. Studio portrait of girl with rooster, ca. 1909. Steven S. Cohen Coll.

a special relationship with the animal, a relationship that likely did not endure.

Most photo postcard images of ambiguous pets were taken on site, at the farm, but on occasion favored animals were brought to the photographer's studio. The resulting images showed the pride people felt in these animals and suggest that their relationships rivaled the affection and tenderness they had for more conventional family pets. This level of feeling was likely the case with the chicken in the studio portrait in illustration 2.24.

Ambiguous pet relationships of a different sort occurred with relatively small, inexpensive, and gentle animals such as pigeons. Some owners raised pigeons for their homing instinct and flying speed, entering them in races. Other pigeon keepers raised breeds for their beauty and treated their animals as art objects. Owners showed their best pigeons at competitive poultry shows in cities like Boston or New York. Their husbandry had an artistic twist—they treated pigeons as living paintings or sculptures. Pigeon fanciers kept birds as pets, but they also sold them. The young man in illustration 2.25 carefully combed his hair and dressed up to take his homing pigeons and the trophies they won to a local photographer so that he could document their victory.

2.25. Fancier with prizewinning pigeons, ca. 1920. Anton van Dalen Coll.

2.26. Woman with dog on lap, ca. 1914. Private Coll.

INTIMACY

Pet owners today express feelings of intimacy and love for their animals by being physically close with them. Owners exhibit this love by touching, gazing at, holding, stroking, or otherwise orienting their bodies to their pets (Katcher and Beck 1983). Early-twentieth-century Americans showed this affection, too. The gentleman pictured in the first illustration in this chapter (2.1) showed how this affection was made evident by body language and other compositional elements of the photo postcard they left for us to examine.

Postcards captured this closeness in different ways. Owners appear with their bodies in contact with their pets or caressing them. The woman in the polka-dot dress sitting on her porch in illustration 2.26 posed, as did many pet owners, with her pet sitting on her lap. Pets displayed this way suggest intimacy as did animals elevated to the same horizontal level as their human companions. Even though pets are sometimes pictured at their owner's feet or at a lower level (see illustration 2.26), a position symbolizing human dominance, bringing the animal to the owner's level was as common.

People also posed by hugging and looking lovingly at their pets. The woman in illustration 2.27 took her pet spaniel with her pup to a photography studio to take this picture. She lovingly holds and looks at the little one while steadying the mother with her touch.

2.27. Woman with dogs, ca. 1924. Private Coll.

2.28. Cradling cat to face, ca. 1909. Todd Weseloh Coll.

2.29. Girl cuddling rabbit, ca. 1911. B. Nelson Coll.

In some images, owners brought their faces close to their pet's heads to make physical contact, making the intimacy that humans feel toward their pets come to life. In illustration 2.28 the owner is smiling as if she were a parent with an infant. In illustration 2.29 a pre-adolescent girl cuddles her pet rabbit, ensuring its safety as it sits on the photographer's stand.

Some of the physical intimacy evident in these images could be attributed to the fact that pets were not easy to pose and owners compensated by controlling them physically. Although there is an element of truth to this claim, there were alternative restraints that could have been used—a leash, a chain, or a strap, or grabbing the animal by its collar. It is telling that if holding was a method of control, the form that it took was loving physical contact rather than harsher alternatives. In addition, the subjects' facial expressions are compatible with the conclusion that the physical touching indicates intimacy.

JOYFUL PLAY

Images of owners playing with pets and having a good time further documented their closeness. Some play involved casual hanging out, petting, teasing, or fooling them with small objects such as cloth tied to a string or a toy. Commercially produced catnip was also available early in the postcard era (Grier 2006). Illustration 2.30 captures a moment of relaxed play on the porch with a mother, her three daughters, and their eleven kittens. Inscribed on the back of the card is the simple but heartfelt message, "The happy family—11 cats, find them."

Dressing up and posing pets for the camera was a form of human-animal play. Anthropomorphizing pets,

2.30. Idle moment with kittens, ca. 1912. Arluke Coll.

treating them as humans, mirrored and mocked the closeness of animals to humans. Although her expression does not reveal it, the girl in illustration 2.31 is having fun playing dress-up with her dog while her cat stands by. She or the photographer has deliberately positioned the dog, who is wearing a dress, in a chair, looking at the camera and striking a pose as if she were a person.

People enjoy teaching "tricks" to pets and getting them to perform for an audience. Photo postcards were the perfect medium to share a pet's accomplishments with friends and family in distant places. Dogs, in particular, could easily be taught to perform simple classic photographable tricks such as sitting or giving a paw. Placed on a chair, the dog in illustration 2.32 offers his paw and at the same time glances into the camera as if he were more interested in the photographer than the woman in the apron. In the next illustration (2.33), the pet is sitting at a piano, paws on the keyboard, singing a duet of sorts with its owner.

As illustration 2.34 shows, some tricks could be elaborate and staged, involving multiple animals and props—a miniature circus of sorts. Here Roderic poses with his pet pony, goat, and dog, reminiscent of trained animals in a circus ring.

2.31. Dog dressed and seated in chair, ca. 1908. Arluke Coll.

2.32. Shaking hands, ca. 1908. Private Coll.

2.33. Dog at the piano, ca. 1915. B. Nelson Coll.

2.34. Roderic and his pets, ca. 1908. Semel Coll.

The next illustration (2.35) of pets and play is unusual and revealing. It is a studio portrait of a man with his back to the camera. His dog is on a chair, apparently interested in something in his master's pocket. It is likely a treat, and the man is tricking or teasing the dog. The owner enjoyed the event so much that he chose to have postcard prints capturing it, despite the fact that we do not see his face.

As with illustration 2.35, you can see in many photos that the trip to the photographer's studio was a joyful outing in itself for owner and pet alike. The woman in illustration 2.36, sitting behind a Model T studio prop with her dog next to her, appears to be having a good time sharing the moment with her pet.

Setting up this next outdoor shot (illustration 2.37) must have been quite a feat, or perhaps the log was a common perch and pose for the dog. Either way, this

2.36. Woman with dog in studio-prop Model T, ca. 1909. Bogdan Coll.

2.35. Man with dog with back to camera, ca. 1919. Private Coll.

photographic encounter was playtime for this owner and his pet and probably was relived again and again by viewing the resulting photograph.

ANIMAL KIN

During the postcard era animals were becoming a more meaningful part of human family life,[11] not merely as workers or showpieces but as significant others and "members of the family."[12] Closer relations brought animals into household routines and rituals, whether

11. "Family" was, and continues to be, an imprecise concept. Although some people use it strictly to refer to blood relations, others use it to include anyone living under the same roof. We use it in the broader sense of the term.

12. Looking at photographs of our pets helps translate this verbal declaration into a specific repertoire of behaviors toward the animal—something that social scientists have failed to do.

2.37. Man in log with dog on top, ca. 1909. Semel Coll.

2.38. Four generations of females, ca. 1918. B. Nelson Coll.

these events were everyday occasions such as gathering in front of the woodstove after dinner or special ones such as the celebration of Christmas. The four generations of females in illustration 2.38 wanted a photograph to capture their family gathering. When they went to a photographer's studio to have the portrait taken, they brought their pet poodle pup to include in the picture.

People who become close to animals in these ways are forced to consider pets as individuals. Humans have long recognized that animals have thoughts and feelings, but during the late nineteenth century people took animals more seriously. Pet owners became freer to express their experiences with their animals and attribute agency and awareness to them (Grier 2006).

Pets' role in the family was changing, and photographers caught this change on film. Both formally taken family studio portraits and informal family snapshots documented that pets were included within the circle of

kin. In the snapshot in illustration 2.39, the family dog sits in the center of the gathering framed by his human kinfolk.

The family on vacation in Seaside, Oregon, took their dog to a photographer's studio that catered to tourists who wanted a "having a great time" family portrait (illustration 2.40). The faux seaside served as the backdrop for the father, mother, daughter, son, and dog. Note how the father is central, with the family dog resting subserviently at his feet. The image illustrates the fact that it was common for families to take their pets with them on vacation trips and include them in photographic souvenirs.

Showing how highly some people regarded their pets, families had studio portraits made of their animals

2.39. Family with dog, ca. 1914. B. Nelson Coll.

2.40. Family with dog at the beach, ca. 1907. Arluke Coll.

was likely placed on the home mantel or in the family album next to photos of grandparents, children, and other relatives. The caption "Eldest Son" might have been placed tongue in cheek on the portrait, but it does suggest that pets were often given the honorary status of child. They could be surrogates for sons or daughters and referred to as "baby" or "child" and talked to and treated as if they were real children.

As members of the family, pets were included in photo postcards of important family events and occasions. Holidays and celebrations were occasions to include pets. They were present at July Fourth festivities, Memorial Day parades, school graduation picnics, and birthdays. Photo postcards were sometimes taken of individual family pets posed on a chair or stool and then mailed as Christmas cards, perhaps with an inscription reading: "Rex comes with Holiday Greetings to you all . . ."

More commonly, holiday pet cards featured family members with their animal companions. The result was a memorable group image for friends and relatives to enjoy and likely keep in the family album for future viewing. Although the scratched "Merry Christmas" message on the photo postcard in illustration 2.42 is difficult to see in the reproduction, it is a Christmas greeting in which the family made sure to include their cat and dog. The dog is perched on the hood of the

alone, with no humans in the picture. We came across hundreds of these portraits. Illustration 2.41 shows a family's undistinguished and not very photogenic dog posed on the top of a cloth-draped table. This picture

2.41. Eldest son, ca. 1909. Arluke Coll.

family's proud new possession, an automobile, while their cat, in order to be seen, is held up in the window. The picture captures the family's pride both in their automobile as well as in their pets.

Pets were not just part of family life at home. Some owners took their pets to work where, in the case of shop owners, the animals could lie in close proximity to owners as they conducted business. The husband and wife photographers in illustration 2.43 took their canine to work and included it in their self-portrait.

The pleasures of making pets a family member came with an emotional cost—owners had to deal with their deaths. The passing of a pet was a difficult experience during the photo postcard era, as it is today. Pets died much more frequently during the first third of the twentieth century than later. Small-animal veterinarians did not come on the scene until the 1920s and 1930s. People used home remedies or patent medicines to treat their pets, but, for the most part, these treatments were ineffective. There was little hope for animals with symptoms of life-threatening diseases, and euthanasia was a common practice.

Owners sometimes wanted token remembrances of their deceased pets. Wealthier people still had the option of having a portrait taken of the dead animal, but this practice, popular in Victorian times, declined after

2.42. Family with car and pets, ca. 1920. B. Nelson Coll.

2.43. Photographers with their dog, ca. 1908. Joel Wayne, Pop's Postcards Coll.

2.44. Spot, embalmed November 28, 1907, by Albert Young, licensed embalmer. Photo taken December 25, 1907. Joel Wayne, Pop's Postcards Coll.

the beginning of the twentieth century (Grier 2006). Increasingly, owners relied on pictures taken when the animal was alive to cherish after the pet's death. We came across one photo postcard of a beloved small black dog sitting on a chair in the family's backyard in Brooklyn. His owners wrote "Gone, but not forgotten" next to his picture as a type of death announcement and memorial after he passed away and mailed the card to a friend in 1904.

Long-term preservation was another possibility. Embalming was experimental at the time and apparently not widespread or lasting. We found only two photo postcards documenting the practice. Illustration 2.44 captures an embalmer with an example of his work, "Spot," who was embalmed approximately a month earlier. Apparently, this studio portrait was produced to advertise the practitioner's services. In another card that pictured two embalmers, the dog had allegedly been dead for close to a year.

A more successful and popular form of preservation was to have a taxidermist mount the pet. Illustration 2.45 is an advertising postcard for a taxidermist and shows two mounts, a white-tailed deer and a pet dog. (We will discuss taxidermy in chapter 9.)

Although embalming and mounting might seem bizarre today, these practices reflect owners' strong attachments to their animals and their desire to have them live on. Far more commonly, people buried their deceased pets in the backyard or in a rural spot, or they simply disposed of them in the garbage or in a dump. But there were burial alternatives. Although they were scarce at the time, animal cemeteries existed. Owners of a pet cemetery in Cheltenham, Pennsylvania, used

2.45. Taxidermist's advertisement for pet mounting, ca. 1910. Joel Wayne, Pop's Postcards Coll.

2.46. Siblings with dog, Clinton, Wisconsin, ca. 1912. Private Coll.

a photo postcard to promote their trade. The printed text on the back of the card gave the internment charge as ten dollars, which included a wooden case and a marked headstone.

CHILDREN AND PETS

The growing willingness to treat animals as kin influenced child rearing. The importance of children associating with animals was strongly embraced during the nineteenth century, a trend that continued throughout the twentieth (Melson 2001). Many children had pets of their own or participated with the family in pet keeping.

This trend can be seen in the overrepresentation of children in the illustrations in this chapter. There are many studio portraits of siblings with their pets. In illustration 2.46, the family dog is included as if he were the fifth child.

We came across hundreds of photo postcards of children and their pets out-of-doors as well. Illustration 2.47 captures two well-to-do sisters with their pet pony in front of their home. The animal is pulling a decorated miniature buggy made especially for their use.

Having pets was thought to be a way to develop a strong sense of self as well as good habits. According to parents of child pet owners, there were important

2.47. Girls' pet, Pleasant Hill, Ohio, 1911. Private Coll.

2.48. Children with pet birds, ca. 1921. Aikenhead Coll.

lessons to be learned from observing the behavior of certain animals. One reason for caged birds' (illustration 2.48) immense popularity was that they were thought to serve as moral models of middle-class life for children because they had prized virtues such as monogamy and devoted parenting skills (Grier 2006).

Pets also provided learning opportunities for children because animals had to be cared for. Children could be taught kindness, compassion, and love for all creatures by assuming responsibility for their pets' welfare. One of the benefits of taking care of pets is that it allows both children and adults to experience the pleasure of nurturing another creature. For children, this important skill could be acquired in the course of attending to their pets' needs. Illustration 2.49 captures the spirit of this learning, as a young boy acts the part of a doctor attending to his pet pit bull.

During the postcard era, children were free to roam their neighborhoods as well as the countryside with minimum adult supervision. It was typical for children to take their pets, especially dogs, with them on such adventures. Dogs were considered ideal playmates, and children were encouraged to include them in their playgroups and leisure pursuits. In illustration 2.50, the neighborhood kids placed their shepherd-mix

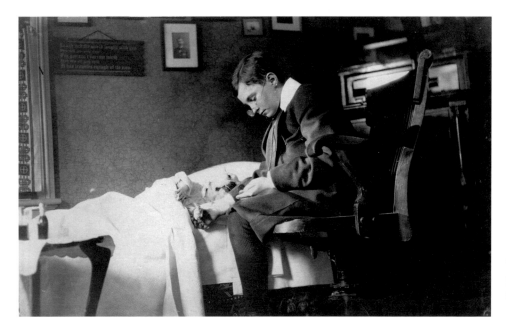

2.49. Boy playing doctor with pit bull, ca. 1908. Tom Gates Coll.

2.50. Children and dog at play, ca. 1920. Private Coll.

buddy on the baby carriage and pointed his face toward the photographer to show that he was a full member of the gang.

By the close of the nineteenth century, many towns in New England had organized children's groups that encouraged and rewarded young people for helping animals. Members of these Bands of Mercy, a youth branch of the Animal Welfare Society, kept a record of their good deeds (Unti and DeRosa 2003). The 4-H began in the early part of the twentieth century, and it encouraged children to learn modern agricultural practices and promoted young people working closely with individual farm animals for competitions that the organization sponsored (Reck 1951). As illustration 2.51 demonstrates, the Boys Scouts of America also sought to encourage kindness toward pets and animals in general and in 1930 began offering a merit badge in pet care; a little more than a decade later, the Girl Scouts followed suit.

2.51. Boy Scouts care for injured dog, ca. 1917. Semel Coll.

Families sometimes chose not to have pets or to delay their acquisition until children became older and more responsible. Toys shaped like animals, stuffed and wooden, served as a substitute for the real thing. These play objects allowed children to rehearse behaviors, such as gentleness and nurturing, that would be important later on when dogs, cats, or other animals became part of the family.

No doll during the early twentieth century rivaled the popularity of the teddy bear, and no doll had its creation and evolution so closely tied to this period. (See chapter 12 for a discussion of the origin of the teddy bear.) Teddy bears and other stuffed animals took on special meaning and importance to children as play and imaginary creatures, becoming both comforter and companion.[13] The toy animal is often the first nonhuman creature infants are given, and they become the earliest companions for children. In illustration 2.52, a young child, held by his mother, holds his teddy bear.

THE BIRTH OF THE MODERN COMPANION

In the past hundred and fifty years, pet keeping has gained widespread acceptance in the United States (Ritvo 1988). Although it began earlier, a significant shift in human-pet relationships occurred during the photo postcard era. Heightened interest in having pets and the development of closer relations with them grew out of increasing urbanization, humans' disconnection from farm animals and wilderness, and the decline in the extended family. Rural dwellers' ambiguous pet relationships gave way to urbanites' emotional attachment to companion animals (Phineas 1974).

13. The bears are also very appealing to older people. In recent years the bears have been used to reduce the stress of patients undergoing dental work or major surgery, as well as those persons coping with pain and loneliness from chronic disease. They also are given to victims of traffic accidents, abuse, rape, and other traumas for their comforting effect and because some people suffering severe anxiety find it easier to communicate by talking through the bear than directly to people. Beyond their therapeutic value, teddy bears now occupy a special niche in American popular culture. Collecting antique bear dolls can be quite expensive, with rare ones auctioning at nearly one hundred thousand dollars. To meet this considerable interest, there are books and magazines about teddy bears, as well as stores and companies specializing in their production and sale.

2.52. Child with teddy bear, ca. 1910. Private Coll.

It was not just that more people embraced pet keeping; human-companion animal relationships changed. Evidence from photo postcards strongly suggests that pet owners treated their pets with more regard, as members of the family and best friends. We saw this closeness throughout the chapter in the way pets were posed and in the interaction between owners and their animals captured in these pictures. Memories of pets were important enough to photograph and then share and display in family albums or place on the mantel. Some pets were treated like people, given humanlike clothing, toys, and furniture, and included in social events. They were interacted with in ways usually reserved for human loved ones.

We do not know the prevalence or depth of these positive sentiments and behaviors. Pet abuse was probably common, but it was not revealed in the postcards we reviewed. Undoubtedly, there were lapses, but the overwhelming affection people had for their pets was real and represents the most affirmative human-animal relationship we will deal with in this book. The positive regard we have reported reflects early manifestations of a trend that has resulted in current human-pet relations described by such phrases as: "Our pet is a member of our family" or "my best friend" (Cain 1983).

The pets depicted in the images in this chapter may have been adored, but life for these animals was created and controlled by their owners, a relationship of dominance that continues today. The physical appearance of some pets and the behavior of most are shaped by human expectations and desires. Owners breed and train dogs to conform to standards of what particular types of dogs should look like and how they should behave. Also, the situation of most pets is confinement—little contact with other animals, sterilization, limited exercise, and artificial food. Their lives are dictated by their owners' lifestyles (Berger 1991, 14). Blissful play with pets masks owners' resolve to control and subdue the potentially unruly forces of nature lying beneath their pets' fur (Tuan 1984). Playfully dominated, pets are patronized, made to act in ways that entertain people at the cost of the animals' freedom. All of this treatment might be considered cruel except to think of the alternative. A world without pets, as we know them, would result in the loss of most dogs, cats, and other companion creatures. We have enslaved them by making them totally dependent on us. Their only hope of survival is our dependence on them.

3

Mascots

3.1. Studio portrait of sailors with mascot, ca. 1915. Brian Buckberry Coll.

The phrase "animal mascot" signifies three aspects of a creature's relationship to a human group. First, it is a companion to many people at once. Mascots play a role similar to the one pets play, but instead of being a friend to a person or a family, mascots become buddies to dozens, or even hundreds, of people, who teach them tricks, take care of them, and lavish attention and affection on them. The second aspect of their relationship is that the animal symbolizes the group and reflects its identity. Mascots become emblems of loyalty, strength, or devotion to the group's mission. They become rallying points around which members can come together, even when tensions exist within the group. And finally, the animal is like a good luck charm. It provides a sense of safety as well as an imagined foot up in competitions, including war. Sport teams have mascots, as do schools. Workers who live in

close proximity, spend long periods of time together, and who are in danger tend to have mascots, too. Fire departments and military units are also good examples.

The mascots most commonly captured on real photo postcards were the ones used in military service. Military men of all countries have kept animal mascots. The practice was especially prevalent during wartime when animals went into the field with soldiers (Keeney 2001; Kramer 1981; Seguin 1998). Mascots were highly prized by Civil War troops. Chickens, bears, dogs, and even a camel held the elite position of company mascot in both the Confederate and the Union armies.

During the postcard era, America finished its engagement in the Spanish-American War, mobilized during the Mexican border war, embarked on World War I, and experienced a military lull before World War II. Early in the century, to demonstrate its position as a world power, the country enlarged and modernized its navy and sent ships to far-off places. A large navy became part of America's military profile. Although animals served as mascots in all branches of the military, they were particularly common during this period aboard navy ships, where they were a pervasive part of life at sea.

Some mascots were publicly displayed as a symbol of the ship they served; they were even dressed up in military attire and marched about during important events. Others were less visible but no less important in building the crew's identity and sense of attachment to their vessel. All were perceived as bringing good luck, good weather, and companionship onboard. They were treated as shipmates, and a special attachment evolved between sailors and their mascots.

The photo postcards taken of mascots with sailors show that these animals were important parts of the crew. In formal portraits done in photography studios on shore, such as illustration 3.1, the animal is typically front and center. Mascots are also prominent in more informal group photos taken onboard. Some of these images were the work of local commercial photographers who boarded ships when they were in port, but amateurs produced many. Amateurs took candid images of daily life, but because of their inferior equipment and lack of skill, their postcards were typically not up to professional standards. Action shots commonly show the mascot as the center of attention. Photographers also posed mascots for individual portraits. Sailors regularly sent these photo postcards to friends and relatives at home, indicating that mascots were an important part of their lives, an aspect they wanted to share with loved ones.[1]

BECOMING A SHIP'S MASCOT

Animals aboard ships were neither officially allowed nor actively prohibited.[2] Navy regulations did not address the issue, so commanding officers made their own rules. Some encouraged mascots, others just overlooked their presence, and a very few banned them (Greene 2008). Even when animals were outlawed, they appeared in secluded places and at opportune times.

Animals were drafted into mascot service through a number of routes. Some officers brought animals onboard knowing that the crew would adopt them. Others were smuggled or openly brought onboard by individuals or small cadres of crew members either at their home port or in ports of call. Also, it was fairly common for cities and states that had navy bases to present animals to ship crews as gifts to support the military's efforts and to wish them good luck. Some foreign governments did the same. These acts of generosity were often accompanied by community presentation ceremonies where the mascot made the transition from land to sea, from civilian to navy life.

Many species served as naval mascots. Although dogs and cats were the most common, other kinds of animals played this role as well, including pigs, bears, snakes, lizards, kangaroos, anteaters, deer, ferrets, turtles, parrots, crows, and goats. Bears were popular mascots during the presidency of Theodore Roosevelt because of the president's association with the teddy bear fad (see chapter 2) and because he launched the worldwide tour of the Great White Fleet.[3] The common name for bear mascots was Teddy. In illustration 3.2 crewmen are posed enjoying the company of their "Teddy."

Goats were another favorite. In early naval history, animals such as goats were brought onboard to be slaughtered and eaten.[4] On occasion, the crew would develop a particular fondness for one, spare it from its sentence, and make it a mascot. Goats became the official mascot for the Naval Academy football team in 1904. This role started in the late 1800s when, the legend goes, a plan to

---

1. It is also possible that sailors sent these postcards because the images softened the war experience, reassuring loved ones at home that they were safe or had playful moments.

2. Internationally, only the British Royal Navy had an official place for mascots by encouraging ships' cats, but in 1975 the Royal

Navy became the first military service in the world to officially prohibit mascots.

3. The fleet consisted of sixteen new battleships from the Atlantic fleet, each painted white. They toured from December 1907 to February 22, 1909.

4. Livestock were kept onboard to provide sailors with food, eggs, and milk, and sometimes pets.

3.2. A teddy bear mascot, ca. 1915. Brian Buckberry Coll.

3.3. USS *Louisiana* mascot Billy with crew, ca. 1920. Brian Buckberry Coll.

have a taxidermist mount the skin of one beloved dead goat was foiled when an officer started parading around during the halftime at a football game wearing the goat's skin. Navy victory that day was attributed to the spirit of this lamented mascot. Billy became the academy's goat's name and also served as the name of many goat mascots on ships (illustration 3.3).

A ship's itinerary influenced the kinds of animals recruited into service. Some species not found in the United States were picked up as souvenir mascots in tropical ports and in other far-away locations. For young sailors, many of whom had not traveled beyond their own states, these creatures were exotic.[5] The mascots represented the adventurous navy life presented in

5. Exotic, wild, or otherwise unusual mascots gave sailors a chance to be close to animals that they could not own as pets for practical and legal reasons.

contemporary recruitment posters: "Join the Navy and See the World." The crew members in illustration 3.4 appear to be in awe of the large iguana mascot they took onboard in Central America.

Monkeys and colorful birds were picked up as ships sailed and docked in Caribbean and South American ports. When the crew of the USS *Arizona* descended on Port of Spain, Trinidad, they found many animals for sale at the local market stalls. Sailors brought back onboard a veritable menagerie, including monkeys, puppies, exotic birds, and reptiles (Stillwell 1991). The USS *North Dakota*'s crew had a similar experience on their Central American dockings. These and other tropical pet-gathering forays are documented on photo postcards.

Kangaroos were acquired as gifts from a port in Tasmania as well as from seacoast towns on the Australian mainland. Illustration 3.5 shows a sailor next to the ship's mascot, identified on the back as a "boxing kangaroo," and taken onboard on the USS *Wisconsin*'s Far Eastern tour. The kangaroo's right paw is bandaged, perhaps resulting from an accident, injury, or even preparation for a boxing match.

ONBOARD DUTIES

Unlike most pets onshore that belonged to a person or family, military mascots were communally owned and regarded as companions by many, even hundreds

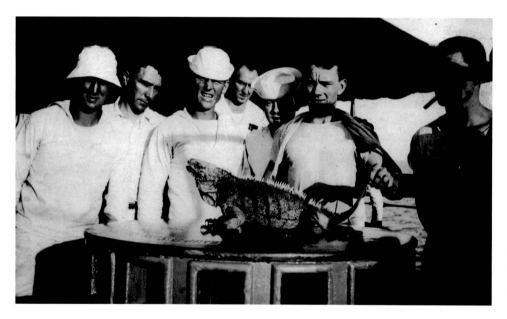

3.4. Iguana mascot collected in a Central American port, ca. 1908. Brian Buckberry Coll.

3.5. Sailor with boxing kangaroo, USS *Wisconsin*, ca. 1911. Brian Buckberry Coll.

or thousands of sailors. Enjoying mascots was not limited to the working sailor; crew members of all ranks enjoyed the companionship. Senior enlisted sailors, officers, and even commanding officers often had their photographs taken with mascots. In illustration 3.6, a chief petty officer proudly holds two kitten mascots for the camera.

Not all mascots served such a large constituency. On a larger ship, a division might have had its own mascot. For example, the galley cooks might have kept their own cat, while the machinist's mates had their dog. Whether the mascot belonged to the whole ship or just a segment of the crew, specific individuals looked after the animal's welfare, feeding and providing a place for it to sleep, often in a sailor's quarters or even bunk.

3.6. Chief petty officer with kittens, ca. 1908. Brian Buckberry Coll.

Illustrating the cooperative nature of animal care, a particular crew member would collect money for a fund to buy special food that a mascot might require. Typically, these caretakers were not considered the animal's owners; mascots belonged to everyone. When caretaker sailors were discharged, they did not take the mascots with them.

More than just symbols and good-luck tokens, mascots served other important functions. Although they were not primarily working animals, a few species accomplished very practical tasks onboard.[6] Cats, ferrets, and in some cases dogs were valued as predators of mice and rats. They were called "ratters." Certain cats were particularly good ratters and earned special pampering as a reward for this service (V. Lewis 2002). In illustration 3.7 the two large cats held by the sailors were likely the ship's ratters.

Some ferrets outdid cats by catching the hated rats in their strong jaws and severing their spinal columns with one bite (J. Fox 1998, 12). Other animals were valued for their cleaning abilities. Goats and pigs had a special reputation for consuming garbage. A 1909 log card on the USS *Charleston* commented that, the ship's mascot, "Bill de Goat assumed his duties as the official scavenger of the Flagship."

Mascots also provided intangible benefits that the crew often valued more than rodent control and housecleaning. They had an uncanny ability to bolster the morale of servicemen.[7] This use was particularly important because of the stressful conditions sailors endured. Stays at sea were long, the living conditions were cramped, ships lacked amenities, and communication with those sailors left behind was limited. Crews in war zones suffered the noise of large guns and the fear of being wounded or killed. The environment challenged the spirits of even seasoned, battle-hardened

6. Of course, the nature of a mascot's military service influenced the functions it could provide. Dogs, for instance, served as army mascots on land and helped to sniff out dead soldiers, track scents, and detect explosives.

7. The morale-raising function of mascots was so important, officers put aside their normal concern for onboard cleanliness (Brian Buckberry, personal communication, September 9, 2009).

3.7. Sailors holding ratters, ca. 1915. Brian Buckberry Coll.

servicemen. Simply being in the presence of mascots and watching their antics was a relief and distraction from the tedium of long journeys, the loneliness at sea, and the tension of battle. A sailor might have a difficult time not smiling when seeing a puppy sticking his head out of the muzzle of a large gun aboard the USS *Georgia* (illustration 3.8).

Mascots provided recreation for all the crewmen who vied for their attention and were friends to anyone who took the time to relate to them. The fact that many mascots had the run of the ship contributed to their popularity. They could visit shipmates everywhere from below to those sailors on the observation deck (All Hands n.d., 78). The bear aboard the USS *Florida* shown in illustration 3.9 amused many a crewman and served as a good buddy to some. In the picture a group of sailors playfully teases a young bear to perform. One of the sailors pictured wrote a message on the postcard's back to a friend stateside: "This is a picture of our bear. It is about four months old; it likes to play and is real funny. In the picture, the bear is trying to get the can in which is milk; he will follow anyone who has something sweet to eat. He climbs all over the ship."

One form of activity aboard ships involved the intense competition between various vessels in fleets over everything from the running of the engines and

3.8. Mascot of the USS *Georgia*, ca. 1915. Brian Buckberry Coll.

3.9. USS *Florida* mascot, ca. 1915. Brian Buckberry Coll.

in some cases animals might have been set upon one another to fight. One image (illustration 3.11) that we came across appears to be a well-organized and well-attended dogfight. It shows a handler restraining his dog as a crowd of soldiers and sailors eagerly awaits the event.[8] Although we cannot draw conclusions from limited and unclear evidence, some mascots may have been used in ways that contradict the kind and gentle care we have portrayed. If true, such inconsistent treatment of animals—being adored one moment only to be harmed the next—has long characterized our relationships with other animals.

CARING FOR MASCOTS AT SEA

Mascots did more than merely distract servicemen from the conditions they faced. With an all-male crew of up to fifteen hundred onboard, a tough-guy, macho culture developed that left little room for tenderness. With animals, servicemen could openly show their softer side, express feelings, and demonstrate their affection without ridicule. In illustration 3.12, a sailor pretends to kiss the ship's dog mascot, as crewmates watch approvingly.

In response, mascots provided servicemen with attention, affection, intimacy, and companionship. Servicemen are seen in photo postcards openly nurturing their mascots, touching, caring, and otherwise tending to their every need. Illustration 3.13 shows two sailors giving a bath to their mascot goat, as fellow crewmen look on with approval written all over their faces.

Beloved mascots engendered tremendous pampering and respect from servicemen.[9] Sailors would go

firing the big guns to the quality of the food and ship cleanliness. There were interfleet boxing and wrestling matches as well as swimming and shooting meets. This sense of competition likely extended to mascots: who had the largest, smallest, strangest, most exotic, or most dangerous animals (Brian Buckberry, personal communication, September 9, 2009)? Most of these comparisons were limited to bragging fests that were carried out in the spirit of jest. This spirit of competition can be seen in the caption in illustration 3.10, where the sailor who produced the image laid claim to having both the biggest and the smallest dogs in the Atlantic fleet.

Competition involving mascots may have gone further than just comparisons. The image of the boxing kangaroo shown earlier (illustration 3.5) suggests that

8. The photo was probably taken of a boxing ring on a ship transporting soldiers to or from France during World War I. The dog in the ring might have been a "war dog" used by soldiers during battles or perhaps an army mascot. Dogfighting might have been used to increase the animal's aggressiveness in combat or to serve as a form of exercise for dogs during long sea voyages (Brian Buckberry, personal communication, September 9, 2009).

9. Although loved by the crew, mascots could be mischievous and cause trouble onboard. Ship's log cards noted, for example, that

3.10. The biggest and smallest dogs of the Atlantic fleet, USS *Florida*, ca. 1915. Brian Buckberry Coll.

3.11. Possible dogfight, ca. 1915. Brian Buckberry Coll.

to extremes to see that mascots were well taken care of. Special sleeping quarters were erected for favorite mascots. Hammocks for cats or small dogs were one example of this kind of treatment. Illustration 3.14

mascots sometimes disappeared, requiring the crew to search for them; occupied off-limit locations like laundry baskets; ate the crew's food; disrupted the crew's work; scratched, bit, or butted the crew; left waste; or were so noisy they awakened sleeping crew members (Brian Buckberry, personal communication, September 9, 2009).

shows a kitten resting comfortably in his hammock, thoughtfully erected by the crew.

Some animals were hand fed by concerned crew members. In illustration 3.15 a sailor bottle-feeds the ship's baby goat mascot.

Sailors thought of mascots as fellow shipmates. A bond develops between creatures living together for long periods of time, especially when they share cramped quarters and a common mission as well as face hardships and dangers together. They become part of each

3.12. Pretending to kiss a mascot, ca. 1915. Brian Buckberry Coll.

3.13. "Billie's morning bath," 1910. Photo by Brown and Shagger. Brian Buckberry Coll.

other's histories. Attributing humanlike characteristics to mascots made it easy for crew members to feel that they "knew" these individual animals and experienced a relationship with them. Mascots were thought of as serving just as their human counterparts—they too displayed courage, honor, and readiness to help fellow crewmen. The result was that some sailors developed deep and lasting emotional connections to mascots, greater than anything they subsequently felt with other animals. Recalling one such relationship, a sailor wrote

of Jim, the dog mascot of the USS *Texas:* "I lost my heart to that dog as I have never done to any other animal" (Schubert 1999, 155).

Crews went out of their way to give mascots recognition.[10] As co-combatants, mascots were considered to be veterans of war, and crewmen were proud to have

10. Since mascots were treated as part of the crew, they were also "punished" in good humor for violating navy regulations. They might, for instance, be given mock trials for running away during

3.14. USS *Wyoming*'s mascot, ca. 1915. Brian Buckberry Coll.

3.15. "One of our mascots," 1907. Brian Buckberry Coll.

served with them. Many mascots were awarded military rank and honors. The ship's company might even feature their mascots when they went on parade.[11] Personi-

fying such contribution is the case of "Tom Whiskers." As shown in illustration 3.16 with its accompanying caption, this cat was considered a "veteran" of World War I, where he was a hospital ship's mascot on the USS *Solace* and then a ship's cat on another hospital ship, the USS *Relief*. Referring to Tom Whiskers as a

liberty onshore and then thrown in the brig for a couple of days (Brian Buckberry, personal communication, September 9, 2009).

    11. When ships arrived in foreign or domestic ports, sailors often marched through the streets. These parades were big events for most communities in the early 1920s and were a chance for the navy to show off its men. In many cases the ship's mascot, sometimes in

"uniform," would be one of the first members of the parade, following behind the ship's banner (Brian Buckberry, personal communication, September 9, 2009).

3.16. "Tom Whiskers—veteran of world war—and still going strong," USS *Relief*, ca. 1920. Brian Buckberry Coll.

veteran highlights the fact that this animal was considered equal to sailors. He was on that vessel when this widely circulated postcard portrait was taken.

Mascots were in danger when at sea. They could be wounded or killed in battle. Even though they were often the first to be rescued, they might go down with their ships. (It was considered bad luck and poor seamanship to abandon a mascot on a sinking ship, and mascots had secure places on the lifeboats.) They also were prone to accidents, like falling down steep staircases or being washed overboard during storms. On the USS *Albany*, one of the goats died because it fell down the chute where ashes were taken from below (USS *Albany*, weekly rough log, December 3–9, year unknown).

Although mascots were pampered, the confines of a ship were not always conducive to an animal's good health. Some mascots died from poor diet and disease. The playful bear pictured in illustration 3.17, basking leisurely in his tub of water while smoking his pipe, died of unknown causes soon after this picture was taken. He was one of sixteen bear-cub mascots presented by the city of Aberdeen, Washington, to the battleships of the Great White Fleet. A former shipmate expressed his grief over the death on the back of a postcard: "This is the Bear that the state of Washington gave us and he died the day we left Japan. We will never forget him. As a shipmate he was added to our death list." When mascots died, they were missed, not merely as pets but also as fellow servicemen. Highly regarded mascots were accorded full military honors when they died while serving, including formal burials at sea.

Mascots that survived their tours of duty went on to lead rather prosaic civilian lives. When they could no longer be kept onboard, some were given to zoos. Others were retired to farms and private homes. Separation from mascots could upset many a toughened, battle-worn serviceman. Although some humor no doubt went into dressing the mascot goat in illustration 3.18, the shipman kneeling to the animal's level proudly, and with regret, shakes its hoof to say good-bye after having served at sea together.

We have covered only the navy in our discussion of military mascots. Although that branch of the armed services was the most active in keeping mascots, other services kept mascots as well.[12] Army units, for example, were known for their mascots. During World War I, mascots hunkered down in the trenches, endured long marches, and occupied cramped tank turrets alongside soldiers. Illustration 3.19 captures a close relationship between an army captain and a crow mascot. Note the expression on the man's face and the responsiveness of the crow. We end this section on military mascots with that photo to remind readers that there is more to the story than we have recounted here and to demonstrate

12. Akin to the navy's official adoption of the goat as their mascot, the army adopted the mule, the marines the bulldog, and the air force the falcon.

3.17. Beloved bear mascot, ca. 1915. Brian Buckberry Coll.

visually once again the importance of close human relationships with animals.

OTHER MASCOTS

Occupational groups other than military units had mascots. Many have them today. The firehouse dog is one that looms large in American culture, both in fiction and in real life (illustration 3.20). Many kinds of dogs served in that capacity, but one breed, the dalmatian, dominated the position.

Although some navy mascots were working animals in addition to having a symbolic function, their jobs were not a crucial part of their presence onboard. It was different for firehouse dogs because they served both as mascots and as workers. An important part of their work related to the history and characteristics of the dalmatian, a breed long associated with horses that pulled large firefighting equipment throughout the early twentieth century. The dalmatian easily adapted to the fire-station environment and to the needs of firemen. Responding to alarms and being on the scene of disasters was stressful for horses. The dalmatian's calming effect on these horses made them excellent coach dogs—staying in their owner's stables and running beside their horse-drawn carriages. Dalmatians provided a

3.18. Bill telling his keeper good-bye, USS *Louisiana*, ca. 1917. Brian Buckberry Coll.

3.19. Captain Pardee and mascot, ca. 1915. Terry Brykczynski and Andrea Miller Coll.

therapeutic companion from the sound of the alarm to the sleep in the stable after a hard day's work. The dogs also served as guards for the horses, the equipment, and the fire station itself. As fire trucks replaced the horse-drawn variety, the dalmatian's usefulness diminished, but they remained as symbols, good-luck tokens, and guard dogs.

Lumber camps provided another environment conducive to having mascots. In the early part of the century, lumber crews established camps in the forest that functioned as the center for logging operations and as the workers' living quarters. The men, and sometimes a few women who served mainly as cooks, lived in these desolate camps for the winter, the season when most logging was done. Rising early in the morning, working all day cutting, skidding, and in other ways harvesting timber, the loggers might return to camp for lunch, but most days they did not return until sundown. Dogs and cats, such as the ones pictured in illustration 3.21, would be there to greet them. The lumber camp's cooks and kitchen crew most often looked after the mascots. They were the ones who stayed at home during the day preparing meals and caring for the living quarters of the laborers out in the woods.

In illustration 3.22 the goat is wearing a cover with the initials "BPOE," which signifies the Benevolent and

3.20. Dalmatian with firemen, ca. 1907. Bryan Hartig Coll.

3.21. Lumber-camp kitchen crew with camp mascots, two cats and a dog, Wisconsin, ca. 1910. Joel Wayne, Pop's Postcards Coll.

Protective Order of the Elks, or, simply, the Elks. This group was a white segregated fraternal organization that existed at the end of the nineteenth century. In 1898 Arthur Riggs, a former slave and Pullman porter who was denied membership in the white Elks, launched an African American version of the organization. The new organization was a duplicate of the old, but they added the word *improved* to *benevolent*.[13] Some Masonic groups, such as the Elks, were named after particular animals. Specific lodges of these organizations adopted mascots that they paraded at special events. As shown in the illustration, these animals were not necessarily the same as the icon symbolizing the group.

We have seen photo postcard images of companion animals traveling with vaudeville troupes and circuses as well. Garages and stores often have pets that are coupled with those establishments. These animal associates hang around particular human groups, gaining occasional attention and favors in return for their simple presence and fleeting friendship. In our search for photo postcards of animals in human groups, we

came across an image of a dog who apparently was a mascot of sorts for an orchestra (illustration 3.23).

THE PUBLIC ANIMAL

The pictures in this chapter signal a whole realm of relationships between human groups and animals that are not adequately covered by such terms as *working animal, pet,* and *companion.* Although the term *mascot* comes to mind to describe these relationships, perhaps a more precise term is *public animal.*

Mascots are public animals in several ways. First, a body of people shares a common interest in them. The mascot's friendship is collectively cultivated, its companionship collectively enjoyed, its care collectively nurtured. In their public role mascots are also the focus of group members' admiration and pride when performing beyond the call of duty as well as group members' sadness and grief when lost in battle or said good-bye to on shore. In addition, group members share a common view of what their mascot means or symbolizes and what can be expected of it. They see reflections of their individual qualities and the group's representative virtues in the jointly owned and cared for animal.

13. The *I* does not seem to be on the goat's cover. We are not sure why there is this omission.

Second, mascots, in their role of public animals, affect the group as a whole. They are very good animals—a synthesis of workers and pets who make contributions, both practical and emotional, that benefit human groups. These animals perform tasks that make life easier, safer, or cleaner for many people. Evidence of the practical side of mascots appears in images we saw of cats that killed rats onboard, goats that ate garbage strewn on ships' decks, or dogs that carried ammunition to the forward gun crews. Photo postcards of mascots also suggest that these animals affected the thinking and feeling of group members in positive ways by representing members as a unit or team, making members feel more cohesive, raising members' morale, and combating members' loneliness. What is interesting about a group's collective interest in and perception of its mascot is that the animal brings together people of very diverse backgrounds in what can be a new community (Tenner 1998), as was certainly the case for sailors leaving port for the first time as novice crew members. That mascots provided these mental health benefits to sailors presages the contemporary interest in therapy animals whose visits provide companionship, nurturance, and stimulation to nursing-home residents, prison inmates, and others (Wood, Giles-Corti, and Bulsara 2005).

And third, as public animals, mascots are available and responsive to all group members, regardless of

3.22. African American member of the Elks with the lodge's mascot, ca. 1914. Coll. of Leonard A. Lauder.

3.23. Orchestra dog, ca. 1918. Private Coll.

number, who come upon them to befriend, pet, or play with as well as to identify with and consider part of the team or unit. By comparison, pets confined within homes or fenced property do not have free rein to entreat new human friendships beyond the immediate family and perhaps a friendly neighbor or two. Mascots are also available to all group members, regardless of their interest in them. Although certain individuals in a group may feel closer to and more responsible for a mascot, the animal truly has a social nature.

But is it inevitable that animals in which groups and communities take an interest are always so warmly regarded? Tables quickly turn in human-animal relationships. As we see in our discussion of vermin in chapter 7, public animals can also be collectively feared and hated.

4

Workers

California Horses just purchased by new Colonists from Nebraska

4.1. Settling California, ca. 1909. Michael J. Semas Coll.

*I*n the illustration that starts this chapter, a team of horses pulls a wagon with supplies for settlers from Nebraska arriving in the early 1900s at what would become the city of Richvale, California.[1] We use it to symbolize all the working animals that labored for humans.

Nineteenth- and twentieth-century Americans and their heirs owe a huge debt to the animals that pulled wagons, harvested crops, built roads, delivered goods and messages, herded cattle, and provided other direct services to humans. These creatures were called various names depending on what they did: draft animals, pack animals, beasts of burden, herders, mousers, guide dogs, and others. We use the generic *working animals* to cover them all. There were many species and breeds that served people as working animals, but in this chapter we concentrate on two animals that contributed most to the growth of nineteenth-century America, horses and mules. To avoid the awkward phrase *horses and mules,* we use *horses* or *equine* to stand for both.[2]

1. Richvale was promoted by con men who sold worthless plots of land to wheat farmers from Nebraska and Kansas. In spite of the trickery, the new settlers made a life there. For that town and others across the nation, horses were crucial because they allowed citizens to build roads, irrigation systems, public buildings, and farms that provided a livelihood for them and future generations.

2. Mules are technically not horses. We borrow the writing convention of combining them with horses from Clay McShane and Joel Tarr's book *The Horse in the City* (2007). In writing this chapter we draw heavily from this book as well as Ann Norton Greene's *Horses at Work* (2008) for both information and perspective. Another equine, the donkey, played less of a role but produced mules

As an unofficial and unintended reminder of the substantial but overlooked contribution equines made to building America, Americans use *horsepower* as the measure of the strength of our engines. During the 1800s steam engines powered the railroad, steamships, and many machines. Energy derived from rivers was another resource. But horses provided most of the energy that moved the country during that century.[3] Their labor helped America to build its cities, farm its land, and fulfill its manifest destiny of exploring, conquering, and settling the West. Humans in partnership with horses determined the fate of the continent. It was equine energy that humans literally harnessed for transportation, manufacturing, construction, timber harvesting, mining, farm production, and other tasks in all parts of the country (Kauffman and Liebowitz 1997).

THE TRANSITION TO A HORSELESS SOCIETY

Work done by horses did not radically change with the eighteenth- and nineteenth-century Industrial Revolution. In fact, the factories and mechanical technology increased the need for horses. They hauled raw materials and finished products, transported people to work, and powered small machines. They helped build railroads and canals (Lang and Marks 1991).

During the first third of the twentieth century, horses were replaced by the main power source of the twentieth century, the internal combustion engine.[4] Like all sweeping technological changes, the complete transition took time. In 1900 the ratio of horses to humans peaked. At that time there was one horse for every three humans (Greene 2008, 41). Even in congested American

cities, the ratio was one horse to every twenty humans (McShane and Tarr 2007, 16). There were 130,000 horses in New York City alone.

By the turn of the century, some forms of transportation that relied on horses were in decline. The canal system that required horsepower to pull barges had been the main conduit for long-distance transportation of goods and people in the early nineteenth century. During the postcard era canals were still in use, and there were even efforts to upgrade the infrastructure of some, but, in general, their importance had been eroded by the railroad. Scenes such as the one captured in illustration 4.2 of horses pulling a barge on the Erie Canal through Rome, New York, became less common.

Another area of early decline in the use of horses was mass urban transport. By 1905 urban horse-drawn omnibuses and trolleys were considered obsolete. The omnibus, a large horse-drawn wagon on wheels that carried twenty to forty people on standard routes in cities or on short interurban runs, was the first form of passenger transportation to be replaced by alternative power sources. Horse-drawn trolleys were similar to omnibuses, but they ran on metal tracks installed on roads. They, too, began disappearing early (McShane and Tarr 2007).

As large cities grew, horse-drawn forms of mass transportation were too slow, caused congestion, and could not handle the volume of people who needed the services. The technology to transform electrical energy into a source of power for trolleys eradicated the need for horses. Although horse-drawn omnibuses and trolleys, such as the one shown in illustration 4.3 operating in Klamath Falls, Oregon, were still in service in small municipalities during the postcard era, by the end of the nineteenth century electric trolleys had almost completely replaced them in large cities (Gillespie 2005).

Declines in the use of horses on canals and in urban mass transportation were minor downturns in American's overall reliance on equine power. Horses were still the main source of power in most sectors of transportation and were a necessary component, if not the major source of power, for industry, commerce, construction, and farming. Compared to steam-powered vehicles,

and served as pack animals, particularly in the West, where they carried equipment and supplies for gold miners.

3. Steam engines were invented in 1775 and were in widespread use, especially in locomotives, ships, and some farm equipment, in the 1800s. Waterpower was important in manufacturing. Still, horses provided all the local transportation and a significant portion of the intercity hauling, construction work, farmwork, and power for machinery in mills and factories (McShane and Tarr 2007).

4. Electric motors and other nonanimal sources of energy were important, too.

4.2. Erie Canal, Rome, New York, ca. 1908. Photo by Brainard. Tom Gates Coll.

4.3. Streetcar in winter, Klamath Falls, Oregon, ca. 1910. Coll. of Leonard A. Lauder.

horses were much cheaper and safer to use for intracity transport of cargo and people (McShane 2001). In 1905 equines were everywhere—on city streets, towns' main thoroughfares, country roads, construction sites, factories, retail outlets, farms, and more. Not a day went by, or even a waking hour, when citizens—no matter their location or social status—would not use or be in contact with equines. This situation, however, would change over the next thirty years.

In 1908 the Ford Motor Company began assembly-line production of the Model T automobile, the first widely affordable car produced in the United States. Ford's move to the assembly line was likely the most influential manufacturing development in the demise of the horse. A few years later low-cost trucks followed. The price paid for horses plummeted around 1916 and never recovered (McShane and Tarr 2007). Aside from a few holdouts—peddlers, junk wagons, and specialized

Hitching Rack, Saturday Afternoon. Commerce Mo.

4.4. Hitching rack, Commerce, Missouri, ca. 1911. C. Trenton Boyd Coll.

delivery services—by 1935 horse-drawn power was a novelty, a thing of the past, old-fashioned. The photo postcard, appearing in the early part of the century, the period of change, captured horse-dependent America and then the almost total replacement of equine power with the automobile, truck, and various petroleum-based fuel-powered machines.[5]

Illustration 4.4 provides a sense of what towns and cities were like during the period immediately before horses started losing ground to gasoline-powered vehicles. The picture was taken in Commerce, Missouri, showing a little girl and her dog in front of a long line of horses tied to the hitching rack on Saturday, a traditional shopping day in small-town America.

For at least twenty years it was common for the horse-drawn carriage and the automobile to be on the same street and for equine-pulled wagons and equipment to be working side-by-side with trucks and other motorized machinery. There are so many photo postcards juxtaposing the old horse-drawn and the new

internal combustion vehicle that it seems photographers understood the significance of the transition and were delighted to catch it on film.

When automobiles first appeared on roads, horses and their owners were not ready for this noisy and intrusive technology. Draft animals were often startled by motorized vehicles and became difficult to control. Jesse Beery, who sold more than two hundred thousand horse-training manuals used in conjunction with his correspondence course, devoted part of his instruction to training horses to deal with the auto problem. Beery also invented and sold special products to help horse owners deal with the change. Illustration 4.5 shows Beery in 1911 demonstrating how to train horses in an automobile environment.

PERSONAL TRANSPORTATION

Substantial decline of horses as transportation did not occur until well into the twentieth century. During the height of photo postcard popularity, outside of cities, people continued to ride horseback (illustration 4.6).

In all parts of the country, equines were still the mainstay for pulling vehicles that transported people and goods. In rural areas and towns people kept their own riding horses and horse-drawn rigs. Until at least

5. Other forms of mechanized transportation beside the automobile also reduced the need for working horses. Trains replaced the draft horses that had towed boats on canals, and engine-driven boats replaced horses that had walked on treadmill-like platforms driving the wheels of paddleboats (Crisman and Cohn 1998).

SPRINGFIELD-STALLION-TESTING-THE-BEERY-SHORT-TURN-BUGGY.

4.5. Beery horse trainer's center, Pleasant Hill, Ohio, 1911. Bogdan Coll.

4.6. Two men and a boy on horseback, ca. 1915. Private Coll.

1910 wealthy people in cities kept stables and used their horses and carriages for jaunts into the country and around urban parks.

The kind of horse you rode or the kind of horse that pulled your carriage was important because, like automobiles today, these vehicles displayed your social status.[6]

6. Until 1920 horse-drawn buggies were a common sight, but fewer people could afford buggies and their equipment than today can afford to own automobiles (McMillen 1992).

Certain horses, because of their breed, speed, color, and comportment, were highly prized. Owning them, along with the ability to afford fancy carriages and expensive outfitting, indicated wealth. Subtle differences, such as a horse's markings or how much brass was on its harness, distinguished upper-class owners from others (S. Jones 2002).

Apparently, Mr. and Mrs. Whiting of Jordon, New York, who are sitting in their horse-drawn carriage in illustration 4.7, were proud of their rig. On the back of the card they identified themselves and their friends, making a point of saying it was "Whiting's horses and carriage." The passengers are all dressed up to attend a local baseball game. The vehicle is furnished with lights, substantial fenders, and a stylish roof. Note the skirts covering the horses.

Merchants, professionals, and other members of the middle and upper middle classes owned respectable but not flashy horses and rigs. Morgans, a type of horse that originated in New England, were considered by many to be the perfect horse because they were thought to embody American values of hard work, courage, thrift, loyalty, and good disposition. Morgans were viewed as smart and reliable, horses that could be counted on to trot all day in good or bad weather (illustration 4.8). They were a favorite choice of physicians making house calls.

4.7. Fancy horses and carriage, Jordon, New York, ca. 1912. Photo by Myer. Bogdan Coll.

4.8. Morgan horse pulling sled, Vermont, ca. 1909. Vaule Coll.

4.9. Light draft horses, ca. 1907. Private Coll.

Dropping down another peg, but still viewed as a better class of draft horses to own, were decent horses used to pull carts for personal transit (illustration 4.9). Individuals often used these light draft horses to get around the city.

At the bottom of the hierarchy were physically flawed horses unfit to pull heavy loads and unattractive owing to age or overwork. Poorer people purchased these preowned hacks. Such horses often received the worst care, pulling loads beyond their capabilities, with less food and water than horses higher in the hierarchy. Their appearance reinforced the low status of their owners.

For those individuals who could not afford to own horses or who lived in population centers where ownership was not practical, renting or hiring horse-drawn carriages was an option. As shown in illustration 4.10, horse-drawn "station wagons" lined up at train depots, street corners, town centers, hotels, and other locations to pick up passengers and take them to their destinations, much in the same way that taxis function today.

Although trains and steamships carried passengers between towns, stagecoaches and other horse-drawn vehicles took passengers to places not served by trains and ships and also carried people from depots and docks to their final destinations.

SMALL BUSINESSES AND INDUSTRY

Some local retailers and traveling merchants conducted their businesses entirely from wagons.[7] Although some had stores, they traveled the streets with their produce and dry goods on board. The ringing of a bell or the seller yelling out a characteristic call heralded their arrival in a neighborhood or town. Illustration 4.11 shows a butcher on his rounds in rural Pennsylvania.

Hauling loads from one location to another within cities and towns, and short hauls between cities and towns, was the work of the horse. All types of supplies, produce, and equipment were transported, including bottled beer from local breweries, such as Radehe Brewing Company in Kankakee, Illinois. Illustration 4.12 shows their delivery wagon. Notice the dalmatian sitting next to the driver.

Horse-drawn wagons distributed manufacturers' wholesale goods to retail outlets, factories, and other industrial locations. Draft horses worked for retailers, delivering produce and other items to customers.

7. Local businesses used small half-ton, one- or perhaps two-horse wagons to deliver merchandise, whereas regional wholesale producers, such as brewers or coal distributors, used large five-ton wagons to deliver their goods (Mom and Kirsh 2001).

4.10. Waiting for the train, Fulton Chain, New York, ca. 1911. Photo by Beach. Private Coll.

4.11. Traveling meat market, Pennsylvania, ca. 1911. Steven S. Cohen Coll.

Traveling salespeople went from town to town and door to door selling their merchandise from horse-drawn wagons.

These draft horses, drivers, and wagons are amply documented on photo postcards. It was common for local businesspeople as well as national companies to have images of their horse-drawn delivery wagons made into photo postcards to give away as advertisements. The preferred composition was a side shot of the wagon on which the painted advertisement and logo of the company could be plainly viewed. Take, for example, the People's Ice Company of Syracuse, New York (illustration 4.13). This image was taken outside the company's office; the caption on the bottom reads "Compliments of People's Ice Co." because it was produced as a handout.

As successful national companies expanded and new companies joined their ranks in the early part of the twentieth century, they used photo postcard advertisements

4.12. Horse-drawn wagon with cases of Radehe beer, Kankakee, Illinois, ca. 1907. Private Coll.

4.13. "Compliments of People's Ice Co.," Syracuse, New York, ca. 1907. Todd Weseloh Coll.

as a method of establishing and reinforcing their brand name. The Borden Company used horse-drawn wagons extensively for retail deliveries. Illustration 2.14 shows a Borden milkman with his horse-drawn wagon making home deliveries. Horses were particularly good in this job because they learned the route and would proceed on their own from the curb of one customer to the curb of the next, while the milkman brought the products to the door without having to climb in and out of the cab. Home delivery of milk and ice were two of the last horse-drawn wagon services to go in the march to a horseless society. These services continued well into the 1920s.

Horse-drawn vehicles were used in all forms of human service, including taking people to the hospital

4.14. Borden's milk wagon, New York, New York, ca. 1907. B. Nelson Coll.

4.15. Ambulance and hearse, Cape Girardeau, Missouri, ca. 1911. C. Trenton Boyd Coll.

and to their graves. The rig in illustration 4.15 did both. The card itself is an advertisement for the Southwest Missouri Undertaking Company. The ambulance sign on the side is removable. The promotional text printed on the back assures would-be users that the company makes prompt calls to accident scenes and to the sick.

Horses were the backbone of many nineteenth- and early-twentieth-century industries vital to the growth and development of American society. Two of these enterprises were lumber and paper manufacturing, both of which depended on harvesting trees from the great American woodlands. Loggers relied on horses to bring logs from deep in the forest directly to saw and paper mills or to rivers or railroads, where they could be transported to factories that made wood products.

The next image (illustration 4.16) shows a fully loaded sled with a team of horses ready to haul the logs out of the forest to a river where they will be dumped on top of the ice, waiting there until the spring when the flowing water brings them to the mill. Lumberjacks had contests as to which horses could pull the largest load. Under the slippery conditions of winter, logging was a dangerous occupation for both humans and their working animals.

Mining was another vital industry where horses served. Miners worked side-by-side with equines from Pennsylvania to Colorado, mining coal and various minerals. Illustration 4.17 shows mules hauling coal three thousand feet below the ground in a Colorado mine.

4.16. Load of timber, Brandreth Lake, New York, ca. 1914. Photo by Beach. Private Coll.

4.17. Coal mining in Colorado, 1912. Photo by Dold and Peacock. Coll. of Leonard A. Lauder.

4 Mule team crossing Tiger.Okla Bridge

4.18. Fourteen-mule team crossing Tiger, Oklahoma, bridge, ca. 1914. Photo by Russell. Coll. of Leonard A. Lauder.

Mules were very popular as draft animals and remained so in the 1920s, when there were more than five million in the United States, mostly in the South (McShane and Tarr 2007). Farmers preferred mules in this part of the country because they tolerated summer heat better and because their smaller size and hooves were well suited for cotton, tobacco, and sugar crops (Sawers 2004). Because mules could work in hot environments, they were also used in mines where temperatures were too oppressive for other equines. On the downside, they were slower and refused to work if underfed, a practice that teamsters commonly used on horses.[8]

Equines were extensively involved in construction, as shown in illustration 4.18—a rural site in Oklahoma where a fourteen-mule team moved heavy equipment to rapidly growing oil fields. Interestingly, horses participated in their own demise, as they worked to improve roads that would better accommodate cars and trucks and set up the infrastructure to extract oil from the ground, providing fuel for internal combustion engines.

8. We now use *teamsters* to refer to truck drivers. Originally it was the name given people who drove teams of draft animals for a living.

HORSES IN PUBLIC SERVICE

Horses also hauled goods and people in the government sector and provided special services such as mail delivery and firefighting. Rural free mail delivery was instituted by the United States Postal Service in 1896, and in 1913 the Postal Service introduced parcel post. Horse-drawn wagons and mail carriers on horseback delivered the mail. The deliverers supplied their own wagons. The woman in illustration 4.19, standing beside her horse, Light Runner, is Lillie Donohoe, the first and, at the time, the only woman mail carrier in the state of Delaware. The card was used by the Illinois manufacturer of her wagon as an advertisement that was sent to rural letter carriers around the country. The message quoted a letter she sent the company praising the product.

Fire departments depended on equine power to get firefighters and their equipment to location. Some of this equipment was heavy steam engines that provided the energy to operate equipment such as pumps. Horses that pulled firefighting equipment had to be strong and fast and have a calm disposition, so as not to be rattled in the tense milieu in which they operated (illustration 4.20).

Horses not only provided the labor to build roads but also kept them drivable in foul weather. In the northern United States heavy snowfall made travel

4.19. First woman postal carrier in the state of Delaware, ca. 1912. Rodriguez Archives, LLC.

4.20. Three-horse team pulling heavy fire equipment, Boston, Massachusetts, 1911. Vaule Coll.

difficult for both horse-drawn vehicles and horseback riders. The snow roller was a popular piece of equipment throughout the Northeast.

Horses also helped to manage roads in another way. In cities dense populations of horses created a sanitary and aesthetic problem by depositing tons of manure on the streets that could create piles large enough to block sidewalks. If not removed, manure would dry and become

pulverized, creating airborne dust that people believed contained tuberculosis germs and other diseases (S. Jones 2002). As seen in illustration 4.21, to control the dust, horses pulled water wagons that would spray streets.[9]

9. Note the caption: "I'm on the Water Wagon Now." The phrase originated at the turn of the twentieth century to refer to a drunkard giving up drinking. A person who had vowed to stop

4.21. "I'm on the Water Wagon Now." Urban dusting wagon, Plymouth, Wisconsin, ca. 1907. Private Coll.

The early part of the century was a time of widespread school consolidation. Before consolidation, children walked or found their own transportation to one-room schools, but trips to consolidated schools were too long to do so. Hence the arrival of the school bus, or should we say school horse-drawn wagon.

Horses aided and abetted the police in many ways. They provided horseback patrols, chased criminals, and, as shown in illustration 4.22, pulled paddy wagons.

Another police function, one that continues today in some cities, was the use of horses to control crowds. Mounted police can strike fear in onlookers and make them disperse because of the show of horsepower and batons and people's dread of being trampled or crushed by the animals. To instill this fear and to command respect from unruly mobs, mounted police prefer horses that are large, muscular, and dark because they are intimidating. Mounted police officers feign that their horses are out of control by shouting, "Watch out, I can't control this horse!" (Lawrence 1985, 133).

Mounted police were often called in to quell violent labor conflicts in steel plants and coal mills in the nineteenth and early twentieth centuries. Police on horseback, such as the ones in illustration 4.23 at the Bethlehem Steel strike in 1910, provided a strong physical presence to handle hostile crowds and mass demonstrations. By calling in twenty-five mounted Pennsylvania state police, Charles Schwab, president of Bethlehem Steel, broke the strike and kept labor unions out of the company for decades.

Mounted horses also policed communities outside the boundaries of conventional government. Marginal groups like the Ku Klux Klan had their own idea of what constituted public service. The Klan had chapters in many American communities and wanted to make its presence known and felt by locals. To appear as powerful as possible, Klan members deliberately exaggerated and highlighted their strength, and the intimidating image of horses helped them accomplish this goal. One way they did so was to create an impression of having many more members than they actually had. Klansmen would march and countermarch very slowly through towns on horseback in single file, unbroken continuity, so it seemed that the parade was not four hundred but

said they would rather drink the dirty water from a water wagon than booze.

4.22. Paddy wagon, Elgin, Illinois, ca. 1907. Coll. of Leonard A. Lauder Coll.

4.23. State police on duty at Bethlehem Steel Company strike, 1910. Private Coll.

four thousand members (Dessommes 1999). Another way they did so was to intimidate townspeople through secrecy. Although in illustration 4.24 the Klansmen's faces are visible, they were often concealed in public, as were their horses' identities. Bystanders watching the Klan parade on horseback usually could not identify riders, even by their horses, because the animals were also successfully disguised (Lester and Wilson 1971).

During the postcard era the American military still had cavalry units, divisions of the army made up of soldiers mounted on horses that would charge the enemy during battle. Although using horses in combat was prevalent in the Civil War, Indian wars, and the Spanish-American War, this use became secondary to transporting supplies and equipment as the United States moved into the twentieth century (Cooper 1983).

4.24. Klansmen on horse-back, Miami, Florida, ca. 1927. Coll. of Leonard A. Lauder.

In the nineteenth century direct engagement with the enemy made some horses heroes, even legends, whose feats were recounted by veteran cavalrymen as well as by current enlistees. Perhaps the most famous cavalry equine was Comanche, who served with Custer at Little Big Horn in 1876, when 225 soldiers were killed. On the cavalry side, Comanche was the sole being to survive. As the story goes, two days after the battle, Comanche was discovered badly wounded. Instead of being shot, the typical treatment for an animal in his condition, Comanche was spared, brought back to health, cared for, and celebrated. By championing the only survivor, the nation was helped to come to terms with the heavy loss of troops (Lawrence 1989a). Comanche also symbolized the end of the era of heroic cavalry charges and the start of an era of a more mechanized army in which horses would serve, though not on the battlefield. Today, Comanche lives on at the University of Kansas, where he, thanks to a taxidermist, stands to remind visitors of Custer's last stand.[10] The photo postcard in illustration 4.25 is of Comanche. It was taken long before the

photo postcard era but was reproduced and sold in that format nonetheless.

Perhaps the most famous cavalry unit was the all-black Ninth and Tenth Cavalry regiments, the so-called Buffalo Soldiers. They were so-named by their Indian foes because of their courage, bravery, and appearance on the battlefield (Leckie 1999). Buffalo Soldiers played a prominent role in westward expansion. They escorted settlers, cattle herds, and railroad crews and fought in two wars—the Plains Indian War and the Spanish-American War. Photo postcards document these units while they were stationed on the Mexican border, while they were in the Philippines, and during their treks from Fort Ethan Allen in Vermont, where they were stationed, to summer maneuvers at Pine Camp, New York.

By World War I the cavalry charge was largely a thing of the past. Battlefields were covered by barbed wire, full of deep mud holes, pockmarked by explosion craters, and guarded by machine guns that easily killed or maimed horses. More than one million horses, mules, and oxen were mobilized for World War I, primarily for

10. The horse's fame also rested on the description of his relationship with his human companion and partner in war, Capt. Myles Keogh. They were remembered as having a remarkable closeness

that some say is an archetypal representation of the universal human desire for unity with the animal world.

4.25. "Comache [*sic*]," sole survivor of Custer's last stand, ca. 1914. C. Trenton Boyd Coll.

4.26. Horses on treadmill threshing wheat, 1907. B. Nelson Coll.

troop transit and hauling supplies, equipment, and cannons. Most cavalry units were officially eliminated by World War II.

ON THE FARM

At the turn of the century most farmers relied on horses for their livelihood. Small family farms were still the mainstay of agriculture, and they would remain so well into the century. Horses were a necessary part of the formula for the successful production of crops. They plowed, fertilized, planted, harvested, and delivered the crops to storage and to market.

Horses on farms and in industry did not serve only as draft animals. Hitched to poles attached to grinding stones or gears, they walked in circles to crush grain and to lift water. As illustration 4.26 shows, they also powered machines by walking on treadmills.

The number of photo postcards depicting working animals laboring on farms and ranches is endless. Each farm in every section of the country had its specific agricultural needs supplied by horses. They might be used for harvesting sap to make maple sugar in Vermont (illustration 4.27) or digging potatoes in Florida (illustration 4.28).

Real photo photographers made house calls in rural areas. Itinerant picture takers stopped at homesteads, ranches, and farms, offering to take photos of families in front of their homes for a fee. Local photographers provided the same service. Because many rural families migrated from their birth homes in Europe and distant states, they were far from old family and friends.

4.27. Gathering sap, Vermont sugar bush, ca. 1907. Private Coll.

4.28. Potato digger, Hastings, Florida, ca. 1912. Vaule Coll.

Postcards were often sent to keep in touch via a visual reminder of the family. The image was sent with hopes that it would convey the message that all was well and the family was prospering. These family portraits regularly included the dog and often a horse or two. Such was the case in illustration 4.29 with a farm family who had settled in Illinois.

The inclusion of horses in such family photos indicates that many farm families were proud of their equines and probably had a close and affectionate relationship with horses. Farmers worked side-by-side with their working animals, often for years, commonly calling them by name and caring about them as living creatures. They were not close enough to be called pets, but they were more than just living machines.

Not all early-twentieth-century farms were the small family type; some were large, verging on corporate, and required large teams of men, horses, and machinery to do the work of planting and harvesting wheat, corn, and other cash crops. More than thirty horses pulled the enormous harvester in illustration 4.30, a machine that included a header, thresher, separator, fanning mill, and sacker. The harvester could cut up to 125 acres and three thousand bushels a day

(P. Fox 1990). These large farms were the precursors of even larger industrial farms that later dominated agriculture. Although some of these farms had their own teams of horses, many used the services of jobbers who traveled from farm to farm during harvest season. With such large-scale production, workers treated horses as machines, much as did teamsters.

Long before the twentieth century, citizens in eastern cities stopped riding horseback for transportation, but it remained a crucial part of people's lives in other parts of the country and in rural America, especially in the West. There, ranchers with large tracts of land relied on horses to help oversee and maintain their cattle. Cattle drives with people on horseback moving cattle hundreds and even thousands of miles to market is part of America's western legend. Women were active ranchers, but men on horseback symbolized the West and represented rugged individualism, challenge, and adventure in the world of the frontier. Although they were merely hired hands, their association with horses and the romanticism surrounding their lifestyle enabled cowboys to be elevated over other people who were just as common and uneducated (Lawrence 1982). We will return to the use of horses on ranches in the next chapter.

4.29. Farm family in front of their home, ca. 1912. Private Coll.

4.30. Harvesting the wheat, Colfax, Washington, 1910. Vaule Coll.

HORSES AS MACHINES

When discussing horses used in urban, rural, and governmental service, we briefly touched on the interpersonal relationships that emerged between horses and humans. Although there were undoubtedly exceptions, teamsters and many owners of fleets of draft horses treated them like machines (McShane and Tarr 2007). Some teamsters owned their own rigs, but most worked for companies. Typically, the boss assigned different teams of horses to employees each day. From the point of view of teamsters and the businessmen who owned draft horses, they were seen purely in terms of the bottom line. The ratio of what the horse produced to what it cost to maintain, feed, and stable it was the crucial factor in whether a horse lived or died. Animals that could do the work were worthy of basic feed and care; the ones that could not were useless and should die.

Equines that were in accidents were killed on the spot. Such was the fate of the horse in illustration 4.31 that would have likely been lame as a result of having his hoof caught in a railroad tie. Most often, horses, especially urban draft horses, did not die of natural causes; they were not put out to pasture for retirement. They were shot (McShane and Tarr 2007).

This depersonalized horse-as-machine approach not only led to premature death among equines but also contributed to their mistreatment by handlers. If horses were uncooperative or could not handle their tasks, they were commonly publicly whipped and beaten. A "how-to" stable manual published in 1912 recommended lighting a fire under horses as a way to get them to start pulling heavy loads (McShane and Tarr 2007). Getting the job done often took precedence over humane care. Regular watering and feeding horses were often neglected, and horses were often worked to death. In the long run this abuse did not benefit the owner. Various campaigns to end animal cruelty and to get teamsters to change their abusive ways reflected such realization. The growth of the anticruelty movement and other efforts to reduce animal abuse will be taken up in chapter 6, where we deal with sick and needy animals.

Most abuse occurred with teamsters, people who used horses they did not own, who did not work with the same horses over a long period of time, and who were at the lower end of the wage scale. In some situations, such as horses used by fire departments and other government services, the humans who drove them were more likely to develop meaningful connections

4.31. Horse with hoof caught in tracks, Galveston, Iowa, ca. 1908. C. Trenton Boyd Coll.

between themselves and the horses. Individual salespeople and delivery workers, those people who worked with the same animals day after day, established personal relations with their animals. They called them by name and were concerned about their welfare. Although we do not know what tasks thirty-year-old horse Old Dock performed for his owner, the eighty-one-year-old Captain Perkins, the card celebrates their long-term relationship—"21 Years Together" (illustration 4.32).

Some horse owners treated their animals more like pets than machines, as our discussion of ambiguous pets revealed in chapter 2. Loving relationships developed between farmers, hunters, and others who relied on animals for their livelihood while forming emotional bonds with them.

SHAPING THE PHYSICAL HORSE

Selective breeding and surgery molded equine bodies and minds to make them more effective machines or better status symbols. The most common and direct intervention was castration or the gelding of stallions. Testicles were routinely removed to increase the strength of horses and make them more docile and therefore easier to handle. Geldings were the workers who lived in cities and other locations where cooperative neutered males did heavy hauling.

By deciding which stallion would mate with which mare, humans could mold breeding stock into specimens that had desirable characteristics, such as strength, endurance, and speed. When horses were in great demand and equine breeding became an industry, stud horses were chosen because of desirable characteristics; they were the best of the males. Some serviced hundreds and even thousands of mares in their lifetimes. Studs lived on breeding farms where mares were treated as foal factories.

Mating was done the old-fashioned way, horse to horse, no artificial insemination, but with some overseeing and help from the human breeders. Although, for the sake of propriety, we questioned whether we should include illustration 4.33, we decided to go against convention because it so graphically documented the human role in breeding as well as the attitudes humans had toward foal production. During our research we saw other real photo images of horses fornicating. These images indicate the degree to which the physical act of impregnation was a taken-for-granted part of equine management and production. It also reminds us

4.32. Captain Perkins and Old Dock, ca. 1908. Steven S. Cohen Coll.

how local photographers documented practices rarely captured by other forms of photography.

Early-nineteenth-century selective breeding was not very scientific, and much was based on folk information. Nonetheless, it produced some of the desired effects. By the mid-nineteenth century selective breeding created horse types with distinct characteristics suited for particular human tasks (McShane and Tarr 2007). Different states or regions of the country became known for the horses they produced: Kentucky for lean breeds well suited for riding and racing, the Midwest for heavy animals best suited for pulling heavy loads, New England for general utility horse such as Morgans, and Missouri for their mules.

Americans were slow to develop their own special breeds; rather, they imported varieties from Europe and then reproduced them in the United States. By the beginning of the twentieth century, imports had seriously declined, and Americans became exporters of horses. They were now the horse sellers.

The Percheron, a particular type of horse from France, is an example of this progression from import to export. Known for their stamina, size, and strength, Percherons were favored in the United States for pulling urban streetcars and other heavy loads. One Percheron named Louis Napoleon, imported in 1851, became a legend by siring thousands of foals and demanding a

4.33. Breeding horses, ca. 1910. Semel Coll.

4.34. Percheron breeder, ca. 1909. Coll. of Leonard A. Lauder.

high stud fee. His offspring were known for their size and pulling power. The powerful and handsome black horse in illustration 4.34 is an imported Percheron named Rotigon who belonged to the Distud family, horse breeders from the Midwest. Note the sign on the barn that heralds the Distuds as breeders of Percheron horses. Although Percherons remained popular well into the twentieth century, new breeds, such as Belgians, made inroads into the draft-horse market.

By the start of the twentieth century, selective breeding substantially increased the speed of trotters and racehorses and greatly increased, as with the Percheron, the size and pulling power of working horses. By 1912 the largest draft horse in New York was double the size of what was produced sixty years earlier (McShane and Tarr 2007).

Selective breeding created competition among owners for the largest, strongest, and fastest horses. Farmers and breeders took their prized equines to fairs and shows to compete and to show off.[11] In illustration 4.35 the owners of a large draft stallion stand proudly next

to their grand-prize winner outside the Oregon State Fair in 1911. The horse, "Bill Taft," was named after the president, William Howard Taft, whose term of office was 1909–13. Taft was the brunt of jokes because he was almost six feet tall and weighed 340 pounds.

As we said earlier, we included mules in our discussion of horses because they were extensively used as working animals in the South and in mines. We bring them up again because their existence is related to our discussion of breeding. Never found naturally in nature, mules are the sterile product of human manipulation. A cross between a male donkey and a female horse, they were first bred in Roman times. Although technically a mule is not a breed of horse, nineteenth-century buyers of working animals saw them as one option when choosing among various breeds of horses (McShane and Tarr 2007).

Breeding, buying, and selling horses were only a small part of the world of horse commerce, supplies, and care. Horses needed to be boarded in livery stables, shoed by blacksmiths, and cared for by trainers and veterinarians. There were thousands of horse-related products, from saddles and bridals, plows and wagons, to feed and tonic that were produced by manufacturers and individuals. The topic is so large and the postcard

11. Fairs were also the sites for horse racing. Various associations evolved, based on producers and owners of specific breeds of both work- and racehorses.

4.35. The grand prize–winning stallion Bill Taft at the Oregon State Fair, ca. 1911. Joel Wayne, Pop's Postcards Coll.

documentation so extensive that we decided not to tackle it here (see chapter 4).

OTHER WORKING ANIMALS

Equines were the most important working animal, but they were not the only species that provided direct services to humans. Other animals performed some of the services horses did, and some provided very different kinds of work. The contribution these animals made to the welfare of humans is extensive. Here we provide a mere sampler of their contribution.

Horses were not the only species to pull wagons and other vehicles. Perhaps the most important after the horse was the ox.[12] Oxen were slower but stronger, cost less, and were in some ways more versatile than horses; females could produce milk, and whatever their sex, they could be consumed, unlike horse meat, which most Americans, like the British, considered taboo to eat. Settlers' covered wagons were pulled across the

country by oxen, and early loggers employed them in the forest to haul logs.

Oxen predate horses as popular draft animals but were largely replaced by equines by the start of the twentieth century. Postcard photographers occasionally captured pictures of oxen at work, although they represent only a fraction of the draft animals appearing on cards. Some cards have captions that suggest that oxen, compared to horses, were an old-fashioned novelty. Illustration 4.36 shows a family with their sod house and their oxen equipped with a prominently displayed yoke, the large wooden collar used to harness and guide pairs. Although the famous photographer, Butcher, printed the card around 1910, he probably took it in the 1890s.

Because of their relatively weak pulling capacity, dogs had limited use as draft animals. Dog teams did provide transport in the snowy northern climates that had poorly developed road systems, such as Alaska and the most northern reaches of the continental United States.[13]

Single dogs were occasionally used to carry light loads and are often shown hitched to carts that pulled

12. There were two uses of the term *oxen*. Some people used it to refer to any bovine (cattle, cows) used as draft animals. Others used it less inclusively to stipulate draft animals that were castrated steers. Colonists and pioneers used *oxen* in both senses.

13. Arctic exploration also relied on sled dogs, and some became famous for playing that role.

4.36. Sod house with family and oxen, Nebraska, ca. 1895. Printed as postcard ca. 1910. Photo by Butcher. Private Coll.

4.37. Fred Vaillancourt with dog team, ca. 1910. Bogdan Coll.

children. Their use with youngsters was more for amusement than transportation. There are more photo postcards of people with disabilities using dog-pulled carriages for transportation than other adults. An example is a series of cards of Fred Vaillancourt, a former railroad brakeman who lost his legs in 1907 in a work-related accident. The card in illustration 4.37 is one of eight or more he sold while touring the United States in his dogcart soliciting money for support.

Small animals pulling wagons as child amusements were popular and commonly found in the United States.

One very common image that appears on real photo postcards is a child in a goat cart. Itinerant professional photographers who traveled from town to town with their own goats in tow took the great majority of goat-cart images. They offered postcard keepsakes. One business, Novelty View Company, shown in illustration 4.38, had a staff of eight who traveled with the group.

Although goats that posed with children were not really draft animals, they provide an interesting variation of working animals. In the history of photo postcards, ponies and donkeys appear in a role similar to

4.38. Traveling goat-cart photographers, ca. 1915. Private Coll.

the goat's, but instead of pulling wagons, ponies have children mounted on them (illustration 4.39). The large number of real photo postcards with children appearing both in goat carts and mounted on ponies suggests that these animals were novelties in the lives of townspeople—an indicator of the decline of real animals in children's daily lives.

Guide or "Seeing Eye" dogs, canines trained to assist people without sight to get about their environment, are an interesting human-animal relationship. The connection between the animal and the owner is complex in that the dog and the human live together and become close companions at the same time that the dog has a real job to perform for its owner. The animal and its owner have to work closely together and get to know each other well (Michalko 1999; Sanders 1999).

Historians of service dogs claim that formal training of dogs to assist people without sight originated around 1916, during World War I, in Germany. Germans trained canines, mainly shepherds, to aid soldiers blinded in the war. After the war Dorothy Eustis, an American dog trainer, observed the German effort and brought the training back to the States, opening the first center in 1929 in Morristown, New Jersey.

What we have reported thus far is the official history of guide dogs. Illustration 4.40 suggests that people without sight used dogs in that capacity long before

4.39. Posing for photo on pony, ca. 1916. Arluke Coll.

the end of World War I. The man in the picture is Mike Shanahan, who lost his sight in a train accident. He, along with his dog, sold newspapers at train depots in the Adirondack region of New York State. The caption reads: "A Wise Dog. He has led Mr. Shanahan Thousands of Miles, N.Y. to Hot Springs, Ark, and Ret. Mr. Shanahan Is Totaly [*sic*] Blind." The caption is written in such a way as to give the dog all the credit for Shanahan's trip, as if the man had nothing to do with it. There are more real photo postcards of Shanahan where other dogs accompany him, suggesting that he trained more than one animal for his use.

Some working dogs were specifically bred for very particular services to humans.[14] The bloodhound is one with a long history in Europe, where it was employed for sniffing out game. Imported to the United States in the 1800s, they were used to track fugitives, including runaway slaves. In the twentieth century they were used to find lost children and adults as well as criminals and escaped convicts. In illustration 4.41 J. A. Landers shows off his bloodhounds with a caption that reads: "On Trail of the Safe Robbers in Grantsville, Md."

During the early part of the twentieth century, some bloodhounds became celebrities because of their sniffing prowess. The most famous was a dog named Nick Carter who supposedly solved more than six hundred crimes. After leading authorities to the body of a little girl in Madison, Wisconsin, the hound Bob La Follet was honored with a studio portrait postcard showing him sitting on a fancy chair.

Dogs also played a part in America's involvement in World War I. However, compared to England, France, and Germany, where more than one hundred thousand dogs were mobilized, the American military did not realize their full potential.[15] Some dogs, especially

4.40. "A Wise Dog," northern New York, ca. 1910. Private Coll.

bloodhounds, were used to sniff out land mines or dead soldiers. Other dogs were pack animals that carried ammunition and supplies. Some served in the medical corps, carrying bandages and medicine to help care for injured soldiers, as in illustration 4.42.

Vehicular and wireless field communication often broke down, and soldiers carrying messages were easy targets, slow, and not agile enough to negotiate barbed wire and difficult terrain. For these reasons, dogs were better at relaying messages than humans. However, pigeons were the messengers of choice—they were the smallest targets and fastest carriers. Both sides used more than one hundred thousand pigeons in World War I, many supplied by pigeon fanciers.

Illustration 4.43 features the most famous American pigeon in World War I, Cher Amie, a bird that

14. There were a number of breeds of dogs that were particularly proficient at herding sheep and cattle, including border collies and various breeds with "sheepdog" or "shepherd" as part of their name. Other dogs guarded livestock from theft and predators. Many mixed breeds performed these functions on farms and ranches quite well too.

15. Many dogs were conscripted from pet owners who expected to have their pets returned after the war if they survived combat, only to find that survivors were shot rather than returned home.

4.41. Bloodhounds on the chase, Grantsville, Maryland, ca. 1913. Coll. of Leonard A. Lauder.

4.42. Jack, military corpsmen dog, ca. 1918. C. Trenton Boyd Coll.

carried out twelve important missions delivering messages from the front. The act that sealed his reputation occurred in 1918. It was then that the bird saved the so-called Lost Battalion of the American Seventy-seventh Division in the battle of Argonne, France. The first day, more than 500 U.S. soldiers were trapped behind enemy lines. By the second day only 200 men were still alive. Two pigeons attempting to deliver messages were shot dead by the enemy. Cher Amie was next. His job was to carry a message giving the soldiers' exact location and informing others at the front that they were in peril. As the legend goes, Cher Amie flew the twenty-five miles to the front, in spite of being shot through the breast, blinded in one eye, covered with blood, and wounded in a leg left hanging by a tendon. Because of the bird's perseverance, 104 soldiers were saved. As a result of his

4.43. Captain of Pigeon Company with Cher Amie, 1918. Anton van Dalen Coll.

gallantry, the French gave him one of their own country's highest honors, the Croix de Guerre. He was celebrated in the United States and after his death in New Jersey in 1919 was mounted by a taxidermist and displayed at the Smithsonian Institution in Washington, D.C., where he presently resides.

THE DREADED COMPARISON

Photo postcards in this chapter capture the work of good animals, those creatures that worked for and cooperated with humans. Postcards also reveal how their masters treated them. Neither beloved as pets nor hated as vermin, good animals did what they were told and served their owners, small businesses, industry, and the community. We saw images of horses hauling

huge logs in frigid weather, mules hauling tons of coal thousands of feet underground, goats towing never-ending lines of children on carts, dogs in dangerous war zones, and pigeons flying over enemy lines while under fire. Humans needed working animals' strength and endurance, but they did not always treat their animals as full partners in work. In too many cases they were little more than machines, worked to death and then replaced. Animals worked hard, suffered, and died for our benefit. The bottom line was not their welfare but ours.

Comparing the situation of most working animals to that of human slaves has been referred to as the "dreaded comparison" (Spiegel 1997). African Americans and other oppressed groups resist having their lives compared to the lives of animals because the comparison trivializes human suffering. Nonetheless, there are striking similarities in the treatment of slaves and working animals in the postcard era. Both slaves and working animals were auctioned off, branded, worked to exhaustion, beaten, abused, and left to die. Ironically, one reason southern planters celebrated mules was because they were perfect animal slaves; they not only worked unceasingly and adeptly in the cotton fields but also appeared to not mind being abused (Renner 1980).[16]

This oppressive relationship—whether of humans or animals—had similar economic and national importance. Working animals, like human slaves, provided an almost unlimited energy resource to fuel America's expansion (Tarr 1999). They were the physical engines needed for businesses to expand, farms to prosper, and cities to grow in the nineteenth and early twentieth centuries.

America's reliance on working animals meant that they were omnipresent. Today many horses spot

---

16. Of course, some owners affectionately regarded their working animals, taxing them less and feeding them better than their more objectified peers. Dogs that led the blind, pulled the disabled, escorted firemen, or served in the trenches with troops were probably viewed as friends as well as machines. However, critics might point out that some slaves were considered members of the family, yet they too were oppressed.

America's rural landscape, but mechanization has made horses largely obsolete as working animals, except for the few that are still used on ranches or in cities to pull carriages for tourists or by the Amish. However, many people still turn to them for other functions. They are pets or ridden for pleasure or sport. In fact, in absolute numbers, more horses now exist in America than there were during the postcard era when they were still a central source of power (Lawrence 1985). Their popularity is a testament to how important they still are to humans for their special physical traits, often considered the noblest of domesticated animals for their grace, beauty, and power. But they also have captured our imaginations, as much or more than any other animal. They are a living symbol of our pioneer spirit and a cherished part of our national heritage.

5

Food and Goods

5.1. Butchering hogs, Ohio, ca. 1908. Vaule Coll.

The most common genus of produce animal, the one that generated more foodstuff for American's consumption than any other, was, and continues to be, bovine. Beef cattle, such as "Straight Goods" in illustration 5.2, were raised primarily for meat but were also an important source of leather and a variety of byproducts.

Dairy cows' primary contribution was the production of milk and other dairy products (illustration 5.3). We came across a number of cards showing farmers squirting cows' milk directly from udders to cats' mouths. The "down-home" appeal of these images made them popular to collect or mail to friends and, today, symbolize a bygone era of the small unmechanized family farm.

In the late nineteenth century pork competed with beef as the meat of choice for Americans (Levenstein 2003). It was the principal raw material for the early meatpacking industry (Skaggs 1986, 5). In rural areas people often raised pigs for their own consumption. Pig skin and lard were important by-products of all hogs, including the ones pictured in illustration 5.1.

Mutton and lamb were not as popular as beef and pork and accounted for only approximately 5 percent of the American meat diet (Levenstein 2003). Sheep were sheared for their fleece, the raw material used to make wool cloth for the manufacture of clothing (illustration 5.4).

Poultry, led by chickens, was another popular source of protein (Levenstein 2003), and chicken feathers were used as stuffing for pillows and garments. Unlike larger animals such as beef and dairy cattle, chickens and other poultry did not need large tracts of land to graze or require heavy-duty processing equipment. Although farmers viewed their poultry as food and income, they also admired the beauty of prize chickens.

*H*orses and other working animals spent their lives serving humans by supplying labor. Cattle, pigs, sheep, poultry, and other domestic creatures contributed to human society in a different capacity. They lived and died to supply meat, hides, milk, eggs, wool, and hundreds of other products to their owners. The bodies and products of these animals were commodities (illustration 5.1).

5.2. Straight Goods, Ewing, Nebraska, ca. 1910. Private Coll.

5.3. Milking cow with cat getting a squirt, Maple Row Farm, Grafton, Massachusetts, ca. 1908. Photo by Davis. Arluke Coll.

The relationship between humans and living produce during the time of real photo popularity was, on the one hand, simple. As commodities, they were produced, raised, bought, and sold for the purpose of feeding the family or generating income. When it came to the treatment and care of their stock, farmers were primarily concerned with maximizing animal production.

On the other hand, the relationship between people and animals used for food and goods was complex. The cold, bottom-line approach was sometimes softened, especially on small farms when people became attached to the very animals they slaughtered, ate, or sold (see the discussion of ambiguous pets in chapter 2). In addition, the production, sales, and consumption of animal

5.4. Women shearing sheep, ca. 1910. Coll. of Leonard A. Lauder.

products varied considerably depending on the type of animal and where and exactly when they were raised and processed. Far greater influences on human-produce animal relations were the changes that occurred in animal husbandry, farming practices, and the organization of the food and animal-goods industry.

KNOWING THE SOURCE OF YOUR FOOD

At the start of the twentieth century consumers knew, firsthand, where their meat and other animal products came from. Times have drastically changed. Recently, a friend told us about his visit with his four-year-old grandson to McDonald's, where he ordered Chicken McNuggets. The friend was flabbergasted when the boy, munching on a deep-fried crispy nugget, asked, "Where does chicken come from?" No matter where you lived in the first third of the twentieth century and how old you were, you knew the source of meat and other animal products.

In the early 1900s close to 50 percent of the population lived in rural areas or small towns where people had direct contact with produce animals. Farm dwellers routinely either participated in or witnessed the slaughtering and butchering of farm animals. The many postcard images of animals, especially of pigs, being slaughtered on farms testify to how common and accepted butchering was. Farmers killing their animals was the culmination of meat production, the finale of their labor, the celebrated harvest. Preserving the moment in a photograph was part of the ceremony. As illustration 5.5 indicates, slaughtering animals was a family affair that children either observed or participated in. Much of the meat that farm families ate came from animals they raised. What they did not eat was sold to local retailers who relied on farmers for their meat. It was no secret where the meat sold in shops came from.

Slaughtering was seasonal in rural locations. In the North meat could be stored unrefrigerated after the first frost in the fall. Before the holiday season farmers brought animals, both alive and dead, to town to sell to local retailers as well as to out-of-town buyers. These market days were public events that marked the holiday season. Illustration 5.6 shows the rear of a buckboard loaded with plucked turkeys. The title in the caption is "Turkey Day, Lisbon, N.Y." This card is one of a series produced of the event that was held each year in the late fall, just before Thanksgiving.

People living in towns and cities bought their meat from local butcher shops or general produce

5.5. Hog slaughter, Abbyville, Kansas, 1913. Photo by Ulmer. C. Trenton Boyd Coll.

5.6. Turkey Day, Lisbon, New York, ca. 1913. Photo by Beach. Private Coll.

stores. Animals sold to local town butcher shops were not always delivered slaughtered. In some cases they were brought to town on the hoof in plain view of the citizenry.

During the postcard era, retail outlets were still neighborhood operations. Although some of their meat was transported from the Midwest, at least some of their meat came from local sources. When you went to buy a cut of meat, even in the heart of a city on the East Coast, it was taken from a carcass that you saw hanging in the shop. Further, many local meat markets had live produce for sale. Urbanites could go and pick out a live chicken that would be killed and prepared by the butcher for your table.

5.7. Christmas card from butcher shop, Sandusky, Ohio, ca. 1910. Don and Newly Preziosi Coll.

The holiday season was a time of year for brisk sales of better cuts of meat. Owners of butcher shops often had the local photographer take pictures of the staff and an array of featured produce for photo postcards that the owner distributed as advertising gifts. In the picture of the interior of a butcher shop in Sandusky, Ohio, a hand-drawn "Merry Xmas" sign hangs on the back wall and crepe-paper decorations hang from the ceiling (illustration 5.7). Meats on display include whole pigs, plucked geese, and turkeys with their heads intact; sides of beef; and more processed meats, such as sausage and ham.

Butchers who owned their own shops, like other town merchants, were well-known local figures who held respected positions in the community. Being a butcher was a standard occupation and a regular part of small-town life. All meat cutters learned their trade through apprenticeships and were proud of their skill, their occupation, and the quality of their meat. This identification with their work is captured in illustration 5.8. The sale and slaughter of unusually large and otherwise prized livestock were moments to celebrate for both butchers and farmers. Very large animals both standing ready for slaughter and butchered were recorded on photo postcards. The elderly butcher

in illustration 5.8 stands with knife in hand next to a huge pig he is in the process of butchering. The caption records the "dressed weight of 506 lbs, a product of Baldwin County, Alabama."

Citizens often marked such prized kills as public events. That was the case with the ox in illustration 5.9. The animal is outside a meat market near Bellows Falls, Vermont, in 1908, and is surrounded by a crowd gathered to see what the caption claims is the largest animal of its kind.[1] Mr. Richards, the market owner, who is standing front and center, had recently purchased the ox. By the time the photo card was printed the animal had been killed and butchered by George Brown, the man holding the creature with a rope.

Richards and other local markets bought wild game for resale too and provided butcher services to local hunters who wanted their game cut and prepared by a skilled craftsperson. Photo postcards of dead deer and other large game hanging outside butcher shops are fairly common, indicating that the public display of local game was a regular part of town life (see chapter 8).

1. Claims like this one should not be taken literally. Such statements were a common boast made about unusually large animals of various species.

5.8. Pig butcher, Baldwin, Alabama, ca. 1910. Joel Wayne, Pop's Postcards Coll.

Chickens and other fowl, such as geese, ducks, turkeys, and guineas, were not retailed in the way we have been describing for cattle, pigs, and sheep. Unlike meat from larger animals, they did not require elaborate butchering, processing, and aging before consumption. Chickens were not exclusively sold in meat markets; in fact, raising chickens was as common in the early part of the century as gardening is today. Chickens required less land and heavy work than did larger animals. Flocks on farms were usually one hundred general purpose–breed hens kept in a poultry house separate from other livestock (P. Johnson 1975). The relative ease of raising chickens meant that they were not raised exclusively on rural farms. Many people keep small flocks of chickens for their own use or to sell to locals. The

presence of chickens in the country, in towns, and even cities was ubiquitous. Rural, town, and even city people were in regular contact with the chickens that produced the eggs they ate for breakfast. If they were not buying eggs from neighbors, people, especially women of the household (illustration 5.10), kept chickens in their backyards, where they were raised to produce eggs and meat for the family as well as to provide a cottage industry (Buckendorf 1993; Striffler 2005). Being responsible for poultry often gave women their sole claim to financial independence. Controlling the chicken money gave the wife some discretion because she decided how to spend this income on the family (P. Johnson 1975).

People in rural areas and small towns saw the cows that produced the milk and dairy products they consumed. Local farmers supplied nearby stores. Families living in rural areas often kept a cow to supply their own needs. Milking was done by hand, which limited the size of milking herds and ensured close physical contact between human and animal. Although town folk might not have directly participated in these activities, they were not far away from where they occurred and were likely to have either experienced them as children or visited friends and family who raised produce animals on their farms or in their backyards. Further, in the early part of the twentieth century milk and cream were processed into dairy products close to where cows produced it.

We no longer go to the local butcher and choose our cuts of meat or see sides of beef and other carcasses hanging from hooks on butchers' racks. Today, meat is neatly packaged before the consumer sees it. Meat is served in fast food restaurants, but their burgers and Chicken McNuggets cannot be identified as coming from living creatures (Schlosser 2001). A similar distancing has occurred for animal produce such as eggs, milk, cheese, and wool. Photo postcards not only document the way it was when animal products came from close to home but also show changes in the production and sale of animal products that made it harder for people to know the source of their food and easier to see farms animals as commodities rather than as individual sentient beings.

5.9. Largest ox in the world, weighing 4,826 pounds. Rutland, Vermont, 1908. B. Nelson Coll.

5.10. Backyard chickens, Pennsylvania, ca. 1908. B. Nelson Coll.

RAISING LIVESTOCK

During colonial times, cattle, swine, and sheep were pastured on unclaimed, unfenced land. In the Northeast this practice was curtailed early in the nineteenth century as land became settled and deeded. In the South the practice lasted longer. During the postcard era there were still vestiges of open-range hog pasturing, as we see in illustration 5.11. Although these animals were free to roam, they were outfitted with yokes designed to keep them out of gardens and other fenced properties.

As settlers acquired titles to more and more land, free pasture diminished and roaming livestock were displaced. People who owned land kept animals confined

5.11. Yoked hogs, Ozark Mountains, Arkansas, ca. 1918. Photo by Hall. C. Trenton Boyd Coll.

within fences and supplemented grazing with feed (Schlebecker 1963). Westward expansion of the frontier resulted in a similar pattern of displacement until stock raisers reached what are now the Great Plains states.[2]

At the end of the Civil War enormous herds of buffalo roamed the Great Plains. By the 1880s they had almost disappeared—victims of hide and sport hunters (Atherton 1961; M. E. Jones 1998, 162). The land was taken over by large herds of rancher-owned cattle. Their grazing land had no boundaries, no fences or markers.[3] Texas longhorns and local mixed breeds dominated the herds. They were known for their ability to survive without tending—they foraged on the prairie—and the poor quality of their meat. Early ranchers sold meat to mining companies, miners, gold prospectors, and work crews, but as the century progressed they began to supply American cities as well (Fletcher 1960). Cattle were delivered by driving the animals long distances, hundreds of miles, directly to market or to cow towns where they could be loaded onto railroad cars.

As the century ended the huge tracts of land where the cattle roamed had been parceled out to farmers who

grew crops, raised farm animals, and fenced their land (Dale 1960). Ranchers also bought large parcels as the open ranges were disappearing. In addition, consumers began to demand higher-quality meat. Ranchers realized that leaving cattle to fend for themselves all winter and subjecting them to long cattle drives was not conducive to delivering high-quality beef to market. A new approach to cattle ranching was required (Atherton 1961).

When the twentieth century began ranchers had completed the transition from open grazing to fenced ranches, where livestock were fed hay and grain during the winters (Jordan 1972). Feedlots, places where livestock were fed corn and grain and other weight-producing food before being sold, became common. Later in the new century a ranch-farm symbiotic relationship developed between western ranchers and midwestern farmers. Farmers bought young improved range stock from ranchers, fed grain and corn to them for a year in confined quarters, and then sold them for a profit (Schlebecker 1963). This last year of specialized production ensured the quality meat desired by more discerning urban consumers. To increase the demand for better meat, dealers tried to move consumers from free-range indigenous breeds to the new feedlot imported breeds. Illustration 5.12 of two rib roasts is a case in point.

2. The West Coast was settled earlier than the plains states.

3. They did not own the land; most of it belonged to the government.

RIB ROAST FROM PURE BRED

AGE 2 YRS. OLD
Gross Weight 1285 Lbs.
Net Weight 774 Lbs.
Weight Rib Roast 9 Lbs.
BRED AND FED BY CAL YOUNG
Pure Bred Short Horn Cattle.

RIB ROAST FROM "SCRUB"

AGE 2 YRS. OLD
Gross Weight 860 Lbs.
Net Weight 352 Lbs.
Weight Rib Roast 4½ Lbs.
EXPENSES OF PRODUCING BEEF ARE
LABOR & FEED. Why not double net
returns by changing from Scrub to Pure Bred

5.12. New and improved rib roast, ca. 1909. Joel Wayne, Pop's Postcards Coll.

A number of activities relating to animal treatment developed during the free-range days of the nineteenth century that carried over to twentieth-century ranching. The roundup was one. Large numbers of cattle spread over thousands of acres of land required some monitoring. Twice a year all the animals would be brought to sites where they were counted, inspected, and sorted. Those animals worth keeping were treated for infection and disease, while the seriously sick and weak were shot. In the spring calves were branded. In the fall those cattle ready for market were separated and transported. Roundups continued after fencing, but they were not as labor intensive as they had been earlier because the cattle were less dispersed and herds were smaller.

Branding was originally instituted during the open-range period. Animals owned by different ranchers mingled together. The brand was a rancher's identifying mark scorched into the hide of the live animal. When free-range ranching diminished, branding continued. Then the brand was used to identify cattle that wandered or were stolen and to establish ownership during transportation and marketing.

Photo postcards document the details of branding and other ranching activities (illustration 5.13). Cowboys on horseback roped each calf and dragged it to the branding area. One person sat on its neck while another

pushed the calf's top hind leg forward. This would stretch the hide taut so the person with the branding iron could apply the sizzling-hot instrument that had been heated in the coals of the fire nearby.

After they had been branded, cowhands castrated young bulls (M. E. Jones 1998, 170). Castration was practiced so that bulls would be easier to manage; it facilitated rapid weight gain as well. A few out of every hundred young bulls, the largest and healthiest, were spared the knife and saved as breeding stock. In addition, when the calf was down an ear was cropped or notched in a pattern that could also identify the animal as belonging to a particular rancher's herd. Testicles and ear parts were thrown in buckets as a method of counting the new stock.

Another activity that often occurred at roundup was dehorning, or cutting the horns of adult cattle. Ranchers did so to reduce injury to other animals, cowboys, shippers, and slaughterhouse workers. Animals were put in a small holding pen, and their hard protrusions would be sheared off with clippers or cruder instruments (illustration 5.14).

An amateur photographer, the same person who wrote the message on the bottom, took the atypical postcard image in illustration 5.15. Pictured is a holding pen used for dehorning with a pile of horns in front of it. The

5.13. Branding a calf, Mandan, North Dakota, ca. 1907. Photo by Holmboe. C. Trenton Boyd Coll.

5.14. Dehorning, ca. 1914. C. Trenton Boyd Coll.

message is unusual in that the author wrote directly of his own experience dehorning and criticized the practice. It reads: "Dehorning cage and the result of one day's work on the ranch. How is this for a scene of cruelty in a state that boasts of protection of decent brutes. Colorado."

Sheep were raised in large flocks and were also subject to spring roundups of a different sort (illustration 5.16). Adult animals were primarily raised for their fleece and were sheared before the onset of hot weather. Many ranches had too many sheep to be handled by

regular staff. Jobbers, groups of skilled shearers who could each complete hundreds of sheep a day, were brought in for this work.

Spring was also a time to review the flock, count the spring lambs, and castrate the young rams. As with other male animals, cattle and hogs, castration of lambs was done routinely. In the case of lambs, some ranches used a technique that seems primitive to current sensibilities. As shown in illustration 5.17, small lambs were set on top of a fence, their legs spread and scrotum cut and pushed

5.15. Dehorning cage, Colorado, 1910. C. Trenton Boyd Coll.

toward the body, forcing the testicles out. They were then bitten off by the worker and thrown in a pail.

BREEDING LIVESTOCK

During the last part of the nineteenth century and first third of the twentieth, ranchers as well as livestock and dairy farmers sought to improve their stock, replacing remaining indigenous and mixed breeds with those breeds suitable for raising higher-quality, more profitable meat. Imported breeds from Europe formed the basis of the breeding pool, but American varieties evolved, too (Byerly 1976). Before the turn of the century, the United States Department of Agriculture created the Bureau of Animal Industry (BAI) to improve animal husbandry and promote superior breeds. The development of new breeds became institutionalized as state agricultural colleges became involved in research and dissemination of new findings. Along with agricultural colleges that offered degrees, special schools that offered short residential and correspondence courses in "scientific breeding" were popular (illustration 5.18).

Scientific breeding replaced the haphazard approach used by ranchers and farmers. During the 1800s breeders tolerated "outcrossing," or producing desirable characteristics in animals without concern for

5.16. Shearing sheep, West Amana, Iowa, 1909. Private Coll.

5.17. Lamb castration, Washington, ca. 1912. C. Trenton Boyd Coll.

5.18. Stock-judging class at a state university, ca. 1910. C. Trenton Boyd Coll.

protecting breed purity. By the early 1900s efforts by breed associations led to restrictive practices that protected breed purity (P. Johnson 1975). Particular breeds became desirable and remain so today. For example, Angus and Herefords emerged as preferred breeds of meat cattle. Angus cattle are a naturally hornless, docile, and fast-growing bovine that produce high-quality beef (illustration 5.19).

Herefords had similar characteristics, but they had horns. At the turn of the century a hornless, or polled, variety was developed and became popular with cattle raisers because they not only had the original desirable characteristics of the breed but also did not require dehorning (Skaggs 1986, 67).

In the early nineteenth century little distinction was made between dairy and beef cattle. However, by the end of that century and accelerating during the postcard era, particular breeding lines of dairy cows were perfected for the purpose of producing large volumes of milk (Byerly 1976). Ayrshire, Jersey, and Gernsey were

5.19. Angus grand-champion prizewinners at stockyard, ca. 1909. Joel Wayne, Pop's Postcards Coll.

5.20. Big Sam, Alva, Oklahoma, 1913. Private Coll.

popular dairy breeds, but Holsteins came to dominate American dairy production. In the various dairy states postcard photographers documented cows that produced record amounts of milk.

When dairy cows declined in milk production they were slaughtered for meat, but their meat was not as desirable as that of beef cattle and brought a lower price. On the other hand, meat from very young bull calves, veal, was and remains highly desirable in some circles. One type of veal, so-called white veal, comes from dairy stock calves that have been fed only milk. Today, production practices including confined housing, antibiotic and hormone use, and the slaughtering of young animals have made veal a high-priority issue among certain animal-welfare and rights groups.

Hogs were also bred for size and other desired characteristics. A. W. Clarke sits proudly astride his prizewinning registered mulefoot hog, Big Sam, in illustration 5.20. The mulefoot is a breed of domestic pig that, unlike most pigs, has a solid hoof rather than a split one. The breed is believed to have originated in the United States from animals brought to the Gulf Coast by the Spanish. They flourished early in the twentieth century but are a rarity today.

Along with cattle and pigs, standard breeds of sheep, chicken, and other livestock came to define animal husbandry. The "Golden Age" of poultry breeding blossomed during the late 1800s and early 1900s. Hundreds of fanciers searched the globe for exotic and highly ornamental breeds (P. Johnson 1975). More economically minded breeders sought the best-producing birds. The marketing of animals bred for specific outcomes became big business. For example, some breeds of chickens were particularly productive as layers, whereas others grew quickly and were ready for market as roasters in a short period of time (Byerly 1976).

Spiffily dressed Mr. Larson, pictured in illustration 5.21, was a chicken salesman who specialized in the sale of the finest breeds of layers. The studio image shows him, sales case in hand, advertising his intention to set up a booth at the Iowa State Fair. Different photo postcards, advertisement novelties, are displayed on each corner of Larson's case. One of them is the image in illustration 5.22. Playing off the double meaning of *laying*—as in laying an egg and laying down—it shows two anthropomorphized hens, one putting the other to bed. The card caption reads: "This is the kind that lays."

Local and state fairs where prize animals were displayed and new breeds introduced have a long history in the East and Midwest. The increased emphasis on quality and more profitable livestock led to renewed interest in these fairs in the early part of the twentieth century, and they flourished (Skaggs 1986, 69). Illustration 5.23 shows a proud midwestern farmer with his prizewinning Holstein that he displayed at a state fair.

5.21. Chicken salesman, Aurelia, Iowa, ca. 1911. Joel Wayne, Pop's Postcards Coll.

Illustration 5.24 was taken in 1910 at the fair in Oneonta, New York. Two farmers show off their prizewinning Dorset horned ram and ewe. While kneeling next to their charges, the two men turn the animals' heads toward the photographer to better expose their curved horns. In illustration 5.25 a group of proud owners of prizewinning chickens displays them before the camera at a local fair.

In many rural areas people appreciated tongue-in-cheek humor. The move toward new breeds and other agricultural innovations was not lost on a number of real photo postcard producers who manipulated photos to create humorous exaggerated images. As shown by illustration 5.26, a tall-tale montage produced by

5.22. Layers, ca. 1911. Joel Wayne, Pop's Post-cards Coll.

5.23. Prize Holstein at fair, ca. 1908. B. Nelson Coll.

William Martin, a Kansas photographer who specialized in the genre, these cards often poked fun at rural pride and the move to modern farming (Rubin and Williams 1990). Typical of the approach, Martin took elements from different photographs and combined them to create the feathered giants on their way to market in "A Load of Fancy Poultry."

LIVESTOCK INNOVATIONS

Agricultural fairs increasingly became venues for selling various animal-husbandry products. For example, stock tank heaters were to prevent cattle water tanks from freezing over during winter months. Another product being sold at the fair was Standard Stock Powder,

5.24. First-place ram and ewe, Oneonta, New York, 1910. Joel Wayne, Pop's Postcards Coll.

5.25. Farmers with their prize chickens, ca. 1908. Aikenhead Coll.

a livestock dewormer (illustration 5.27). The salesmen in the picture lined up in a way that does not block the view of the jars filled with parasite specimens in formaldehyde. This display of intestinal worms was designed to attract farmers to the booth.

There was great demand for products to ensure the health and robust growth of livestock. Larger businesses entered this market. One of these companies, the Council Bluffs Remedy Company of Iowa, specialized in hog remedies that allegedly helped to produce half-ton hogs, as advertised by "one of our users" painted on the building's side (illustration 5.28).

When farming moved from pasturing to grain and feed mixtures, feed industries grew and prospered. As

A Load of fancy Poultry.

Copyright 1909 by Martin Post Card Co.

5.26. A load of fancy poultry, ca. 1909. Private Coll.

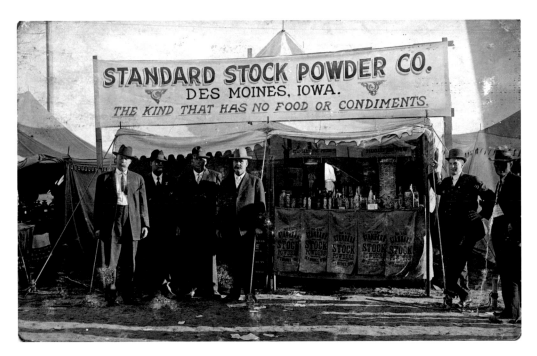

STANDARD STOCK POWDER CO.
DES MOINES, IOWA.
THE KIND THAT HAS NO FOOD OR CONDIMENTS.

5.27. Standard Stock Powder Company at Iowa Fair, ca. 1909. C. Trenton Boyd Coll.

the century progressed, a variety of products emerged to support a new form of farming—an approach away from grazing and local production to production based on manufactured feed. Various manufacturers competed for their share of the market, and salespersons traveled in automobiles and trucks selling their products from farm to farm.

One of many innovations was the development of cows' milk substitutes that could be fed to calves. Such early weaning made cows commercial milk producers soon after birth. A 50 percent increase in average annual yield between 1850 and 1910 can be traced to advances in the quality of feed (Bateman 1968). Illustration 5.29 is a photo postcard advertising Blatchford's Calf Meal,

5.28. Council Bluffs Remedy Company salesmen, Council Bluffs, Iowa, ca. 1920. C. Trenton Boyd Coll.

5.29. Calf and calf meal, ca. 1914. C. Trenton Boyd Coll.

a product that claimed to be the perfect substitute for cows' milk.

INDUSTRIALIZATION

By the early twentieth century the industrial model had taken hold of animal production, and by the late 1930s the model was on its way to dominating the way we eat. The industrial approach meant large-volume operations, centralization of processing and sales, assembly-line handling, and far-flung retailing products. The large Armour plant in illustration 5.30 is emblematic of this industrial model.

As we have said, the transition from local to industrial meat production started before the postcard era was under way. A number of factors moved America in the industrial direction in the late nineteenth century and continued into the twentieth. As cities grew, population

5.30. Armour plant, St. Paul, Minnesota, 1919. Bogdan Coll.

density increased, especially in the East, and the local supply model just could not meet growing demands. Another factor was that the grazing land of the prairie states had the capacity to sustain very large herds of beef cattle and sheep that could supply the urbanizing population (Dale 1960). Midwestern farmers developed the capacity to do the same for hogs. Ranchers and farmers saw the opportunity for large profits and took advantage of their open spaces. The third factor was the railroad. Having expanded across the country, the rail system could provide trains to bring animals raised in the West and Midwest to meat-processing plants in large cities to be slaughtered and processed (Schlebecker 1963); the Union Pacific stock car in illustration 5.31 is a case in point.

The development of refrigerated railroad cars toward the end of the nineteenth century made railroad transport an even greater enabler of industrialization (White 1986). This innovation eliminated the need to ship live animals across the country. Livestock could be shipped shorter distances to meatpacking centers where they were slaughtered and dressed before being shipped by rail across the country. This improvement limited the death of cattle in transit and reduced the cost of shipping.[4] Soon the West and Midwest were dotted with meatpacking plants.

The card in illustration 5.32 was sent by a Swift meatpacking employee in 1908 to a friend back home to show him what it was like in a Chicago meatpacking plant. The photo shows a skilled worker butchering a hog. In addition to those workers who actually did the killing and butchering, there were many unskilled assistants who led the animals to slaughter, moved and positioned the meat, removed the intestines, cleaned up the blood, and washed the carcasses (R. Horowitz 2006). They can be seen in the background. In the employee's message, he is not critical of the operation; in fact, after he proudly reports that they killed two thousand hogs a day "on the killing floor" of his building, he invites his hometown friends to visit.[5]

By the start of the twentieth century many companies were involved in transforming meat from a local product to an industrial good. Two companies that are now household names stand out in the change: Amour and Swift.[6] Both came to prominence in the 1870s and

4. The sale, slaughter, and butchering of livestock also became less seasonal.

5. Apparently, two thousand a day was not an exceptional number. Skaggs reports that large plants processed three to five hundred an hour (1986, 127).

6. Armour, along with other meatpackers, set up the National Packing Company to fix prices, divide the market, and fight efforts to unionize the workers. The Supreme Court ordered the group to disband the monopoly in 1905. Gustavus Swift is credited with developing the refrigerated railroad car. Although he met with resistance

5.31. Loading sheep, New Salem, North Dakota, 1910. Photo by Holmroe and White. Private Coll.

documents Armour paying record prices in 1912 for steers in the Chicago stockyards. Note the huge area in the background that holds cattle waiting to be sold and then slaughtered.

In 1906 Upton Sinclair published *The Jungle*, a muckraking classic that described the working conditions in these early plants. Although Sinclair and others revealed worker exploitation in the meatpacking industry as well as unsanitary conditions, these authors were not moved to comment on the treatment of animals.[7] Despite silence on this issue, there were many shocking instances of cruelty by today's standards. Cattle were hit in the head with sledgehammers to stun them. The creatures' hind legs were then hooked to a moving chain. Hanging upside down, still alive, their throats were cut and then they were bled. Hogs missed the sledgehammer step. Instead, a chain attached to a conveyor rail was looped around their back leg, lifting the hogs into the air. Squealing, they approached the "sticker" who severed their carotid artery that eventually ended their lives (Skaggs 1986, 125).

Besides the image in illustration 5.35, we did not encounter any candid interior images of large processing plants taken by local photographers. Plant owners were under attack by reformers and were not open to having outsiders with cameras shoot their operations. Meatpackers such as Swift and Armour mounted publicity campaigns to counter negative portrayals (Levin 2001). Some of their propaganda was in the form of photo postcards, but bulk production for wide distribution required that images be printed rather than photographed. However, Swift did a series of sanitized, touched-up, and otherwise manipulated photo postcards to show the cleanliness of the operation as well as the good working conditions. Ironically, one in the series showed the stables where the draft horses that pulled delivery wagons were kept in luxurious quarters. The condition shown for the horses greatly exceeded the well-being of the

early 1880s and were instrumental in Chicago's Union Stock Yards becoming the center of the American meatpacking industry (Wade 1987). They were two of the first to employ assembly-line techniques in their factories or, more accurately, "disassembly"-line techniques (quoted in Burt 2006, 124). Illustration 5.33 shows the final stage of the disassembly of a pig—a window display of ham for sale that is labeled an Armour product.

They were the big players in buying premium livestock from all over the country. Illustration 5.34

from local butchers on the East Coast who questioned the safety of dressed meat being transported over long distances, he was successful in setting up a nationwide distribution system.

7. Nor were people particularly concerned about alleviating the plight of migrant workers in these factories. Improving the quality of meat was much more important to the public than improving the horrific working conditions of the meatpacking industry (Burt 2006).

5.32. Interior of meat-packing plant, Chicago, Illinois, 1908. C. Trenton Boyd Coll.

5.33. Armour ham for sale in shop window, ca. 1908. Joel Wayne, Pop's Postcards Coll.

workers, not to mention the cattle and hogs being processed nearby. The series of postcards was an attempt to rebut the attacks made on meatpackers by muckrakers for the poor sanitary conditions animals faced and the horrific assembly-line environment workers endured. Illustration 5.35 was meant to show that the conditions in the Swift meatpacking plants were fine.

Industrialization of cattle, hog, and sheep production grew quickly during the first third of the twentieth century. Small growers and processors continued to dominate chicken production and processing until the 1930s. Although there was some movement toward larger poultry producers, these operations were minuscule compared to the larger animal operations.

HIGHEST PRICED TWO LOAD STEERS EVER SOLD UPON AN OPEN MARKET AUG 21-1912 SOLD BY CHAS.H.WOOD OF WOOD BROS C° FED AND SHIPPED BY R.E. % A.L.HILL MORRISONVILLE ILL. BOUGHT BY ARMOUR & C° AVG WGT. 1531 PRICE 10⁶⁰ PER CWT.

5.34. Highest-priced steers bought by Armour, 1912, Chicago, Illinois. Vaule Coll.

Beef Dressing Department
Swift & Company

F.R. 238

5.35. Swift Dressing Department, Chicago, Illinois, ca. 1910. C. Trenton Boyd Coll.

Illustration 5.36 shows a Pennsylvania chicken farmer standing with his flock. The chicken coops are to the right. Either the owner had the card produced as an advertisement or the local photographer took the view to sell the cards to town merchants. In either case, the caption suggests that the large scale of production was unusual for the time, something to boast about. It reads: "Pride of the Valley, Poultry farm. Raised 1,500 Chickens on ½ acre." The appearance of farms like "The Pride of the Valley" indicates that flocks were growing larger and larger and chicken processing was moving from a "mom-and-pop" enterprise to a factory model.

In another postcard (illustration 5.37), a group of men is plucking chickens in the poultry department at the North American Storage Company in Alexandria,

5.36. "Pride of the Valley poultry farm. Raised 1,500 Chickens on ½ Acre." Scheeklyville, Pennsylvania, ca. 1910. Photo by Welsh. Private Coll.

5.37. Poultry Department, North American Storage Company, Alexandria, Minnesota, ca. 1915. Semel Coll.

Minnesota. Judging from the feathers on the floor, they must have processed a large number of chickens using old-fashioned methods rather than a mechanized disassembly line.

After World War II the poultry business evolved into an industry in which a few companies accounted for most of the country's chicken production. Feed mills, hatcheries, farms, slaughterhouses, and processing plants were consolidated into huge conglomerates that managed all stages of production.

Ambiguity surrounded the treatment of certain species, though. Rabbits were both popular house pets and raised to be killed to supply fur for the garment industry and meat for consumption. Rabbit fur became fashionable in hat design as well as trim on coats. Rabbit meat was more popular in the first third of the twentieth century than it is today. During World War I and the Great Depression, as well as during World War II, the government encouraged people to raise rabbits for their own table and to supply soldiers.

The Flemish giant rabbit (males can grow to twenty-two pounds), the breed shown in illustration 5.38, was imported to the States in the early 1890s and began appearing in livestock shows around 1910. The National Federation of Flemish Giant Rabbit Breeders, formed in 1916, promoted the breed. It is referred to as a "universal breed" suitable for eating, fur production, and pet keeping. The man in the illustration poses with his prizewinning Flemish giant outside his rabbit coop at the "Imperial Rabbit Farm" in Owaosso, Michigan. Illustration 5.39 shows Mr. Fenner in his rabbitry checking on the growth of his rabbit crop in Pennsylvania. However, raising rabbits for meat declined after World War II, saving it from the industrialization experienced by other meats.

Industrialization also occurred among dairy farmers. During the early years of the postcard era, creameries dominated milk processing. Farmers brought small quantities of milk in cans to these local centers that dotted the landscape. In addition, there were small-scale cheese producers close by. The Borden Company has its origins in the nineteenth century as a manufacturer of condensed milk. In the early decades of the twentieth century it expanded rapidly, buying local dairies, ice cream manufacturers, and other producers of dairy products.

As refrigeration replaced ice as a method of cooling, dairy products could be stored, shipped, and sold bottled in stores. Starting in the East and extending across the country, by the 1920s Borden and other large companies dominated the industry. Despite this dominance many areas had regionally based dairy industries that continued to function. Although companies like Borden dabbled in farming, they mainly bought milk from small family farms.

Between 1900 and 1920 several companies manufactured milking machines, but they were poorly designed and not widely used. However, in the 1920s improved machines reached the market, and in the 1930s and 1940s they became more common (illustration 5.40). By

5.38. Prize Flemish rabbit, Owaosso, Michigan, ca. 1912. Aikenhead Coll.

the 1930s milk cans began to be replaced by bulk tanks for storage. Dairies evolved from small farms with only a few cows to operations with larger herds.

THE INDUSTRIALIZATION OF LIVING CREATURES

Discussions of the industrialization of American agriculture usually focus on the economic impact of this sweeping change on farming and how it altered rural America. Small, labor-intensive family-owned farms that produced an assortment of animals were replaced by large, mechanized operations that concentrated on single animal products (Dimitri, Effland, and Conklin 2005). Images in this book of local butchers, backyard flocks, children posing with their farm animals, and farmers slaughtering their own hogs document a rural past that was on the path to obscurity. As economic power shifted from small farm owners to large

5.39. Fenner's rabbitry, Boyertown, Pennsylvania, 1911. Maslan Coll.

5.40. Surge bucket milking machine, ca. 1932. C. Trenton Boyd Coll.

companies, the number of family farms declined and the ones that survived lost their autonomy in exchange for easy access to the mass market (Pew Commission on Industrial Farm Animal Production 2008). Because of these changes, American agriculture became more efficient and fueled the country's twentieth-century growth. Human-animal relations paid the price (Pollan 2006).

Beyond its economic significance, the implementation of the industrial model influenced almost every aspect of human and animal life. This point was documented in photo postcard images of animals, human workers, and the changing face of America. Brutal slaughterhouse killing was only one part of the complex and extensive picture of the disregard for animal welfare, or what Jonathan Burt calls a "cumulative horror" (2006, 121). Increasing reliance on an industrial model transformed animal bodies into sellable products, changing how humans both interacted with and thought about animals. Americans changed grazing living creatures into stock that were confined to small spaces and fed a foreign diet, slaughtered, and turned into carcasses and finally into packaged meat.[8] For most Americans, especially those persons living in urban areas, contacts with produce animals became limited to wrapped meat in retail stores. As animals became things to consume, it became harder to think of them as living creatures. The image of the Armour ham is a case in point (see illustration 5.33). This growing distance between living animals and finished products reflected our culture's increasing exploitation and domination of animals, a process that firmly took hold and even accelerated during the photo postcard period.

Although we currently live in a world with a huge gap between consumers and animals used for meat and goods, Americans express more concern with animal rights and the abuses of the animal-produce industry than ever before. In recent years some Americans have started a "buy local" movement. Inherent in its proponents' point of view is a critique of the industrial approach to farming and other aspects of the produce-animal industry. Accelerated by the rising cost of fuel, consumers are beginning to see that the industrial model is not good for humans, animals, the environment, or the economy (Mason and Finelli 2006). Although this chapter does not provide an answer to the questions people are raising about the way we eat, it does remind us of a time when produce animals were raised closer to home and how we got to where we are.

The big question this chapter raises is how such large-scale, systematic, and brutal alienation of humans and animals was allowed. We have already addressed how the very process of industrialization distanced humans from animals. The notion of "out of sight, out of mind" offers some explanation. Another factor was the concept of industrialization itself. As Americans

moved into the twentieth century, they were enthralled with ideas of efficiency, productivity, large-scale production, and assembly-line organization. These characteristics of modern industry influenced the character of all American businesses from automobile manufacturing to animal processing (Licht 1995). In addition, having grown up around farm-animal slaughtering, killing of animals for substance was taken for granted. Although there was some concern for the humane treatment of working horses, the public's consciousness about and concern for animal welfare in general was minimal. The fledgling American humane movement was more concerned with protecting animals in scientific laboratories and working animals that were abandoned and abused than it was with farm animals (Frazer, Mench, and Millman 2001).

Ironically, probably another factor behind the emergence and tolerance of industrial brutality toward farm animals was the growing closeness felt by middle-class Americans to one kind of animal, pets (Grier 2006). Owners expressing love and kindness to pets allowed them to see themselves as humane. At the same time, they turned their backs on farm animals, dismissing them as commodities unworthy of concern.

8. By the 1930s hog producers referred to their animals as "machines" (Mayda 2004, 21).

6

Patients and Needy

6.1. Dr. Sass, veterinary surgeon, Toledo, Ohio, ca. 1914. C. Trenton Boyd Coll.

People exploited animals for their own gratification in most of the human and animal relationships we have described thus far. In this chapter we look at animals as patients and as objects of humanitarian concern. We focus on veterinarians' services as well as humane workers' efforts to prevent the mistreatment of animals. Although veterinarians also championed humane care, they often compromised that concern in their own practice. After all, veterinarians had to make a living, and animal owners paid the bills. What owners wanted was not always compatible with the well-being of their animals.

American veterinarians experienced exciting times during the late nineteenth and early twentieth centuries. Their occupation was beginning to professionalize and gain respectability. There were medical discoveries to observe and implement. Pasteur proved that anthrax in cattle and sheep, cholera in chickens, and other similar diseases of animals could be prevented by vaccination. Antibiotics, anesthesia, and aseptic operating conditions were being introduced.

Times were not as good for animals. Despite scientific advances, many animals suffered and died because of lack of effective treatment. Veterinarians and other animal caretakers often failed to bring relief and to heal their patients (Stalheim 2003). Even the best veterinarians did not know how to address some diseases. In addition, their service was not available to all, and their fees were too high for the budgets of many owners. Hogs had cholera; cattle got tuberculosis, brucellosis, and anthrax; and horses died from the mysterious "bottom disease." Crowding and other conditions associated with industrial livestock production facilitated the spread of diseases and exacerbated other medical problems.

Technological and other societal changes resulted in dramatic shifts in veterinary practice. The rise of the automobile threatened the profession that focused on caring for working horses. As lumberyards, dairies, construction crews, coal-and-ice companies, movers, and retail stores turned to cars and trucks for transportation, "horse doctors" were no longer needed. Engine-driven combines and thrashers required mechanics, not veterinarians. The same was true for a wide variety of previously horse-driven machines and vehicles (Thompson 1984).

The need for equines declined, but Americans were still dependent on other animals. At the start of the new century and with the trend toward more scientific animal husbandry for produce animals, veterinarians were increasingly called upon to care for cattle, sheep, pigs, and poultry. Later in the century, as urban pets became more common in people's lives, the care of small companion animals became central to the profession.

Some of the trends we have been discussing are evident in illustration 6.1. Dr. Sass poses in his new automobile in front of the facade of his extensive veterinary facility. Earlier, the sign would have read "Horse Hospital," not "Horse and Dog Hospital," and his patients would have been exclusively equines. Dr. Sass sits solidly in the middle of the transitions from the age of horsepower to the gasoline engine and from large animal veterinary medicine to companion animals.

THE BIRTH OF THE AMERICAN VETERINARY PROFESSION

For much of the nineteenth century animal owners did not employ formally trained veterinarians to care for their creatures. Few trained veterinarians were available, and their fees were high. Owners typically treated their own animals or relied on friends, employees, or townspeople who had practical experience. Most were fatalistic about their ability to effectively treat certain diseases and injuries; owners regularly "put down" their animals or "let nature take its course."

There were people who had no real formal credentials who called themselves horse (also known as "hoss") doctors or animal doctors. These practitioners were a far cry from what we now think of as veterinarians, but they set broken bones, helped with difficult deliveries, and tried to cure the "fever" and other diseases. Blacksmiths who shoed horses, or farriers, provided some of this early veterinary care. Years of experience working with horses taught them more than how to shoe an animal and file its teeth. Illustration 6.2 shows a blacksmith holding a "nail ripper," used to remove the nails that secured shoes to horses' hooves. His toolbox also included a horse tooth rasp and other instruments that helped him deal with various horse maintenance concerns as well as with medical problems.

Farmers and ranchers learned about the ailments and injuries of horses and livestock by observing their own animals. Illustration 6.3 shows a self-taught farmer using a dosing syringe to inject some sort of herbal or patent medicine into the sick horse's mouth. The medicine jar and the box holding the syringe can be seen in the photo. The sick horse is unrestrained as it lies in a field. The man to the left in the picture is holding a shotgun, the treatment of last resort.

On farms, in liveries, and in other places where horses were common, a hired hand sometimes took on responsibility for caring for sick animals. In illustration 6.4 the workman wearing a laborer's hat and smoking a clay pipe is using a dosing syringe to administer a pill to a horse. His surroundings suggest that he was working in a ship's hold, perhaps a boat on a river, canal, or one of the Great Lakes.

Until the postcard era anyone could hang out a shingle claiming to be a "veterinarian." There was no licensing or legal regulation of the work. Some practitioners were charlatans, but others developed considerable expertise (Smithcors 1975). A few became widely known just for doing particular procedures, such as horse castration, and appeared to be as proficient, or even better, than many legitimately trained veterinarians.

6.2. Blacksmith at work, ca. 1910. C. Trenton Boyd Coll.

6.3. Farmer veterinarian, ca. 1907. C. Trenton Boyd Coll.

Toward the end of the nineteenth century formally trained veterinarians banded together to stop untrained interlopers from treating animals. To regulate veterinary education and enforce their role as animal experts, veterinarians formed, in 1863, the United States Veterinary Medical Association and, in 1884, the government Bureau of Animal Industry. The USVMA changed its name to the American Veterinary Medical Association (AVMA) in 1898.[1] These bodies

1. Its membership now exceeds sixty thousand.

6.4. Worker veterinarian, ca. 1907. C. Trenton Boyd Coll.

labeled nongraduate practitioners "quacks" and tried to eliminate their practice.

During this period increasing numbers of practitioners who called themselves veterinarians received their formal training in schools of veterinary medicine.[2] By 1900 about 40 percent of the approximately eighty-two hundred veterinarians in America graduated from North American veterinary colleges, although fewer than 5 percent belonged to the AVMA (Dunlop and Williams 1996). Most of these schools were privately owned. By 1913 eleven private veterinary schools existed of varying educational quality along with several academically sound programs at state universities and land-grant colleges. Despite the growing importance of veterinary training, graduates still had to compete with nongraduates for customers (Smithcors 1975).

Veterinary colleges required students to take lecture classes and work in laboratories. Accredited schools required courses in anatomy, pathology, and bacteriology, thereby ensuring that veterinary education would be based on laboratory science. This emphasis made it possible for graduates to care for animals and to act as qualified meat inspectors and scientists as well (S. Jones

2002). The crucial role of the horse in society ensured that the care of those animals would be emphasized in veterinary training until after World War I.

Illustration 6.5 shows what must have been a familiar scene at every veterinary college of this era. A student sits in a classroom devoted to horse anatomy filled with teaching aids, such as a horse's skeleton, skull, and various diagrams of its musculoskeletal and gastrointestinal systems. In this case, it was the veterinary training course at Fort Riley, Kansas.

Study of these anatomical drawings and models was a prelude to dissecting real bodies in gross-anatomy class. Cutting into dead animals was considered the best way for veterinary students to understand the structure and function of the body in ways that textbooks, diagrams, and models could not explicate. Students got to work on "real" patients, albeit dead. As a rite of passage, they had the opportunity to act like surgeons slicing through skin, spreading ribs, cracking bones, and removing organs. Cadaver dissection was sometimes a messy process because noxious body fluids were everywhere, but students were proud to get dirty because it was a vivid reminder that they were becoming veterinarians. In illustration 6.6 long blood-spattered lab coats covering dress shirts and ties suggest that the students performed the dissection shortly before the photograph was taken. They appear to know

2. Veterinarians who did not receive formal training could still practice if they could pass the state veterinary board examination.

6.5. The anatomy of the horse, Fort Riley, Kansas, 1915. Don and Newly Preziosi Coll.

6.6. Veterinary students with horse cadaver, ca. 1909. C. Trenton Boyd Coll.

that they have entered a special fraternity of experts, the satisfaction of which is suggested by the wry smile on the student's face on the far left.

It is not by chance that all the above images show only male students. It was highly unusual for women to attend veterinary school at the beginning of the twentieth century (Slater and Slater 2000). Veterinary work was dirty and physical, more akin to being a farmhand than

a professional. The label of "unladylike" was attached to those women entering the profession (Drum and Whiteley 1991; Lawrence 1997b). This stigma is exemplified by the following quote from an 1897 editorial in the *American Veterinary Review:* "No lady . . . would like to perform these operations which are almost daily work of the veterinary practitioner . . . [unless she] is prepared to unsex herself completely" (quoted in Brahm

6.7. Cornell veterinary graduation class with Florence Kimball, Ithaca, New York, 1910. C. Trenton Boyd Coll.

2003, 37). Until the 1940s the AVMA openly denied admission to women, and as late as the 1970s some veterinary school deans did the same (S. Jones 2002). Bias against women practicing veterinary medicine is still seen today among some ranchers and farmers.

Women first entered veterinary colleges as early as 1898. Most were enrolled in private schools that have long been out of business. Illustration 6.7 shows a lone female standing on the left among her fellow male veterinary students, as they pose for a 1910 graduate-class portrait at Cornell University. Now considered a veterinary "pioneer," her name was Florence Kimball, the first female graduate of a state-supported veterinary school. Dr. Kimball graduated with twenty-one men in her class. She returned to her native Massachusetts where she opened an unusual practice for the time, a small-animal hospital. The horse in the picture is wearing a cover with the class date in bold, 1910.[3]

REIGN OF THE HORSE DOCTOR

As we have discussed, at the turn of the century veterinarians spent most of their time treating horses. Horses were worth more than other animals to owners, so they

were more likely to seek veterinary care for them (S. Jones 2002). In many ways, the work life of a "horse doctor" was a lot like the proverbial country physician. Their occupation was certainly respectable, but they were a far cry from being elite professionals. Like country physicians, rural veterinarians did not make much money and survived by making house calls. Some bartered for their services, getting vegetables or even livestock instead of money. And like country physicians, horse doctors were solo practitioners who worked long hours.

It was difficult if not impossible to bring horses to veterinarians' clinics. They were just too big to transport. Veterinary ambulances that could accommodate horses were rare. Farms and ranches were far from town, so veterinarians had to drive great distances to see their patients. Until the introduction of the automobile, veterinarians traveled by horse and buggy to make house calls. In illustration 6.8, Dr. C. H. Powell sits atop his mule-driven cart on his way to visit ailing animals.

Once veterinarians arrived on site, their work was often dirty, physical, dangerous, and carried out in unpleasant conditions. Before advances in restraint technology, horse doctors needed strength to maneuver their burly patients. They often stood for hours in cold barns or outside in the baking sun (Dinsmore 1940). Working with horses was dangerous—veterinarians could be bitten, stomped, or kicked. In illustration 6.9, a horse suffering from blood poisoning and with extensive necrotic tissue is treated by Dr. Robert Walsh.

3. Only sixty years later there was a dramatic increase in the number of women attending veterinary schools. Now, women constitute almost three-fourths of the graduates of veterinary schools (Slater and Slater 2000).

6.8. Dr. Powell, veterinarian, ca. 1908. C. Trenton Boyd Coll.

6.9. "Blood Poison." Dr. Robert Walsh, Trent, South Dakota, ca. 1909. C. Trenton Boyd Coll.

Walsh exposed himself to blood and other discharge as well as the danger of getting kicked by his patient. Nevertheless, with his sleeves rolled up, as if to say that no work is too tough or dirty, he pulls aside the tail for the camera to record the diseased skin.

Some of the danger to veterinarians came from their sharp instruments combined with the patients' unpredictable, often sudden moves. These doctors often wore leather aprons to protect their bodies from an inadvertent slip of a surgical tool. That was the case for the veterinarian in illustration 6.10. He poses next to his patient with a case full of sharp instruments at his feet.

Early veterinarians were, like their country-doctor counterparts, jacks-of-all-trades. They were called upon to prescribe medicine, perform medical and surgical procedures, help with deliveries, and give advice and consolation when necessary. In some ways, what was required of them exceeded the expectations of physicians who served humans. Veterinarians also served as animal dentists and treated many animal species, including an occasional human (Dinsmore 1940).

Into the 1920s spokespersons for the profession decried specialization and called for veterinarians to remain generalists (Gardiner 2006). One past president of the AVMA admitted in 1922 that it was a "Herculean

6.10. Veterinarian in protective dress, ca. 1908. C. Trenton Boyd Coll.

task" for one person to accumulate all the knowledge needed to treat every species and every infirmity, but that doing so was a necessity for the profession's successful future. Indeed, animal doctors had to do everything because there were no specialties in veterinary schools (such as internal medicine or orthopedics) and their animal patients had a wide range of medical problems.

Photo postcards captured some of the many services offered by veterinarians at this time. A common problem faced by equine owners was the lifelong and constant growth of horses' teeth. Whereas wild horses eat fodder that is abrasive, domestic horses eat soft grain and alfalfa that allow excessive and uneven tooth growth. If not filed, teeth can cut into the horses' cheeks, causing pain and injury. The procedure was called "floating" and consisted of using a special dental rasp, or float, that was drawn across the teeth.

Veterinarians were also orthopedists. Horses with cuts, bruises, sprains, or broken legs were lame, unable to perform tasks required of them. In illustration 6.11 a veterinarian wearing a suit and dress shoes is making a house call to bandage a horse's leg as it stands patiently in an open field.

As we stated in chapter 4, owners of urban draft horses commonly had their animals shot if the injury limited their work capacity and could not be easily and

inexpensively fixed. Ironically, veterinarians were often the people who pulled the trigger. Laws allowed them to do so. If veterinarians certified that the horse was seriously injured and that killing was justifiable, insurance claims were more likely accepted. Death was not inevitable, though. Owners called for the healing services of veterinarians, if injured horses had utilitarian or sentimental value, if they were likely to respond to treatment, and if they could afford the veterinarian's services.

Animals had many injuries and diseases that were best treated by surgery. The horse with the massive tumor protruding from his chest in illustration 6.12 was such a case. The two veterinarians who are posed beside the animal are preparing to remove the growth. It was unlikely that they used anesthesia because it was not widely available and considered unnecessary. People thought that animals did not feel pain the way humans did.[4] Even if the surgeons were skilled and well trained,

4. It was not that veterinarians were inhumane so much as the fact that anesthesia was relatively new, not widely available, hard to properly administer, and expensive. Though sometimes available, chloroform and ether were dangerous to use on horses. Chloral hydrate was available at this time, and it might have been used as a sedative depending on how forward thinking and up-to-date the veterinarians were. However, chloral hydrate is a sedative and not an

6.11. Treating a horse's lameness, Philip, South Dakota, ca. 1910. Photo by Johnson. C. Trenton Boyd Coll.

6.12. Preoperative horse with large tumor between front legs, Sioux Falls, South Dakota, 1909. C. Trenton Boyd Coll.

given the size and location of the tumor, the horse likely died after the surgery. In general, horses did not tolerate operations well, and large wounds led to infections. Antibiotics were not available, and infections easily spread to other organs or involved major blood vessels.

anesthetic, so it would have paralyzed the animal but not killed the pain or made it unconscious (Smithcors 1957).

The veterinarians in the illustration wanted to capture their surgery on photo postcards for a few reasons. The tumor's massive size made it worthy of scientific documentation. And, if they were successful and the horse lived, the picture would be a testimony to their surgical skills. Accompanying the photo postcard in the illustration was a postcard of the removed tumor. We did not find a postoperative picture of the horse, dead or alive, so we are unsure of the outcome.

Another surgical procedure performed by veterinarians and documented on postcards was horse castration, or gelding. As mentioned in chapter 4, this procedure was not performed out of medical necessity or for the horse's well-being; rather, geldings were easier to manage than aggressive and troublesome stallions.

Castration involved a number of strong hands to accomplish. The first step, called "casting," was to take the horse down to the ground and immobilize it by tying its legs to its head ("hog tied") (illustration 6.13). Then, as shown in illustration 6.14, the veterinarian and his assistant would use an instrument resembling a large pair of pliers with two sharp blades to cut off the horse's testicles.

At the start of the century, before horses were completely displaced by motor-powered vehicles, emergency

6.13. Castrating a wild one, Ainsworth, Nebraska, ca. 1909. Photo by Phelps. C. Trenton Boyd Coll.

6.14. Dr. J. L. Myers, ready to operate, Illinois, 1912. C. Trenton Boyd Coll.

6.15. Fire ruins East End sheds. Twenty-one horses and one man burned. Battle Creek, Michigan, July 15, 1911. Private Coll.

calls increased for veterinarians to service horses involved in accidents. Crashes with cars were common, as were falls on slippery asphalt roads and trolley and train tracks. Horses were also hurt and in need of care after fires. Stables, barns, or sheds that kept horses ignited easily, and the fire would spread rapidly to other wooden structures. Animals that survived needed attention, even if only to be euthanized. Illustration 6.15 captures the aftermath of a fire in Battle Creek, Michigan, that killed twenty-one horses and one man. Curious boys and men survey the fire's aftermath. One of the horse victims lies at the stable's entrance, where it succumbed to smoke.

World War I stimulated the demand for equine veterinary care (Dethloff and Dyal 1991). Horses, mules, and donkeys were used extensively as draft animals to pull light artillery, ambulances, ammunition, engineering equipment, and water carts, as well as to deliver food for the American and Allied armies.[5] The United States used almost 250,000 horses and mules during

the war. The Army Veterinary Corps was established in 1916 to maintain these animals, and more than 2,000 veterinarians saw active service (Merillat and Campbell 1935; Smithcors 1975).

There were virtually no veterinary instruments, medicines, and supplies available to care for army equines. To meet these needs, the War Department asked that the American Humane Association (AHA) do for army animals what the American Red Cross did for soldiers. In response, the AHA created the American Red Star Animal Relief (Red Star) program to raise money for drugs, tents, food, bandages, blankets, and ambulances for the thousands of horses and mules injured each month.

More than 120 Red Star branches operated out of humane societies throughout the United States (Unti 2002). To raise money and awareness, Red Star branches produced postcards featuring an appealing collie named Beauty that were mailed to potential donors. Although most of the cards produced were printed for mass mailings, at least one of the Red Star branches used the real photo format in their campaign (illustration 6.16). "Beauty," a collie mix, is featured on the card along with a Red Star worker. The banner on the wall reads: "Be Kind to Animals."

5. See Stout (1986) for details on the use of equines at one army fort. The war also stimulated massive increases in demand for hogs, beef cattle, and dairy cows that required veterinary services on the ranges and farms within the United States.

6.16. Red Star promotion, ca. 1917. MSPCA Archives.

THE TRANSITION TO LIVESTOCK CARE

The displacement of horsepower by motor vehicles created a crisis in veterinary education, practice, and research. Agricultural changes presented the profession with an opportunity for a new emphasis. Ranchers and farmers needed veterinarians to help manage their improved cattle stock, poultry, swine, and sheep in the Midwest, western prairies, and plains. The early twentieth century was also a time of rapid expansion of the dairy industry. The demand for milk grew rapidly following safety improvements like pasteurization and refrigeration. Livestock needed to be vaccinated, helped with complicated deliveries, mended when injured, quarantined for infections like tuberculosis, or euthanized when they were untreatable, lost their utilitarian value, or became a contagious risk (Dunlop and Williams 1996).

Real photo postcards captured some of the services provided by veterinarians who worked with livestock.

Some of the difficult deliveries veterinarians were asked to assist with involved calves with rare congenital deformities. The availability of the postcard camera enabled veterinarians to document these "freaks of nature." The veterinarian in illustration 6.17 adopts a stern pose, pipe in mouth, as he stands next to his opened roll-up case of obstetrical instruments and a mounted two-headed calf that he delivered.

Some animals with profound abnormalities that might be of interest to the general public were sometimes spared death and exhibited as freaks at county and state fairs (Nickell 2005). But most animals born with profound anomalies offered no potential as producers or workers for farm owners, so typically they were killed. This outcome was likely the fate of the two-legged calf in illustration 6.18 who suffered from thoracic amelia. Vernacularly called a "kangaroo calf," the deformed animal was immobilized by its physiology.[6]

As the American livestock industry expanded in the early twentieth century, veterinarians found an important role beyond the everyday mending of injuries and routine ailments. They were called to stop the spread of highly contagious livestock diseases. By defining themselves as experts in the management of infectious diseases, veterinarians found work to replace their waning equine business.

A major livestock disease was Texas fever, a parasite transmitted by tick to cattle, sheep, and horses. Left untreated, it threatened the welfare of the American livestock industry. Infected animals suffered from high fever, emaciation, bloody urine, and anemia, and they eventually died (Hutson 1994). In 1906 the BAI moved to control Texas fever by eliminating the carrier tick from all cattle south of the thirty-fifth parallel (Stalheim 1994). The method employed was a process known as "dipping," or submerging cattle in vats of a weak arsenic solution at two-week intervals, demonstrated in illustration 6.19 (Strom 2004). More than one hundred BAI veterinarians were sent into the field to implement and oversee this campaign. At first, angry

6. Whether genetic or environmental factors cause this problem is still being debated (C. Trenton Boyd, personal communication, September 4, 2008).

6.17. Veterinarian with two-headed calf, ca. 1914. C. Trenton Boyd Coll.

6.18. Two-legged calf, ca. 1909. C. Trenton Boyd Coll.

farmers were leery of the procedure and formed antidipping associations. Dipping vats were blown up, and a few veterinarians were killed during the conflict (Strom 2000). With greater acceptance of the procedure, farmers and ranchers carried it out themselves. Healthier livestock resulted, but it was not until 1943 that the ticks were eradicated from the United States.

Other meat-producing animals were plagued with fatal diseases that were difficult and often impossible to control. Hog cholera, also called swine fever, is a highly infectious viral disease that plagued pig farmers throughout the United States with devastating losses. More than 10 percent of the hogs in the country died in the 1913 outbreak. Spread by direct and indirect contact, people and vehicles that transported the animals spread it to others, as did one pig to another. In the early part of the century, feeding healthy pigs raw garbage containing pork scraps from infected pigs commonly caused the infection. Having pigs without cholera was very important for good business, so it is not surprising that the farmer in illustration 6.20 posted a prominent sign indicating the health of his livestock.

Fallen pigs were burned; during epidemics the countryside was spotted with smoke ascending from

6.19. Dipping cattle, Elgin, Kansas, ca. 1914. C. Trenton Boyd Coll.

6.20. "No Cholera in Premont. We're All Well. Come and See Us." Premont, Texas, ca. 1916. C. Trenton Boyd Coll.

farms forced to burn their dead animals. Veterinarians from the BAI oversaw eradication programs that relied on large-scale slaughtering and used an anti–hog cholera serum that was successfully tested in 1907 (S. Jones 2002). To some extent, veterinarians were actually helping to spread hog cholera because the vaccine they used contained a live virus (Jack Horton, personal communication, August 27, 2009). Despite these efforts, cholera among pigs was not eradicated in the United States until 1978 (Stalheim 1988).

Foot-and-mouth disease was the most feared of all contagious livestock diseases. Stricken animals could suffer not only from high fever but also from mouth blisters that led to heavy drooling, foot blisters that

6.21. Foot-and-mouth-disease killing, ca. 1913. C. Trenton Boyd Coll.

could rupture and cause lameness, weight loss, testicular swelling, decline in cow milk production, inflammation of the heart, starvation, and death. Major outbreaks occurred in 1902, 1908, 1914, and 1924. The 1914 outbreak spread to twenty states before it was curtailed. Rather than risking the spread of the disease, infected animals were rounded up, led to a trench, shot to death, and buried (Clements 2007).[7] Thousands of animals died that way (Smithcors 1975). BAI veterinarians played a key role in identifying infected herds. To quell farmers and ranchers, and compensate them for their financial loss, the government reimbursed them (Spear 1982). Illustration 6.21 shows stoic farmworkers in the Midwest holding infected heifers that they were about to kill. The long trench in the background is filled with dozens of dead animals being inspected by government officials. Soon after their slaughter, the animals were either doused with gasoline and burned or covered with dirt and lime to form a mass grave (Clements 2007).

7. Thirty-six states also imposed severe quarantines on many animal and vegetable products from California, including armed roadblocks to prevent shipment of potentially infected meat (Kendall 1973).

THE TRANSITION TO COMPANION ANIMALS

Working with farm animals and horses was not sufficient to support the number of veterinary practices after the close of World War I. With increasing urbanization and with pet owners willing to pay for veterinary care, companion-animal practices or specialties began to fill the gap. Pet care, almost nonexistent before the war, gradually assumed a larger role in veterinary practices. The dog at the side of Dr. H. L. Pool in illustration 6.22 was probably his own pet or office mascot, but it is unlikely that he limited his practice to pets.

The Great Depression further encouraged small-animal veterinary practice. During this period fewer students enrolled in veterinary colleges, and former large-animal clients were finding it hard to pay for veterinary care. The price of livestock dropped so much, it was cheaper to let the animals die than to pay for a veterinarian's services (Bryant 1985). Veterinarians who had not done so earlier expanded their practices to include both small and large animals (Burnett 2007). Others adopted small animals as their specialty.

After the war Americans in general showed a growing interest in pets, especially dogs, and particularly in cities. As these animals established more intimate

6.22. Dr. H. L. Pool, veterinary surgeon, ca. 1918. Private Coll.

6.23. Veterinary students examining dog cadaver, ca. 1920. Joel Wayne, Pop's Postcards Coll.

roles in families, owners became more willing to spend money for their pets' health care.

Veterinary training changed to reflect the profession's shift. At the start of the century few veterinary schools offered classes in small-animal medicine or had suitable hospital facilities to accommodate them. At this time anatomical study of small animals was for students' general biological education. Only in later decades did it assume practical importance. Classes began to cover topics such as the dog's anatomy and physiology. Illustration 6.23 shows a group of students huddled over a dog cadaver they were dissecting.

Hospitals attached to veterinary colleges also changed, first only including and then later concentrat-

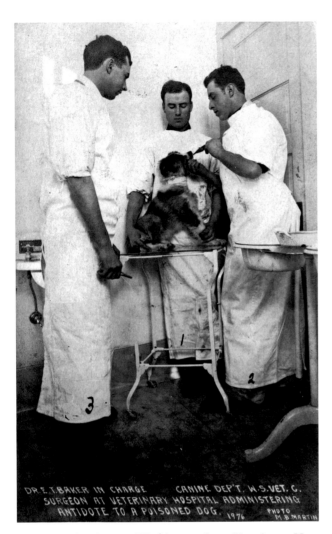

6.24. Veterinarians at Washington State Veterinary Hospital administering antidote to a poisoned dog, ca. 1918. Photo by Martin. C. Trenton Boyd Coll.

ing on small-animal care. In illustration 6.24, taken in the "Canine Department" at Washington State College of Veterinary Medicine, veterinarian Dr. E. T. Baker gives an antidote to a poisoned dog as two colleagues look on.

Urban veterinarians increasingly committed more or even all of their practices to small-animal care. Whether called "veterinary hospitals," "pet clinics," or "cat and dog hospitals," these venues began appearing in the mid-1920s as small-animal medicine established itself as a veterinary specialty (Dethloff and Dyal 1991). Horse operating tables were replaced with small examining stands (Stalheim 1994), and boarding and

6.25. Veterinary-clinic dog kennel, ca. 1926. C. Trenton Boyd Coll.

recovery kennels became common (illustration 6.25). A few of these specialized practices even introduced pet ambulances in the 1930s for emergency calls and to bring small patients to clinics.

HUMANE WORKERS

The Progressive movement, during which reformers demanded improvements in the welfare of children and the poor, also raised questions about the status and treatment of animals. In 1866 Henry Bergh founded the American Society for the Prevention of Cruelty to Animals. During the nineteenth and the first years of the twentieth centuries, horse abuse was its primary concern (Beers 2006). The ASPCA joined with George Angell's Massachusetts Society for the Prevention of Cruelty to Animals to pass anticruelty laws and to develop humane law enforcement departments to enforce these regulations (Carson 1968). Early in their history they fought both to get horse owners to stop beating their working animals and to stop the wanton killing of lame animals.[8]

Perhaps the most important contribution humane societies made to equine welfare was the campaign to provide water to working horses. Henry Bergh spearheaded this effort in 1867 when he started the "fountain movement" (Unti 2002). In summer's hottest months, dehydration commonly caused equine suffering and death. In one hot spell in Philadelphia more than one hundred horses died from heat-related causes in a twenty-four-hour period. Following Bergh's idea, humane societies across the United States started to install fountains with troughs for horses.[9]

In some cities and towns the fountains met with community resistance. Claiming water shortages and dismissing the needs of horses as a waste of resources, officials shut off fountains when they were most needed. Municipal art commissioners even rejected some fountains' designs, calling them unattractive. To remedy these problems, fountains were reengineered to conserve water and redesigned to copy some of the architectural splendor of their European predecessors.

The granite fountain in illustration 6.26 met those standards quite well. Installed in Carson, Washington, it served hundreds of equines each day. At the fountain's base were four small water bowls for dogs, cats, and other animals. Similar fountains were shipped to cities across America, where they were installed with great ceremony. By the mid-1930s, as horses were displaced, troughs began to disappear from city streets. Some of the National Humane Alliance fountains still stand in prominent urban locations as historic landmarks of the humane movement.

At the same time that New York and Boston formed their humane societies, the first humane shelter

appeared in Philadelphia and became a model for other organizations that sought to find homes for unwanted animals. Animal welfare societies and shelters sprouted throughout the country, with women often taking the lead in the nascent humane movement (Beers 2006). Adoption was their goal; if it could not be arranged, euthanizing was the last resort.

Early humane societies depended on donations for survival. To make their presence known and to promote their cause, these societies participated in town parades across the country. Such was the case with the Hillsboro County Humane Society float in Dade City, Florida, where a white papier-mâché horse towers over the female humane society workers. The horse pulling the display is wearing a banner that states, "Water Frequently" (illustration 6.27).

The humane movement allied with the veterinary profession. One AVMA president proclaimed that all graduates of "modern" veterinary schools were "honorary members of humane societies" (quoted in Smithcors 1975, 99). He argued that veterinarians should encourage humane behavior in their clients and speak out against abuse. Humane organizations also advocated for regulation of the veterinary profession in order to prevent charlatans from practicing.

As part of their alliance with veterinarians, humane societies in major cities such as Boston, New York, and San Francisco began establishing animal hospitals to serve neglected animals and owners who could not afford professional care. These facilities had up-to-date equipment and promoted modern procedures. In 1912 the president of the MSPCA decided to honor its founder, George Angell, by naming its first animal hospital after him. Doing so would embody a humane ethic by providing a facility where sick and injured animals, even if owned by poor people, would receive care comparable to that which humans received. Like the ASPCA's hospital in New York, Angell Memorial had horse, dog, and cat wards; isolation areas for all three species; lethal chambers; mange and distemper wards; and exercise areas. The hospital was associated with a number of advancements, including anesthesia, aseptic surgery, radiology, and fracture repair.

---

8. They also promoted the use of slings to lift injured horses and more humane procedures in slaughterhouses.

9. In addition, some fountains even had cups for people. Humane workers also supplied bonnets or straw hats for horses to wear, wet sponges to people working with horses, and the occasional bath when it became unusually hot.

6.26. Equine drinking at fountain, Carson, Washington, ca. 1912. B. Nelson Coll.

6.27. Humane-society float, Dade City, Florida, 1914. C. Trenton Boyd Coll.

ALMOST A PROFESSION

During the early twentieth century American veterinarians tried hard to professionalize by following in the footsteps of physicians who were successfully establishing their authority, legitimacy, prestige, and power (Starr 1984). Like human medicine, veterinary medicine underwent a dramatic transformation from a profane trade populated in the nineteenth century by low-status practitioners, such as quacks, folk-medicine advocates, healers, and farmers, to the profession of highly trained specialized practitioners we recognize today as veterinarians. But unlike their physician counterparts, veterinarians achieved only ambiguous professional status in the twentieth century, never reaching the high status, income, and prestige achieved by human doctors.

Photo postcards seen in this chapter suggest why this disparity occurred. Images of veterinarians working in the fields, wearing protective smocks to ward off kicks by horses, castrating animals, moving large animals, and facing the possibility of being bitten or scratched show their work as physically challenging manual labor, or what sociologists call "dirty work" (Hughes 1958; Sanders 1994). Further compounding the low status accorded to dirty workers, and further explaining veterinarians' clouded professional status, is the fact that their patients were, after all, "only animals," having less stature and significance than they do now. The budding animal-rights movement, exploding interest in companion animals, and growing understanding of and respect for animal consciousness have helped to change that.

The growth of veterinary medicine mirrored society's conflicted perception and use of animals. Veterinarians, especially in their work with farm and working animals, dealt with animals as expendable commodities whose lives were valuable only for what they produced. The profession's shift from working with large agricultural animals to small companion animals, and from treating them as utilitarian objects to pets, meant that animals were no longer sheer commodities to euthanize when no longer productive; they were sentient beings with whom people developed deep and long-lasting attachments and to whom people projected human traits.

Although this shift in veterinary emphasis from large to small animals is usually depicted as a post–World War II trend, photo postcards tell a different story about the importance of companion animals in the early decades of the twentieth century. The veterinary profession was playing catch-up to a groundswell of interest in pets.

7

Vermin

7.1. Children with dead coyotes, Alexandria, Nebraska, 1913. Joel Wayne, Pop's Postcards Coll.

*A*dimension of human-animal relationships that we have not explored is hatred for particular species. At the beginning of the twentieth century most mammals were greeted with positive regard or at least considered benign creatures, but there were exceptions. Some animals were perceived as a threat, as enemies of the common good, despised and demonized as vermin. Large predators such as cougars and occasionally bears fitted that category, but particular hatred was reserved for coyotes and wolves. They were especially targeted for extermination.[1]

The goal of exterminating particular animals was not new to Americans. Widespread killing of coyotes and wolves in an attempt at extermination was a common practice first in colonial New England (Coleman 2004), then in the Midwest (Lopez 1978), and, during the postcard era, in the Great Plains states and beyond (McIntyre 1993).

At first glance, the picture in illustration 7.1 appears to be rural youngsters with canine pets. Look again. Those animals are dead coyotes. A few of the children are smiling, while others are more somber, which is

---

1. In the plains states, *wolf, prairie wolf,* and *coyote* were and still are often used interchangeably (W. Johnson 1922, 41). With some real photo postcards it is difficult to tell whether the animals in the picture are wolves or coyotes. Cards use *wolf* in the caption

where the animals appear to be coyotes. Using *wolf* to label an animal that is actually a coyote raised the kill's significance and the hunter's status. Even given the difficulties, we try to maintain the distinction between wolves and coyotes in this chapter.

probably more a function of the chill in the air than the animal corpses at their feet. The picture was taken by a local postcard photographer in Nebraska and sold to citizens in the area as a souvenir of an event they celebrated, a coyote kill, or "roundup," as locals called it.

WOLF HUNTS

Real photo postcards document how wolves were trapped and hunted by individuals for bounty. Illustration 7.2 depicts a wolf caught in a steel leg-hold trap. Animals caught in these traps suffered lacerations, joint dislocation, broken bones, or starvation, and sometimes chewed off the clamped leg to free themselves. To save ammunition, hunters often clubbed trapped wolves to death. Local government-sponsored wolf bounty killing started in colonial times. In the mid-1800s many western states introduced the practice for wolves, mountain lions, and other carnivores (Sweet 2002). After 1890 state legislators institutionalized ranchers' killing of wolves by ranking wolves at the top of the list of animals to be destroyed. They believed wolves preyed on game and ranch stock and were the most destructive canines (Zmyj 1996). By the beginning of the twentieth century the federal government joined the states in declaring warfare upon predatory animals. The U.S. Forest Service, for example, killed wolves until the job

was taken over by the U.S. Bureau of Biological Survey (Robinson 2005).

The most dramatic images of wolf killing were produced at events where citizens of rural communities teamed up for community hunts. The goal of these forays was specicide—the intentional extermination of a species by killing as many as possible—in this case the wolf. Although the exact procedure varied from area to area, the general approach was for people to meet at a location where wolves roamed. Captains would organize the day. The area covered was often large, miles in diameter. One of the largest wolf hunts on record took place in Osborne County, Kansas, in 1908, where more than eight hundred people participated and covered more than forty-eight square miles (F. Wood and Daymond 1988). The crowd of hunters would disperse to form a huge circle. At the designated time they would move toward the middle, rustling the brush, shouting, and making other loud noises as they drove the confused wolves toward the center. There, wild canines would be clubbed, shot, and stabbed. Although men dominated, women and children were part of the congregation, too. Some wolf roundups used horses and then cars and trucks later in the century. Illustration 7.3 shows a line of humans supported by horse-drawn carriages and cars joining a wolf drive in Holstein, Nebraska, in 1922. In the next image we see the result

7.2. Trapped wolf, ca. 1917. Arluke Coll.

7.3. "The Drive." Holstein, Nebraska, 1922. Dingman Coll.

7.4. Display of killed wolves, Holstein, Nebraska, 1922. Dingman Coll.

of the Holstein, Nebraska, hunt: nine dead wolves displayed with a small segment of the hunting party. Note the boys dispersed throughout the crowd.

Illustration 7.5 documents a different sort of community wolf hunt. In this case, dogs, selectively bred and highly trained as wolf hunters, are prominently displayed along with a dead wolf. The dogs were mixtures of greyhounds, Irish wolfhounds, and other breeds. In small packs they were capable of outrunning wolves and killing or mutilating them until the hunting party

arrived on horseback to finish them off. This form of community hunt involved groups of riding townspeople following the dogs until they caught their prey. Note the two young women holding guns to the right and in back of the dead wolf.

Dogs not only were used for community hunts but could also be hired to outsiders who wanted to kill wolves for sport. Illustration 7.6 shows two local guides with their dogs and two dandies, urban outsiders, with a wolf hanging from the saddle. In the

7.5. Dogs, townspeople, and a dead wolf, Great Plains, ca. 1920. Dingman Coll.

7.6. Wolf hunters with guides and dogs, Independence, Kansas, 1909. Ruth Hanchett Coll.

message to the writer's cousin on the back of the card, the writer says, "We caught 9 wolves, eight small ones with their mother."

Illustration 7.7 introduces a different practice in townwide community wolf hunts. It shows the result of a 1921 Isabel and Sawyer, Kansas, competition over which town could kill the most wolves in one day. It looks like Sawyer beat Isabel by one wolf.

Photographers who took images of wolf hunts sold them to the participants shortly after the events. These

visuals document, and other accounts confirm (Coleman 2004), that participants developed a moblike mentality similar to what happened at a lynching (J. Allen 2000). Many experienced the mass and indiscriminate wolf killing as "fun" or "sport." Part of the ritual of the hunt was for everyone to gather and shoot their guns into the air at the closing. At the end of the day the hunt evolved into a community gathering where people ate, drank, and socialized, with the pile of killed wolves nearby (W. Johnson 1922).

7.7. Wolf-killing competition between Isabel and Sawyer, Kansas, 1921, Kobel Coll.

THE BIG BAD WOLF

Although community wolf hunts often took on a festive atmosphere, participants would tell you that the killing was not just for fun. Those individuals involved believed that wolves were murderers, a menace and a threat to their way of life. One rancher and well-known wolf hunter declared that wolves were the "enemy of civilization." Local people recall that wolves were seen as evil as killers of game, cattle, sheep, and even fellow wolves. Anthropomorphizing wolves—attributing human qualities to them—fanned fear and hatred of them because the qualities attributed to them were uniformly negative: savagery, lack of mercy, unfair hunting practices, and cowardice (Emel 1998). These attributes were contrary to important frontier ideals of morality, civilization, and progress.

Wolf hysteria gripped the land as ranchers and hunters preyed on the public's fear of wolf attack by spreading unverified reports of children and elders being savagely attacked by wolves. Although no official records exist of documented cases of unprovoked attacks on humans on the North American continent (Coleman 2004; Lopez 1978; McIntyre 1993), humans hated wolves and feared them.

Wolves hunted in packs, and their natural food was game—deer, elk, and buffalo. As settlers moved west, game diminished, and land was taken over by ranchers and farmers who converted it to pasture and farm. Wolves competed with human hunters for the declining game population. By the beginning of the twentieth century people believed that wolves would render large game mammals extinct in areas of the United States, and hunters were convinced that there would be nothing left for them to hunt. The settlers brought livestock, cattle, and sheep to the area. Soon, the wolves were killing them as a substitute for what had been their natural diet. Even today, people argue about the degree to which wolves threaten livestock. Some say the number of reported killings is an extreme exaggeration, that facts about these animals were deliberately distorted to justify their suffering and death (Serpell 1986). Others stand by the assessment that wolves are destructive killers of livestock.

Postcards both documented wolf killing and incited the hatred that promoted the hunt. By using the title "Deer Slayers," the image of killed wolves in illustration 7.8 recalls the glory of the legendary hunters described in James Fenimore Cooper's novel of the same name.

7.8. "Deer Slayers." Wolves shot by bounty hunters, Great Plains, ca. 1916. Photo by Rice-Maid. Jim Matthews Coll.

Wolves were often so hated they were slowly tortured to death. Estimates are that hundreds of thousands of wolves in America were poisoned, dynamited in their dens, burned alive after being soaked with kerosene, scalped, had their mouths wired shut or their eyes burned out with branding irons before being released to starve to death, tied up with leather belts and eaten alive by hunting dogs, or bound with ropes and then tied to opposing horses that ripped them apart (Hampton 1997).

The extreme hostility toward this carnivore was based not just on the harm they caused to the farmer or the actual threat to human life. Although wolf hatred reached its zenith in early-twentieth-century America, it originated elsewhere. When Europeans came to the United States, they brought with them deeply held fears about wolves. Folklore from the Middle Ages told of a special type of blood-sucking canine whose bite could transform humans into wolves. Werewolves continued to be a part of Americans' mentality (Lopez 1978, 228). Fairy tales that were read to children, such as *Little Red Riding Hood* and *The Three Little Pigs*, cast the wolf in the role of a clever, deceitful, and ferocious flesh consumer. Settlers developed their own folktales, with vicious wolves attacking innocent farmers and killing their children (Coleman 2004). The wolves were not just a real-life threat; they loomed large as symbols of the evil forces of nature that threatened human life. Killing wolves was a way for people to assert dominance over the natural world and over their own anxieties.

Some wolves became local legends for their killing prowess and skill in avoiding humans' attempts to do them in. Some demanded inflated bounties from hunters who tracked particular wolves for years. These high-profile wolves—often given names—acquired infamous reputations as "outlaws," "monsters," or "mass murderers." Such was the case with the large and notorious Buffalo Wolf shot in Oneonta, Nebraska, in approximately 1910 and shown in illustration 7.9. Such wolves could grow as long as six and half feet from snout to tail and weigh more than one hundred pounds. This wolf allegedly killed much valuable stock, justifying the $180 reward for his death, a "good night's work" for the hunter, Walter Brown.

Wolves became nearly extinct in the Lower 48 in the twentieth century. The once prolific wolf, estimated to be in the millions, dwindled to several hundred. Many parts of the country celebrated their "last wolf" (Robinson 2005). We came across a 1907 photo postcard showing a taxidermy mount of what was claimed to be the "last wolf" in Washtenaw County, Michigan.

Although none of those wolves pictured on postcards was truly the last wolf, the hatred and attention they received doomed them (Hampton 1997). Wolves were killed with more passion and determination than any other animal in American history. Even after

7.9. Buffalo wolf shot and killed by Walter Brown, Oneonto, Nebraska, ca. 1910. Photo by Butcher. Private Coll.

national parks were created to conserve and preserve natural resources—including wild animals—wolves along with other "bad animals," such as bears and ravens, were considered a threat to "good" animals and were systematically extirpated from park areas (K. Jones 2002; Tardona 2007). The Endangered Species Act of 1973 finally protected wolves (Robinson 2005). Today, more than two thousand wolves live in the wild in Minnesota, a few hundred in Michigan's Upper Peninsula, a similar number in Wisconsin, and about twice that many in the northern Rocky Mountains of Montana, Idaho, and Wyoming. In the spring of 2008 the Federal Endangered Species Act that had protected wolves was lifted in Idaho, Montana, and Wyoming.

Not everyone has welcomed the return of wolves to our natural landscape; opposition serves as a stark reminder that wolves' image as vermin continues today. There was considerable local resistance to the reintroduction of gray wolves to Yellowstone National Park in the mid-1990s (K. Jones 2002); some of the released wolves have been illegally shot.

OTHER ENEMIES

The wolf takes precedence for the most hated of animal foes, but there were others that were targeted for extermination as well.[2] As we have said, the coyote (see illustration 7.1) was subjected to the same community hunts and government-sponsored systematic killing as the wolf (Antle 1997; Dunlap 1984). Some of the activities that we have described as wolf hunts may have involved coyotes.[3] Cousin to the wolf but more diminutive, not a pack hunter, and a predator of smaller prey, coyotes were not as hated as the wolf. Coyotes' diet was rich with rodents and light on livestock. They were tolerated, at least more so than wolves, and are still found in many areas of the United States, including New England.

In illustration 7.10 an elderly man smoking a pipe stands outside the bank on the main street of Lebanon, Iowa, with a string of dead coyotes. The message on the back of the card reads: "Coyote hunting is the game here. This is a picture of about half of the coyotes we got in one roundup. . . . About 800 people at this hunt. Some sport."

The mountain lion, or cougar, once inhabited most of North America. Unlike the wolf that roamed and hunted in packs, mountain lions were loners or traveled in pairs. Much less prolific than the wolf, and never as abundant, they were less of a threat and less vulnerable to mass killings. Nonetheless, their extermination followed the pattern of the wolf: gradually killed off in the East and Midwest until, state by state, locals could claim that the last cougar had been killed. Illustration 7.11 shows the alleged last cougar killed in Wisconsin.

Large predatory animals were not the only species that rural people sought to eliminate. The jackrabbit

2. We do not touch on other animals hated and pursued by human beings as vermin—types of insects such as locusts (Lockwood 2004), water creatures such as sharks (Wallace and Gisborne 2006), or birds such as pigeons (Jerolmack 2008) as well as other warm-blooded animals, such as black bears (Stith 2007).

3. Because some locals used the terms *wolf* and *coyote* interchangeably, some of the illustrations used earlier in the chapter to depict wolf hunts might actually show coyotes.

7.10. Dead coyotes, Lebanon, Iowa, ca. 1916. Private Coll.

7.11. Alleged last cougar in Wisconsin, ca. 1912. Private Coll.

was another. According to zoological classification, the jackrabbit is not actually a rabbit, but a hare. Hares are considerably larger than rabbits, have huge appetites, and have long legs that allow them to run at high speed. They are extremely prolific. Their voracious eating habits combined with their large reproductive capacity made them a threat to farmers' crops. They, like wolves, were subjected to various attempts at annihilation, including rabbit drives, poisoning, shooting, and mass community hunts (Lovin 1979). The procedure was similar to the town wolf hunt, only the rabbits were typically driven into a large wire-mesh funnel that directed them to a wire corral. At the conclusion of the drive, men and boys would enter the wire enclosure and club hundreds, even thousands, of hares to death. Such hunts were common throughout the Midwest and West (F. Wood and Daymond 1988, 276). Early in the century the products of such kills were thrown away or destroyed. As fur farms developed as an industry, farmers bought the dead hares to feed the fox and other fur-bearing animals they were raising.

Illustration 7.12 of the jackrabbit hunt was taken in Kansas in the early 1920s. It shows the piles of dead jackrabbits that had been clubbed to death inside the carrel. In illustration 7.13, hunters in Stockton, Kansas, proudly display the results of a day's work—scores of jackrabbits.

Another widely shunned animal was the snake. The very sight of snakes could repulse people, leading them to avoid these reptiles with a vengeance. Some say human aversion to snakes is deep, even genetic. Unlike other vermin, snakes did not directly affect the livelihood of humans by killing livestock or eating grain. Farmers even appreciated the fact that many snakes had an appetite for rodents, creatures that really posed a threat to agricultural productivity.

7.12. Western Kansas rabbit drive, ca. 1919. Private Coll.

7.13. One-day hunt near Stockton, Kansas, ca. 1919. Ottaway Coll.

7.14. The king of the rattlers, South Dakota, ca. 1916. Photo by Leeland. Cynthia Elyce Rubin Coll.

Only a few kinds of American snakes were poisonous and posed a direct threat to human life. They were the direct subjects of human wrath. The most feared snake in the United States is the poisonous rattler, and it is this snake that is most photographed by postcard photographers. Ole Leeland, a Norwegian immigrant photographer known for his views of South Dakota, took the image in illustration 7.14 of two men displaying the huge skinned rattler.

Rattlesnakes have long been subjected to systematic campaigns of extermination. Illustration 7.15 provides a graphic visual of a hunt in Dupree, South Dakota. One hundred and twenty-eight rattlesnakes were killed in a single day on one farm. A correspondent who sent a copy of this card to a friend in the East wrote on the message side: "How would you like to side step rattlesnakes. That's what this country is noted for" (Morgan and Brown 1981, 134).

In Boston's nearby Blue Hills, rattlesnake bounties were so successful that they were discontinued when the number of snakes dropped markedly by the mid-1800s (Palmer 1992). In the early twentieth century, rattlesnake hunts, or "roundups," were common throughout the United States and even exist today in some states. Sweetwater, Texas, claims to hold the biggest annual roundup in the world, which includes a rattlesnake-re-

7.15. "One Days [sic] Catch of Rattlers." Dupree, South Dakota, ca. 1914. Joel Wayne, Pop's Postcards Coll.

view parade, a Miss Snake Charmer pageant, and deep-fried rattlesnake meat.

Other animals were correctly characterized as threats. Rats, for example, were a significant hazard. They consumed the grain meant for horses and livestock, spread disease, crawled over slum dwellers, and stole the bread of people of all social classes (Sullivan 2004). Even though some strains of white rats were caged and kept as pets for children of the elite, the street and barn varieties were hated. The loathing was so ingrained that comparing a human to a rat was an extreme insult, and applying the rat image to describe people of other cultures was a way of dehumanizing them and justifying their mistreatment and colonization.

Despite this intense hatred, we did not find any real photo postcards of rats or rat-eradication programs in our search of images for this book. One would expect to find pictures of piles of rats produced by proud exterminators after successful urban crusades, but we found none. Perhaps they were too despised or too elusive even to be photographed?

COUNTERPOINT

We end the chapter with an irony, a contradiction to the picture we have painted of humans hating certain animals. We end with an about-face from images of killing and death to a brighter side of human-animal relations. Although we emphasized how wolves were the most despised of all creatures, there are a number of cases documented on real photo postcards of people who had working and even loving relations with wolves. Apparently, they lived together with them in harmony, albeit after their owners tamed them. Illustration 7.16 is one example from South Dakota. It shows a man holding up his pet wolf so the photographer can get a better shot. Another counterintuitive example is that of Professor J. Damrell, pictured in illustration 7.17 with his small wolf pack driving from Seattle to New York City. The team, trained to pull the professor's wagon, hardly looks like the ferocious creatures portrayed by farmers and ranchers.

Undoubtedly, the examples of the South Dakota cowboy with his pet and Professor Damrell and his team are unusual. There are also documented cases of

7.16. Western South Dakota pet, ca. 1908. Cynthia Elyce Rubin Coll.

wolf pups being taken from their dens and raised as pets (Thiel 1993). Although we do not know the fate of the cowboy's pet or Dr. Damrell's wolves, we do know that wolf pups usually did not fare well. Hostility on the part of strangers often led to their deliberate killing. In the end, wolf-pulling teams or pets were mere exceptions to America's unrelenting pursuit of the wolf that led to its near demise during the real postcard era.

THE DARK SIDE

The idea that animals can be objectively ranked with lesser species on the bottom and humans at the top has

7.17. Professor Damrell with his team of wolves driving from Seattle to New York City, ca. 1914. Coll. of Leonard A. Lauder.

dominated Western thought since Aristotle and the Old Testament. Humans not only cast themselves as different from and better than other animals but also create further divisions among animals. "Good" animals are the ones that benefit people, are subordinate, and "fit in" the human world, whereas "bad" animals are cast as a threat to the human race.

This bold distinction existed a century ago and was apparent in photo postcards of that era. In earlier chapters we saw many examples of the very best animals who were almost regarded as kin and were treated accordingly—they not only knew their place in the social order but were invited into it. We also saw many examples of good animals who worked ceaselessly for humans—sometimes literally worked to death. This chapter's images show evidence of a darker side of human-animal relationships. Animals were not just killed but also deliberately tortured, not just disliked but also feared and hated, not just worked to death but hunted almost to extinction.

Yet not all hunted and killed creatures were considered bad animals. Other kinds of animals were deliberately killed, not out of loathing but for sport, profit, or subsistence. Whereas fear and hatred fueled the cruel treatment of vermin, what was the allure of

killing game? To what extent, if any, was hunters' attitude toward their prey different from the perspective of those individuals who hunted vermin? We turn to these questions next.

8

Game

8.1. Studio portrait of hunters with dead mule buck, ca. 1907. B. Nelson Coll.

The image that launches this chapter may seem strange to people who live in this age where cities dominate and an active antihunting movement exists (illustration 8.1). What contributes to its unreal quality is the painted studio backdrop, an artist's romantic rendering of the western wilderness. As we will see, the background is not the only illusion that characterized hunting and fishing during the postcard era. The hunters' serious masculine pose, weapons at hand and kill on the floor, foreshadows our discussion of the pursuit of game in the first third of the twentieth century.

Whether they were urban or rural, elite or working class, male or female, young or old, native citizen or immigrant, many Americans during the postcard era considered hunting and fishing important in their everyday lives. Young boys saw their older counterparts go off

to hunt with adults and expected one day to be included. Women sometimes accompanied men on the excursions and, as we shall discuss, even hunted. The rich and poor went to the forests and lakes to take part in the wildlife bounty, albeit with different motivations and under different codes. Fishing was more ubiquitous, and participation was even more widespread than hunting.

The types of game pursued varied from region to region, but different species of deer—white-tailed east of the Rocky Mountains and mule deer in the West (see illustration 8.1)—were the most popular large game and were most often pictured on photo postcards. Other hoofed animals taken in the hunt included moose, elk, antelope, mountain goats, and wild boars. Grizzly and other variations of the brown bear were shot in the West, and black bear were hunted in the East. Cougars, also known as panthers or mountain lions, as well as wolves and coyotes, as we discussed in the last chapter, were hunted because they were vermin. Small game, including rabbits, possum, raccoons, and squirrels, were the delight of some, as were various waterfowl and game birds, such as turkey, prairie chickens, grouse, pheasant, bobwhite, and quail. In addition to mammals and game birds, a few reptiles were on the wanted list, with alligators at the top. The names of the variety of fish pursued, both freshwater and salt, are too abundant to include here.

Since our focus in the book has been warm-blooded animals, fish do not get the same attention in this chapter as other game. However, we include them because there are so many images of fish as game on photo postcards and because hunting and fishing are so closely linked. We also include alligators because they were important in the South and we do not want to neglect that region of the country.

Unlike today, hunters at the beginning of the twentieth century did not have to deal with a vocal animal-rights lobby that calls for curtailing or eliminating hunting. Although questions about the propriety of hunting have been raised for centuries, the intensity of moral outrage against this practice has never been so widely embraced by critics or so strongly defended by proponents as it is today.[1] Fishing, however, has not been attacked to the same extent as hunting.

Our goal is not to attack or defend hunting and fishing. We use real photo postcards to understand the perspective of American hunters toward game at the beginning of the twentieth century. Who hunted and what did they hunt? How did they define their activity? Why were they were drawn to it? How did it fit into their family life? What were they trying to convey about themselves and their experiences by documenting them in this manner and sharing them with friends and family? We try to answer these questions through photo postcards.

SUBSISTENCE VERSUS SPORT

Most nineteenth-century Americans hunted and fished primarily for meat and fur. Most killed to feed their families, harvesting game in the fall to eat during the long winter or venturing into the forest during the cold months to replace dwindling provisions. Others killed for the money their catch could bring. Market hunters supplied wholesale and retail businesses with meat as well as with skins and fur. (Trappers and fur suppliers are discussed in chapter 9.) A for-profit hunter is pictured in illustration 8.2 with an array of raccoons, skunk, and birds he shot with the aid of his dog.

Photo postcards such as the one in illustration 8.3 of a small-town market in Lowville, New York, with dead deer hanging out front, show the kill of local "market hunters" being sold by a local butcher shop.

People of lesser means, known among townspeople as "crackers" or "pineys," killed certain animal species for food that more prosperous citizens would not consider game worthy of the hunt (Sitton 1995). Possum, badgers, and woodchucks are examples. Illustration 8.4 shows a subsistence hunter carrying his day's catch of rodents.

In some quarters the purely utilitarian function of the hunt was partially eclipsed in the latter half of the nineteenth century by a different perspective. Hunting acquired an honorable halo by emphasizing sport rather than meat, pleasure rather than subsistence (Proctor 2002). This approach took hold and came to define hunting during the twentieth century.[2] Shaped by upper-class sensibilities and a desire to connect with genteel and elite British hunters, the ideal of the sportsman appealed to the increasingly urban and educated middle- and upper-class American.

Those persons embracing the sportsman ideal, known as "sports," believed that they belonged to a special fraternity whose members had a moral way of thinking about hunting and fishing, a code of conduct about doing it.

1. Not all scholars oppose hunting. Paul Shepard (1997), for one, maintains that hunting has always been a legitimate way to be intensely involved with nature and wildlife and that without hunters Americans would be overrun by some species. Several other scholars also defend hunting (Dizard 2003; Rivers 2002; Strange 1997). Yet others, like anthropologist Matt Cartmill (1991), are distinctly anti-hunting, dismissing conservation efforts by some hunters and equating hunting to slaughterhouse work.

2. Ironically, as sociologist Jan Dizard observes (1994), this emphasis is now a major criticism of hunters. Some antihunters acquiesce to the value of hunting as a utilitarian activity, but not as recreation.

8.2. Catch near Elkton, South Dakota. T. J. Waterhouse, ca. 1909. Joel Wayne, Pop's Postcards Coll.

8.3. Singer's Market, Lowville, New York, ca. 1911. Pierce Coll.

Part of this ideology was that true sportsmen gave game a sporting chance. The assumption behind sport hunting and, to a lesser extent, sportfishing, was that a fair match existed, more or less, between the hunted and the hunter. Their prey was wild, capable of tricking and in other ways avoiding the pursuer or even, in the case of predators, striking back. Hunters' lore is filled with tales of wise prey who foiled all human attempts to kill them no matter how skilled the hunters or extraordinary their effort. The creed stated that in order for sportsmen to be successful, they either had to hire guides or had to have the special skills and knowledge of nature to outwit the animals themselves. In addition, the chase required physical endurance and inner strength. Killing also involved marksmanship

8.4. Groundhog hunter, ca. 1910. B. Nelson Coll.

and knowledge of weapons. There was some truth in the sportsman's claims, but the extent to which hunting was a contest between equals was exaggerated.

In their ideal form, sports also championed and appreciated the natural environment. They did not disrupt the tranquillity of the wilderness or upset the balance of nature; they were part of nature. True sportsmen also made sure that the deaths they caused were "clean kills," with as little suffering as possible. In the case of fishing, the "catch-and-release" approach arose.

Being a sportsman meant more than just having a special attitude or code toward hunting and killing animals. It also was a way of life. Magazines like *Field and Stream,* produced for the sport hunter, advertised expensive equipment and special hunting and fishing getaways where hired guides were available to help pursue prey. Sports clubs for the wealthy were founded, and their members collectively bought huge tracts of land on which to pursue game (Lynn 2002). The well-dressed sportsman holding the large salmon in illustration 8.5 fits the profile of the wealthy sportsman. Like this man, sportsmen would sometimes pose for studio photos fully dressed in their hunting or fishing outfits, while holding their gear and trophies.

The work of guides, local people who hired out their hunting and fishing skills to outside hunters who could afford such individual service, became a seasonal occupation that brought sports together with rural people. Some guides became attached to particular hunting clubs and hotels where they served regular customers who came year after year. Others freelanced.

Local photographers understood the uneasiness between natives, rural people who were mainly meat hunters, and sports, who were outsiders. This point is evident in the portrait of Mr. Bateson, his guide, and a five-pound trout (illustration 8.6). Their placement in the picture, in addition to the fact that the guide is holding the trout, accentuates the status difference between the two men. The guide appears relaxed, whereas Bateson's fingers and hands divulge discomfort. Bateson's white city-slicker suit catches the light, making him glow like an alien against the rough-cut vertical logs. The photographer, Henry Beach, wrote in the caption that Bateson was from New York City, a dead giveaway to his derided outsider's status among locals.

Another example of local photographers capturing the tension between locals and sports is illustration 8.7. It is a widely distributed exaggeration card, a form of trick photographic montage that was especially popular in the Midwest. A few, such as this image, captured the hunter's tall tale—the oversized superimposed rabbit—while conveying the swagger some local hunters displayed toward

8.5. Sportfisherman, ca. 1920. Joel Wayne, Pop's Postcards Coll.

8.6. Five-pound trout, Wawbeek, New York, ca. 1911. Photo by Beach. Tom Gates Coll.

the hunting dudes. The card shows a sportsman trying to catch a rabbit by pouring salt on its tail, an approach to hunting that locals conveyed to naive hunters. No matter how inexperienced, it is doubtful that anyone would believe that tale, but old-timers would laugh, telling about the time an outsider or a local youngster went out and actually tried.

In certain ways the sportsman's code was challenged during the photo postcard era. New technology and other mechanical advances changed the odds even more in favor of the hunter, questioning the general belief at the time that the match between hunters and animals was somewhat equal. Rifles fired quicker and more accurately and began to be equipped with sophisticated sights. The internal combustion engine and four-wheel-

drive truck allowed hunters easy access to hunting and fishing sites. So did the outboard motor.

The Evinrudes, a husband-and-wife team, were pioneers in the development of engines that could be attached to rowboats, thus allowing hunters and fishermen to travel to previously unreachable locations. Ole and Cary Evinrude introduced their 1.5-hp model in 1909. Illustration 8.8 shows one of the company's products on the back of a small boat carrying alligator hunters in Florida. The image is one of a set produced to promote the Evinrude. The caption reads: "Evinrude Hunters Don't Row, They Go Where the 'Gators Are and Get 'Em."

The growth of private game preserves where animals, raised to be killed, are released in fenced-in areas or ponds to be shot or caught by sportsmen and -women who can

8.7. "Salted. So Easy. Put Salt on Their Tails." Midwest, ca. 1912. Photo by Martin. Private Coll.

afford to pay the high fees also redefined hunting. This practice stacked the deck for the hunter and represented a clear drift from the sportsman creed. Whereas advanced equipment and fenced hunting preserves increased hunters' odds of bagging game, some species' populations declined, making them more difficult to find and decreasing the likelihood of a successful hunt (Dunlap 1988).

The sportsman's code also spread throughout the population during this period. Although the notion of hunting and fishing as an honorable pursuit was originally a way for upper-class American hunters to separate themselves from the common hunter, this thinking gradually trickled down the class hierarchy (Miner 2001; Reiger 2001). Middle-class hunters and fishermen, and some from less privileged backgrounds, sometimes followed the sportsman's creed and were just as proud of their kill as were upper-class "gentlemen" hunters. They, too, would often capture their hunting and fishing success on photo postcards that could be mailed to friends and family or placed in family albums.

Whether for sport, food, or profit, the passion behind hunting is complex. The excitement of the hunt meant different things to different hunters depending on their status, age, and experience. Whereas many hunters sought the thrill of stalking and killing animals,

8.8. Evinrude gator hunters, Florida, ca. 1923. Bogdan Coll.

8.9. Hunting season, Adirondacks, New York, ca. 1907. Private Coll.

8.10. Fishermen with catch, Forest Lake, Michigan, 1931. Joel Wayne, Pop's Postcards Coll.

shooting the biggest buck or the most ducks, outdoing other hunters with the size and number of their prey, others just enjoyed the forest and the outdoors (Cohn 2007). Clues to hunting's and fishing's deep appeal—what hunters loved about them—can be seen in the postcard photographs they left behind. Five elements appear again and again in photo postcards that suggest the lure: the abundance of game, trophies, guns, dogs, and hunting companions (Cohn 2007).

ABUNDANCE

Postcard depictions of both sport and market hunters often show hunters posed with a multitude of dead animals—piled in front of them, hanging from trees, strapped on cars, or stacked on carts and wagons (illustration 8.9).

Fishermen as well as hunters enthusiastically had pictures taken of their abundant catches. Fishing poles were included in some photos, but not as commonly as

8.11. "One Days [*sic*] Work with Dog and Gun." Nebraska, ca. 1910. Arluke Coll.

were guns in hunting photos. The crew in illustration 8.10 took their catch and poles to a photo studio for this group portrait. The photographer's backdrop simulates a lake in a forest scene.

Images flaunting the dead game not only visually confirmed the prowess of the hunter but also served to foster the impression that the land and water provided an endless bounty of wildlife. Showing the plenitude of game suggested that any journey by properly skilled hunters into America's backwoods would provide game for the taking. In illustration 8.11, "One Days Work with Dog and Gun," the rural photographer arranged the hunter's shotgun diagonally across the image with an abundance of waterfowl and other game birds placed neatly in line atop ammunition boxes with his dog asleep in the background, resting after a long day's hunt. In illustration 8.12 the dead ducks spill over the chairs in front of the hunter in a virtual waterfall of kills. He stands above the ducks, hands on his hips, as if to say, "Isn't it obvious there are a lot of ducks to be shot and I have had a good day's hunt?"

In addition to postcards showing hunters posed with their abundant kills, many depicted hunters transporting scores of dead game out of the forest. Illustration 8.13 shows hunters' dead deer stacked up at a railroad depot in northern Michigan waiting to be shipped home after

8.12. Duck hunter, Midwest, ca. 1909. Private Coll.

8.13. American Express shipping deer, Cheboygan, Michigan, ca. 1918. Photo by Johnson. Private Coll.

8.14. "Hunting Is Good in Colorado." Idaho Springs, Colorado, ca. 1925. Semel Coll.

a fall hunt. Note the American Express logo and the tags on the deer identifying the hunters who bagged them. The image suggests a seemingly endless supply of deer.

Some hunting and fishing postcards were produced to entice hunters to a region by showing how abundant game was in that locale. That allure was the case in illustration 8.13 as well as in illustration 8.14, which is captioned: "Hunting Is Good in Colorado. A Bag of Elk at Idaho Spring." Although those individuals pictured

appear to be locals rather than sport hunters, such images were made to attract the latter.

Lighthearted exaggeration cards reinforced the idea that an endless supply of wildlife existed. Some of these cards show hunters and fishermen bagging scores of larger-than-life animals and fish. Legendary tales of catching the largest fish, so much a part of the lore of abundance and the language of the braggart, were an easy target for photographers who made postcards (illustration 8.15).

8.15. "We Had a Team to Haul 'Em Out." Schenevus, New York, 1913. Photo by Beach. Private Coll.

At the same time photos were showing an unending supply of game, westward expansion and urban growth were encroaching on the frontier and eastern and midwestern forests, jeopardizing wildlife and calling into question the greedy behavior of some hunters and fishermen.[3]

TROPHIES

Quantity was not the only lure of hunting. Quality or significance of a kill—the trophy animal—was equally important. Although some hunters held aesthetic or even reverential attitudes toward the animals they sought to kill, many saw animals as trophies, symbols of their personal achievement and manliness (Proctor 2002). Some animals were singled out to photograph because of their large size or weight or other special features. Deer, moose, elks, and other hoofed animals with mature racks were flaunted over spike horns and antlerless females. For others it was the wingspread, weight, or length of the dead beast. A local area record or an individual hunter's

personal best was often captured in a picture. So was the large number of animals shot on a given day.

Illustration 8.16 captures the importance to hunters of bagging a relatively rare trophy. In this case, the buck lying front and center in the image is a piebald (with white patches) eastern white-tailed buck. When one looks at the way the men are dressed, the group appears to be composed of a mix of sportsmen and guides. Their guns are prominently displayed, as are the baskets that they carried on their backs into the hunting grounds. The hind legs of another dead deer protrude from a basket.

The next illustration (8.17) represents a different kind of trophy—a "personal best" for the most game bagged of a particular kind. The image shows a veteran bear hunter with his 101st kill, the victim of a leg-hold trap clearly visible in the photograph. Here, the significance of the trophy and the photograph is its marker of the aging hunter's prowess.

Anglers cared about their trophies, too. The biggest, heaviest, or rarest catch served as testimony to the fisherman's patience and skill. Recording these successful outings on a photo postcard provided evidence for future bragging rights among anglers. The thirty-five-pound buffalo fish in illustration 8.18 must have been quite a catch for the two fishermen. They put on their best clothing and carried their prize trophies to a photographer's studio to make a permanent memory of this event.

3. According to American studies scholar Jay Mechling (2004), this picturing coincided with the rise of commodity capitalism. He claims that these images resemble period photographs of department store displays or fair displays of goods that testified to the belief that goods were abundant and life was good in the United States.

8.16. Hunters with piebald buck, Adirondacks, New York, ca. 1911. Pierce Coll.

8.17. M. E. Robbins, veteran bear hunter of Vermont, with his 101st bear caught, ca. 1914. Jim Matthews Coll.

GUNS

In our search for photo postcards of hunters, we found very few without firearms. Hunters posed with their firearms in many ways, cradling them in their laps, holding them diagonally across their chests, straddling them on their hips, or resting against them as they stood. Whatever the pose, their guns and rifles seem far more than mere killing instruments or simple tools.

Weapons appear as extensions of hunters' identities and symbols of important American male values, including power, independence, self-reliance, and dominance over the natural world.

Hunters cherished their rifles and shotguns. They took great pride in them, sometimes decorating their weapons with etchings of hunting scenes as well with fancy inlaid grips. Hunters competed and argued with each other over what were the best models and who

8.18. Thirty-five-pound buffalo fish, Michigan, ca. 1919. Private Coll.

8.19. Winchester guns and ammunition salesman, ca. 1910. Joel Wayne, Pop's Postcards Coll.

owned them. This competition was flamed by rapid technological innovations that made weapons more deadly. The breech-loading hammerless shotgun and center-fire cartridges made weapons more reliable and more user-friendly compared with earlier weapons. Other refinements, including different-size double-barreled shotguns and repeating and automatic rifles increased the pleasure and effectiveness of shooting for both sport and market hunters (Marks 1992). Manufacturers such as Remington and Winchester courted hunters to buy their guns and rifles. Illustration 8.19 is an advertising postcard for a Winchester salesman.

The proud hunter in illustration 8.20 stands between a large buck and a smaller doe while holding a Winchester level-action rifle that was popular during the late nineteenth century and all of the twentieth century. It was the weapon of choice used by John Wayne's characters in his movies. Teddy Roosevelt boosted its fame by using it on his famous 1909 African safari. The Winchester 94 was one of the most popular deer rifles in the twentieth century. The rifle was made by the Winchester U.S. Repeating Arms Company in New Haven, Connecticut, which closed in 2006.

Ironically, the increasing effectiveness of weapons resulted in shooting more wildlife, a loss bemoaned by conservationist-minded sportsmen. Occasionally, photo postcards include a message bragging about how quickly the writer killed animals with his new rifle or shotgun. One card that we came across shows a hunter holding dead ducks and his gun with a message across

8.20. Hunter with gun, northern Maine, ca. 1915. B. Nelson Coll.

8.21. Hunters with dog, guns, and game, Midwest, ca. 1911. Bogdan Coll.

the front: "Ten ducks in four shots with a Marlin repeating shotgun."

DOGS

Dogs were another element of a hunter's joy. Many hunters cherished their canine hunting partners. A good one, a dog that could track and run game, point, or retrieve fresh kill, was almost as essential to some hunters as their rifles. Not all hunting dogs were created equally, nor could all breeds serve the purpose of every hunt. There were coonhounds that could run down and tree their prey, field dogs that could search out and retrieve game birds, and other retrievers that could fetch downed water

fowl. Some individual dogs were better than others in picking up a scent and following it, some had more determination and endurance, and some had more instinct and wherewithal to pursue and bring down wounded prey. Highly talented dogs became legendary and sometimes became valuable as profitable breeding lines.

Postcard images confirm the assertion that hunters' dogs were more than instrumental hunting accessories. The affection between hunters and their dogs comes through in human-animal body language. Illustration 8.21 shows hunting buddies with their game (raccoon, fox, ferret, mink) and cherished guns crossed over their legs in the picture's foreground. An equally important photographic element in the image is the dog, who peers into the camera's lens as he is tenderly cradled by one of the hunters.

The composition of many images suggests that dogs were part of the party, partners in the hunt. In illustration 8.22 the two men on the right demonstrate their connection by nestling their canines under their arms. In one case the hunter puts down his gun in favor of his dogs. The dead bear, impersonally strung from a tree, provides a stark contrast to the closeness the dogs had with their human companions. There was no emotional attachment to the wild game, whereas dogs occupied a unique social place between humans and the wild.

The hunter-dog relationship, however, was, and remains to this day, an ambiguous one. On the one hand, some hunters enjoyed the companionship of their dogs and reciprocated their service and affection with kindness. On the other, some hunters treated their dogs with disregard or even meanness.

COMPANIONSHIP

Hunting, especially for sports, was an occasion for men to be together with other men where they could be buddies. Hunters with their male companions account for a common element in hunters' photo postcards. Some local hunters were loners, but many hunted with buddies close to home and on more extended trips into the wilderness. Sportsmen ventured into the countryside with their friends for annual hunts where they escaped from their normal routines and work constraints, and from city and town life. Such trips lasted anywhere from a long weekend to several weeks. For them, hunting was a rural hobby. Away from work and family, they did not have to stand on proper etiquette or worry about being censored for engaging in male evening activities such as drinking, smoking, playing cards, talking business, and telling stories and off-color jokes.

Such carefree time built bonds among like-minded men. The resulting camaraderie is evident in postcard photographs that documented these excursions. The group of hunting buddies in illustration 8.23 hunted together yearly in northern Wisconsin, roughing it by using a freight car as their residence. In addition to the five deer hanging on the side of the car, there is a large dead owl on the sliding door. The cookstove, used both to prepare food and to keep the hunters warm, can be seen through the open door.

Nothing pleased a hunter more than returning to his lodge with evidence of success after a day in the woods. The satisfied deer hunters in illustration 8.24 stand proudly outside their cabin with their kill. There, they shared stories about their day's hunt, their success

8.22. Bear hunters with dogs, eastern United States, ca. 1909. Bogdan Coll.

8.23. Hunters with freight-car camp with deer and owl kill hanging on boxcar, Manawa, Wisconsin, ca. 1912. Photo by Quimby. Private Coll.

8.24. Hunters' lodge, Maine, ca. 1914. B. Nelson Coll.

in bringing the deer in, and their pleasure in being outdoors with nature and friends.

Hunting lodges and hotels catering to sportsmen shooting ducks, deer, grouse, or even bear grew in popularity toward the close of the nineteenth century. Some of the larger resorts had more than one hundred rooms for guests, with lobby and drawing room walls covered with hunting trophies. Hotel furniture might even be made from animal horns and hides. The duck hunters in illustration 8.25 sit on the porch of the Jacks Reef Hotel, located in the hamlet of Van Buren, New York.

A sense of fraternity among hunters could be experienced for more than an annual getaway to the country. Hunting clubs rose in popularity during the nineteenth century, with as many as one thousand existing by the late 1890s. Many clubs catered to wealthy and prominent patrons, but not to subsistence hunters with whom club members felt no kinship. In fact, clubs sometimes campaigned for game laws that revealed the antipathy

8.25. Hunters at hotel, Jacks Reef, New York, ca. 1909. Photo by Myer. Private Coll.

members felt for backwoods hunters. Club members deepened their friendships with middle- and upper-class hunters, as they participated in events that might last for days. Some of these clubs had dogs and hired hands, known as "drivers," to find and force deer out of the woods into the shooting range of club members. Grouse and ducks might be baited with corn. After an exhilarating day in the woods, club friendships flourished during evenings filled with drink and hearty dining, along with ample singing, storytelling, and bragging.

BECOMING A MAN

The connection between hunting and manliness exists in many cultures (Maybury-Lewis 1967). Hunters are "real" men—brave, strong, resourceful, and able to kill (Kimmel 1996). This link is so ingrained in the United States that it now serves as a rhetorical device to criticize both hunters and antihunters alike. Prohunters call animal-rights activists "sissies," while antihunting proponents claim that hunters cope with the fear of not being "man enough" by killing animals (Emel 1998).

During the late nineteenth and early twentieth centuries, there was an increasing fear that men were losing their virility (Rotundo 1993). People believed that increasing urbanization and the growth of the middle class took males away from masculine pursuits, such as manual labor, nature, and hunting and fishing. Men were becoming domesticated dilettantes. President Theodore Roosevelt's appeal was in part a function of the manliness he displayed as a rancher and hunter (Herman 2001). People believed that sustained immersion in the wilderness while hunting could remedy the loss of characteristics like courage, aggression, or mastery caused by overcivilization (Loo 2001).

As it had been for centuries, the use of hunting to acquire manly virtues started early in the lives of young boys during the photo postcard era. The first step was to play-hunt. Getting one's first rifle, even if only a BB gun, was sought after and relished as a Christmas or birthday gift. Handling the weapon and shooting at targets were good practice for what was to come—full-fledged participation in hunting and male adulthood (Herman 2001). In illustration 8.26 we see three brothers out for an adventure armed with play rifles and their trusty pug dog.

Boys were introduced to hunting early, and their success in the field was celebrated on photo postcards. In illustration 8.27 the smiling eleven year old strikes the pose of the hunter with his gun, dog, and game.

8.26. Young boys on outing with guns, ca. 1908. Arluke Coll.

8.27. One morning hunt, Maine, ca. 1911. B. Nelson Coll.

Hunting was, and still is, a family ritual handed down from generation to generation. According to the ideal, bonding occurs as fathers teach sons, and now increasingly girls, skills and an honorable code for hunting. Illustration 8.28 shows family members proudly posing with their fresh kills, a trophy moose and calf. Although the boy's presence does not necessarily mean he actually participated in this hunt, including him in the photo acknowledges his place alongside his father, uncle or friend, and trophies. Imitating the adults, the boy holds a pellet gun on his shoulder.

In many parts of rural America, when a boy kills his first buck it is a significant achievement that elevates his status from youngster to man. The young man in illustration 8.29 hides his exuberance with an expressionless face after bagging his first buck. Although his kill was an important achievement, he knew that the specimen he shot was only a forked horn, an animal that did not measure up to the higher standard for a trophy deer.

Many parents thought it important for their sons' healthy development as young men to have this outdoor experience. For young boys, especially those boys living in the countryside, learning to hunt was considered a rite of passage into manhood. This attitude still prevails in certain parts of the country. In one rural town in North Carolina, 91 percent of the men interviewed agreed that hunting provides boys an opportunity to identify with the world of men (Marks 1992).

8.28. Father and son with game, St. Paul, Minnesota, ca. 1911. Photo by Kregel. Private Coll.

8.29. Young adult with buck and gun, Vermont, ca. 1911. Jim and Kayce Dimond Coll.

Building on these early attempts to encourage children to hunt, groups like the Sons of Daniel Boone, later taken over by the Boy Scouts in 1910, taught boys how to track and trap animals, as well as how to mount them (Marks 1992). These organizations also tried to teach adolescents to respect the wilderness and wildlife. Boys belonging to these organizations kept a record of their good deeds, whether protecting the forest or the animals within it. As they participated in these outdoor activities, young frontiersmen also found themselves enjoying the company of like-minded friends. Just like their hunting fathers, they discovered new friends, told stories, sang songs, competed for trophies, and camped together.

FEMALE HUNTERS

So far, images of male hunters have dominated this chapter. This prominence reflects the content of the photos we found in our research, but there were some images that countered this trend by showing that frontier and rural women hunted, often as successfully as men (Herman 2001). Women were less involved in sport hunting than their rural counterparts, but there is evidence that there was more participation in sport than we might expect (Smalley 2005).

Although in most parts of the country girls were not generally taught to hunt, those girls who grew up in rural areas or small towns were routinely exposed to hunting, and some did participate. In the family portrait show in illustration 8.30, taken in upstate New York, it is clear that the female child in the family was as comfortable holding a rifle, albeit a smaller version, as her brothers.

Girls expected their fathers and older brothers would bring home their kills, where they were dressed, eaten, and sometimes worn. They inevitably heard menfolk spin tales of their hunting adventures that detailed the challenge and excitement of each kill. Undoubtedly, these tales excited some women's interest in hunting and fishing.

The bizarre "Compliments of the Season" card pictures two sisters in front of their home with one of them astride a propped-up small dead white-tailed deer (illustration 8.31). The pose documents how comfortable girls were with dead game (and how uncomfortable we

8.30. Family portrait with girl holding gun, ca. 1907. Pierce Coll.

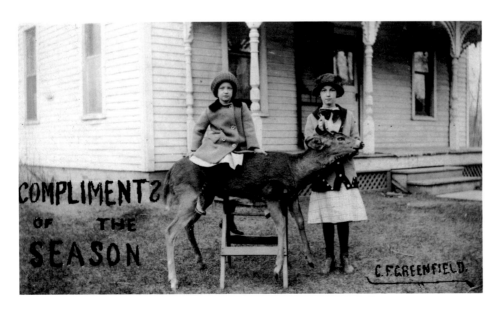

8.31. "Compliments of the Season," ca. 1910. Photo by Greenfield. Ziegler Coll.

are in viewing such a display today). There is no message on the back, so we are left to wonder who shot the deer and whether it might have been the older sister.

We did find a few postcards of sportswomen involved in hunting and fishing, and these women might have been forerunners of what was to come. Indeed, by the end of the twentieth century, women were the fastest-growing segment of hunters in America, making up 11 percent of the fourteen million hunters, up from 4 percent. The woman in illustration 8.32 strikes a familiar hunter's pose on the porch of a rural hotel, holding her rifle and standing next to a large white-tailed buck. Note that she is wearing a regular female dress rather than hunting gear. In many of the early images we came across, outdoor women wore long skirts.

Some men encouraged women's participation in hunting and fishing, but most resisted their intrusion into this masculine domain. To protect their virility, men argued that it was not ladylike to hunt, and, besides, the activity required a man's mental and physical strength. Learning to handle a weapon represented a reversal of the stereotype that depicted women as having an antipathy to guns (Strange 1997). Occasionally, women were permitted to join men on their expeditions, but their activity was often limited to observing, not shooting (Herman 2001).

Of course, there were exceptions. Some women embraced hunting and fishing, rivaling male counterparts in their skill and enthusiasm for killing game (Kalof and Fitzgerald 2003). Like the men pictured in other photos, the woman in illustration 8.33 brandished her weapon, along with her dogs and prolific kill, for the photographer to capture. And like men, women often discovered the same pleasures of hunting—it was fun, exciting, and invigorating, and it provided a social escape with like-minded women.

Women also learned how to handle a fishing rod, work with bait and tackle, make lures, and cast with the best of their male counterparts on the banks of America's streams. Although women have fished for centuries, angling became particularly popular toward the close of the nineteenth century among American women. Some even rose to celebrity status and made important contributions to the sport through invention or cataloging (Duncan 2004).

The fisherwoman in illustration 8.34, dressed according to the fashion of the day, gazes at her large catch while she holds her pole in the photographer's studio. Note that the photographer provided a stand to steady the fish for posing.

Women derived an additional pleasure from hunting not experienced by men. Although hunting by

8.32. Woman hunter with buck, Adirondacks, New York, ca. 1908. Pierce Coll.

8.33. Woman duck hunter, ca. 1910. Joel Wayne, Pop's Post-cards Coll.

8.34. Woman with catch, ca. 1910. Joel Wayne, Pop's Post-cards Coll.

rural women was probably understood as a practical requirement of life, there was a different attitude when it came to middle- and upper-class women who hunted for sport (Duncan 2004). After listening to and learning from the hunting tales of their husbands and fathers, they too wanted to hunt for adventure, competition, and companionship. Those females who challenged this prohibition broke down social barriers that women faced at the same time women were challenging other barriers in the workplace, at the voting booth, and in the home. Engaging in these forbidden activities may have given women a sense of accomplishment and exhilaration from the sheer novelty of doing something they wanted to do that was considered taboo.

WHALING

Hunting took place at sea as well as on land. Whaling, in particular, played a prominent part in America's growth and prosperity. Rather than people going out alone or in small groups to hunt, this form of hunting was an industrial activity that required large boats, heavy equipment, and a paid crew. Without international conflict or restriction, and with growing demand, the United States developed the largest whaling fleet in history (L. Davis, Gallman, and Gleiter 1997; Dolan 2007). Although we now think of whales as a scarce and highly valued sea mammal that needs protecting, they were plentiful in the mid- to late nineteenth century; more than eight thousand were killed by American whalers in 1853. It was common, for instance, to see a dozen or more whales spouting and blowing off the California seacoast on a given day.

Whale hunting continued during the postcard era, and technological advances made it possible for whalers to kill more efficiently and easily. Hand-thrown harpoons became a thing of the past. The development of firearms technology set the stage for building devices that could shoot harpoons farther and more accurately. A typical early instrument consisted of a cannonlike gun that operated on a swivel and fired a harpoon with a rope attached. These devices were mounted in the bow of the whaling boat. The goal was to stick the harpoon deep enough into the blubber to "make fast" the line to the whale. Attached to the lines were heavy buoys that were designed to tire the whale as it attempted to dive to

8.35. Harpooned whale, California, ca. 1932. Vaule Coll.

foil its pursuers. After the whale tired, seamen got near enough to kill it with a slender blade that was thrust into its vitals.

Later, a lance with a bomblike head that exploded on contact replaced the harpoon. If it struck in a critical location and deep enough, it would kill the whale promptly (Ellis 1991). Illustration 8.36 shows a gun that fired a barbed harpoon that would hook into the whale and explode seconds later. The dead whale would be retrieved with a winch. Once alongside the ship, the whale was pumped full of air to keep it afloat as it was towed back to port.

In the latter half of the nineteenth century, at least fifteen whaling stations were established along the California and Oregon shores to process as many as four thousand dead whales per year (Ellis 1991). A dozen or more men manned each station, where they harvested gray whales, humpbacks, and fin whales that swam close to the coast. Because these stations were fixed sites, whaleboats often cruised within a radius of about ten miles. Captured whales towed back to the station would be drawn up on the platforms, tail first and belly up. The whale in illustration 8.37 is being hauled up at the Trinidad, California, whaling station, established in 1914.

Once inside the whaling station, teams of about a half-dozen workers had the job of cutting up cadavers, as shown in illustration 8.38. Blubber was quickly stripped using longitudinal cuts made with knives on long poles called "blubber spades." This step was the first in the manufacture of diverse products, including oil, soap, margarine, and lubricants. For Americans, the whale trade was primarily a commercial industry to obtain oil and bone (Shoemaker 1996). Shoemaker believes that Americans' reluctance to incorporate whale meat into their diets opened the door for them to embrace whale-preservation efforts when petroleum and plastic came along.

The golden age of American whaling reached its peak by the mid-1800s. The dramatic rise of petroleum caused a steep decline in demand for whale oil (Dolan 2007; Shoemaker 1996). In addition, steam-powered boats and harpoon cannons were so effective that the whale populations near shore were severely depleted by the mid-1920s. By the close of the postcard era, whaling in the

8.36. Harpoon canon, California, ca. 1934. Vaule Coll.

8.37. Humpback whale, Trinidad, California, whaling station, ca. 1935. Elvrum Coll.

United States had virtually disappeared, becoming a part of its mythic past. With the exception of the one near Eureka, the once highly productive whaling stations on the California coast closed. The occasional whale hauled into Eureka for processing became a tourist attraction.

CONSERVATION

At the beginning of this chapter we listed the most commonly hunted game in the United States during the early part of the twentieth century. Other species, including some that are now considered endangered, were hunted for sport and profit, too. These species include the trumpeter swan, whooping crane, and bald eagle.

The youthful hunter in illustration 8.39 went to a photographer's studio in the Midwest to have his picture taken with a magnificent bird, what we believe to be a trumpeter swan that he recently shot. The shotgun he used for the kill is displayed on a specially rigged board along with his catch. These swans were common

8.38. Cutting up a whale, California, ca. 1915. Coll. of Leonard A. Lauder.

8.39. Young man displaying dead swan, Midwest, ca. 1920. Aikenhead Coll.

throughout the northern United States and Canada in the early nineteenth century but were nearly eliminated by the start of the twentieth. They were victims of market hunters who indiscriminately shot them to satisfy the fashion desires of wealthy women who favored the swan's feathers for powder puffs and adornments for fancy hats. It was believed that the species had become extinct, but 69 were documented in the northwestern United States in 1932.

Illustration 8.40 shows another hunter with his prey. This one is a large whooping crane. Whooping cranes were on the brink of extinction during the early part of the twentieth century (Collins 1969; Dunlap 1991). In 1941 there were only 16 known birds. The population has been gradually increasing since then. As of April 2007 there were 340 whooping cranes living in the wild.

The photo card in illustration 8.41 is of a father and son holding a bald eagle that they shot at Kintnersville,

8.40. Hunter with whooping crane, ca. 1918. Don and Newly
Preziosi Coll.

Pennsylvania. The handwritten notation on the front of
the card indicates that the bird's wingspread was six
feet, nine inches. Bald eagles were still plentiful during the postcard era, but they fell victim to widespread
spraying with the pesticide DDT, declining habitat, and
illegal shooting.[4] By the 1950s only 412 known pairs
existed. The U.S. and Canadian governments first protected them in 1918.

The last decades of the nineteenth century were the
heyday of market hunting. Game was indiscriminately

4. There was a division between conservationists and hunting
advocates who believed birds of prey were major contributors to the
declining population of game birds (Barrow 2002).

massacred. In addition to the danger of overhunting,
urban growth and western expansion became a concern of conservationists, as humans encroached on the
animals' wilderness. Whatever their class background,
sportsmen who hunted and fished for pleasure rather
than for profit or necessity increasingly realized that the
country's wildlife and natural resources were dimin-
ishing. Most understood that without a strong and
enforced conservation policy, some animals would be
hunted to extinction (Dunlap 1988). This realization
inspired conservation-minded sportsmen to do more to
protect vanishing wildlife (Casto 2006). Market hunters who violated the sportsman's creed were one of the
targets of reform efforts (Marks 1992; Smalley 2005).

The most infamous exploitation of American wildlife occurred in the last half of the nineteenth century
with the relentless hunting of the American buffalo.
Although it is estimated that at one time 60 million
roamed the prairies, by 1893 approximately 300 animals remained. These magnificent animals were virtually eliminated from the Great Plains by 1900 (Haines
1970). Illustration 8.42 shows a bison about to be butchered on a privately owned preserve in South Dakota.

To protect the few existing buffalo and preserve
the species, the American Bison Society was formed in
1905 with Theodore Roosevelt as its honorary president. This group succeeded in stocking a number of
wildlife preserves with bison donated by private owners (Plumb and Sucec 2006). By 1929 estimates put the
American buffalo population at about 3,400; today
there are about 150,000.

Roosevelt was concerned about the extinction of the
buffalo and acted to restore its presence. His attempt to
do something about the buffalo massacre represented
only a small fraction of his larger effort to curtail unbri-
dled hunting and exploitation of natural resources. He
persuaded Congress to create several wildlife preserves.
In one of his more celebrated acts, Roosevelt used his
influence to create Yellowstone National Park in 1872
(Franke 2005). He traveled there in 1903 to dedicate an
archway marking an entrance to the park. During this
visit the beauty of the wilderness and the abundance of
game inspired him, including one mountain lion that
he shot. Roosevelt was a conservationist, but a major

8.41. Bald eagle (six-feet, nine-inch wingspan), Kintnersville, Pennsylvania, ca. 1910. Marder Coll.

8.42. "Christmas Meat for the Capital City of S.D." A fat buffalo on western South Dakota range, 1909. Photo by Leeland. Cynthia Elyce Rubin Coll.

reason he promoted wildlife preservation was to ensure hunters would have game in the future.

Despite efforts by Roosevelt and others, conservation efforts were slow in coming. When regulations were enacted to put limits on hunters—creating hunting seasons, limiting killing to mature animals, stopping the killing of others, setting a limit on how many could be killed in a season, restricting the hunting of deer at night with lights—many hunters ignored these restrictions (Herman 2001).

Some backwoods meat and market hunters were hostile to the new rules and purposely ignored them. This attitude exacerbated a conflict between local meat hunters and sportsmen that still exists today. Hunters who made a living by selling their catch did not want the source of their livelihood infringed upon by the government, which they saw as an illegitimate outside influence.

During the nineteenth century and early twentieth, anglers expressed increasing concern for the loss of natural habitat and exhaustion of fish stock (Mighetto 1995). This distress led to various fishing restrictions, such as enacting temporary bans on fishing in certain areas or at certain times of the year and limits on the number of fish and size that could be caught. As with game laws, though, local people resisted these restrictions.

THE ALLURE AND AMBIVALENCE OF HUNTING

At the start of the twentieth century hunting appealed to many people for many reasons that seem simple and straightforward. Photo postcards showed meat hunters gathering their kill and sports hunters proudly displaying their trophies, both showing their guns, enjoying the pleasures of human companionship, relishing the plenitude of wildlife, displaying their kills, and showing affection for their dogs.

Lurking behind hunting's surface appeal were ironic and inconsistent human-animal relationships. When it came to hunters' dogs, these animals were valued as tools, just as were guns, but they could also be valued emotionally as companions. And although some hunters treated their dogs kindly, even lovingly, they simultaneously abused them, driving them in pursuit of game to the point of exhaustion. When it came to hunters' prey, some hunters saw these animals as a source of income or means of survival, whereas others respected them as game and part of the natural habit. Those individuals who were drawn to hunting because they wanted to be in the presence of wild animals and nature derived pleasure from watching animals as they flew overhead or ran through the bush. Yet they too chose to kill the objects of their admiration for many reasons, including furthering their sense of masculinity. From the contemporary perspective of many, the idea that one can respect, even love, an animal but still kill it seems old-fashioned and morally thorny. Nevertheless, hunters a century ago and also today embody this contradiction at the same time they unambiguously and unapologetically express joy in the hunt (Nelson 1998). People learn to live with apparent contradictions in many aspects of their lives, including, but certainly not limited to, their relationships with other animals.

Yet fewer and fewer Americans hunt. This decline has occurred while humans have increasingly encroached on animal habitat. Natural predators such as the wolf and other carnivores who kept the population of deer, turkey, and other large and small game under control have been eliminated in many areas. Whereas some species are in decline, many, such as deer and turkey, are so abundant that they create a danger to motorists as well as serious health and property challenges to suburbanites. Despite the decline of some species, hunting continues to be firmly anchored in American culture, deeply so in rural areas. To some, this practice is like apple pie or motherhood—a valued and cherished tradition built into our way of life.

When searching for photo postcards of hunting, we found many of hunters displaying mounted heads, deer racks, or fish on the walls of their homes. Why did they do so? Were there other ways of transforming dead animals into valued objects in the early decades of the twentieth century? And what uses were served by these disembodied and unreal animals, so far removed from their prior home as part of nature? With the help of photo postcards, we turn to these questions in the following chapter on trophies, specimens, and clothing.

Trophies, Specimens, and Furs

9.1. Taxidermist advertisement, Clarissa, Minnesota, ca. 1910. Photo by Teller. Joel Wayne, Pop's Postcards Coll.

The most common reason for killing wild animals was to consume their flesh or to engage in outdoor sports. But there were other justifications. During the postcard era preserving animals was another reason to kill them (Desmond 2002, 159). It was fashionable to display mounted animal trophies and specimens, as well as skins and horns, in homes, museums, and other establishments (illustration 9.1). Another reason to kill wild animals was to use their coats and skins to make stylish and protective garments and fashion accessories.

Taxidermy is the art of creating animal sculptures from dead creatures.[1] The most common way to create a specimen is to skin the dead animal, cure the hide, and either stuff the pelt or fit it over a mold that has been shaped to approximate the size and contours of the dead beast. Horns, hooves, beaks, teeth, and other body parts, as well as glass eyes, are installed during the process.[2] Fur garments are produced by skinning the animal and treating the pelt with chemicals to make it soft and manageable for tailoring.

1. Most definitions of taxidermy are broader and include the preservation of hides and insects and the mounting of horns.

2. In some forms of taxidermy the dead animal is used to make a mold from which a casting is made and then painted and decorated. In these cases no flesh, skin, or other parts of the animal are actually incorporated into the finished product. This procedure is commonly used in mounting fish. When taxidermists create rugs from dead animals, the entire pelt is not stuffed or mounted. As with bearskin rugs, the head may remain attached.

Contemporary young American urbanites would regard these practices as strange, even barbaric. How did they originate? Far back in human history, hunters and gatherers used animal skins to keep warm as well as to create crude creature look-alikes used in ceremonies and as decoys. Later, royalty and rich landowners adorned themselves in furs and decorated their castles and estates with animal horns and mounts.

SCIENTIFIC AND EDUCATIONAL TAXIDERMY

In the eighteenth and nineteenth centuries the roles of European scientists and hunters often overlapped, both engaging in dead-animal preservation.[3] As explorers and naturalists toured the globe, they encountered new lands and previously unknown species of animals. To develop schemes for the scientific classification of animals, as well as to show their finds to people at home, naturalists killed animals, skinned them, and cured the hides. In some cases, they stuffed the pelts, attempting to simulate lifelike figures, sometimes placing the animals in carefully reproduced dioramas that included particular plants or rocks native to their natural environment (Nyhart 2004). The more skillfully produced figures were displayed in early museums, widespread in England and other European countries. Such museum displays began appearing in the United States soon after the American Revolution (Irmscher 1999), but their number and size increased greatly toward the end of the 1800s and the early 1900s with the widespread development of public natural history museums.[4]

Museums needed the most lifelike and realistic mounts for the public to see and learn from.[5] Although amateurs and local craftspeople created dead-animal sculptures to produce trophies for hunters, they were

usually inferior to the ones produced by professional naturalists. As taxidermy began to evolve into an occupation that used more sophisticated techniques and formal instruction, public museums employed people trained as taxidermists and naturalists to create high-quality mounts for display (Kohler 2008).

The Society of American Taxidermists, a professional organization for the improvement and advancement of taxidermy, was established in 1880 (Desmond 2002, 162). Exceptional natural history pioneers who were associated with that organization laid the groundwork for these advances. In the United States, Carl E. Akeley and William Hornaday (Hornaday 1891) were the most exalted and influential. They and others were responsible for dramatic animal displays in museums, such as Washington's National Museum, New York's Museum of Natural History, and Chicago's Field Museum, that are still the centerpieces of these institutions. They are credited with turning taxidermy into an art guided by scientific knowledge and technical expertise (Haraway 1985). Rather than stuff skins, they and others created pelt-covered mannequins molded into artistically pleasing poses that were lifelike and natural for each species.[6]

In some cases, taxidermy was displayed in privately run museums. Arguably, the largest was established by Ira Morse and his son Philip, successful owners of a chain of New England shoe stores who amassed an enormous collection of specimens from their around-the-world hunting safaris (illustration 9.2) (Morse and Morse 2003).

In late 1928, when their holdings outgrew their home, the Morses opened a museum in Warren, New Hampshire (Morse and Morse 2003). Visitors attending could stand beside hundreds of different mounted animals (and animal parts), including lions, tigers, leopards, hyenas, hippos, antelopes, giraffes, wildebeests, zebras, baboons, monkeys, impalas, rhinoceroses, elephants, and crocodiles as well as other exotic curios collected on their trips (illustration 9.3). Admission was free; the family wanted the public to see their prized

3. This chapter draws heavily on Bryant and Shoemaker's (1988) typology of American taxidermy, with some modification.

4. Charles Willson Peale started a museum that included stuffed specimens in 1786.

5. Then, and continuing today, formally trained taxidermists distance themselves from old-school taxidermists by insisting that the word *stuffed* be erased from descriptions of their work and replaced with the word *mounted*.

6. Although Akeley and Hornaday are given credit for the mannequin and naturalist approach to taxidermy, Charles Willson Peale employed them in the late 1700s (Irmscher 1999, 73–74).

9.2. Dead elephant's ear held by Ira (*left*) and Phil Morse, ca. 1926. Arluke Coll.

9.3. Ira Morse standing next to lions he shot in Kenya, Warren, New Hampshire, ca. 1929. Private Coll.

possessions. The museum hosted its last visitors in 1992 when the whole collection was sold at auction.

Mounted species were also displayed in schools, where they were favored in science classrooms and libraries. The American buffalo and armadillo in illustration 9.4 were located in the science room at Fort Hayes Normal School, Kansas, a teachers' training college.[7] The

7. The American buffalo is also known as the American bison. Although widely used, the term *American buffalo* is a misnomer in that the animal is only a distant relative of true buffaloes, found in Asia and Africa.

man posing as a hunter with the specimens was one of the instructors.

Monsters, the medical term for creatures with congenital abnormalities or deformities, were also mounted and kept for student viewing and study. Although we are not sure who owned the mounted conjoined lamb in illustration 9.5, it was common for such specimens to be on view in educational institutions.

Schools and biomedical organizations used mounted animals and dead specimens as lifelike educational illustrations to teach science. Not officially part of taxidermy, middle and high school dissection classes were

9.4. Mounted buffalo at Fort Hays Normal School, Fort Hayes, Kansas, 1914. Bogdan Coll.

soon to become a rite of passage for most American children. The smell of formaldehyde and the sight of impaled, desecrated frogs became a standard feature of biology classes by the middle of the century. More advanced high school and college classes routinely featured anatomical dissection of fetal pigs and cats without much thought to the morality or educational value of the practice. Not until the end of the twentieth century did dissections come under scrutiny and schools begin offering students alternatives or even abolishing the practice altogether. Seeing the dead cats nailed to boards outside an anatomy class at the National University of the Philippines when the United States occupied that country would make most contemporary pet owners cringe (illustration 9.6).

ENTREPRENEURIAL TAXIDERMY

Early professional taxidermists were connected to museums (Bryant and Shoemaker 1988). They learned their trade as a craft through apprenticeships with old-timers or by trial and error. But in the later decades of the nineteenth century, expertise in this craft gradually

spread to individual, noninstitutionally affiliated taxidermists who observed these changes in taxidermy technique and incorporated them into their own practices.[8] Also influenced were taxidermy schools that proliferated during the postcard era. The quest for the creation of mounts that looked alive became the guiding principle of these schools (Desmond 2002). Although they offered diplomas and certificates, very few schools had residency requirements; the majority consisted of correspondence courses.

The earnest young taxidermist in illustration 9.7 proudly displays the products of his craft along with his diploma from the Northwestern School of Taxidermy. The school was established around 1902 in Omaha, Nebraska, and offered thorough and reasonably priced correspondence courses in the art of animal mounting and preservation.

8. Taxidermy rapidly diffused throughout American culture, becoming institutionalized as a folk craft. By 1911 the Boy Scouts created a merit badge for taxidermy that was not dropped from the *Handbook* until 1954, and then because of "lack of interest" (Bryant and Shoemaker 1988, 195).

9.5. Freak lamb, LaMoille, Illinois, 1911. Arluke Coll.

Northwestern graduated well over five hundred thousand taxidermists who completed studies by following the forty-lesson instruction booklets sent to enrollees, who completed them at their own pace. Although the photo postcard of the man with his diploma was probably produced for the purpose of advertising his new taxidermy business, students of the school were encouraged to send in pictures of their work as part of the instruction.

In addition to the school, the company supplied taxidermists with millions of dollars of tools and accessories, including glass eyes, mounts, stands, plaques, and preservation chemicals. They also provided taxidermy services to those persons who did not want to do it themselves. They boasted of serving such clients as Theodore Roosevelt, Buffalo Bill Cody, and the Prince of Wales.[9]

The Northwestern School of Taxidermy became a huge company that had a major impact on taxidermy in the United States. Period advertising literature for the institution hailed it as "a school for nature lovers and sportsmen" and suggested to potential enrollees that taxidermy was a way to "eat your trophy and have it too." Additionally, common with the logic of other taxidermy campaigns, the advertisement advanced the notion that having animals mounted was a way of preserving endangered species. They meant it both in the literal sense that mounting kept animals physically present but also environmentally: if trophies were mounted, there would be less need to shoot them. This counterintuitive advertising slogan does not fit well with modern logic or sensibilities. The company went out of business in the early 1990s.

Local entrepreneurial taxidermists went to their town photographers and had photo postcard advertisements made to promote their businesses. These illustrations are some of the most interesting images available that document the occupation. Illustration 9.1 is an example. Glen Sarff created this advertising postcard displaying an assortment of his work. Note the head mount of the white hare at the top of his arrangement. The wildly flamboyant card in illustration 9.8 was Rudolph Goller's way of telling potential clients about the quality of his work. Those full-figured deer, arranged so they look like they are pulling the wagon, are products of his craft. Were you fooled into thinking they were alive? That was what Rudolph wanted you to think. It showed that his products were "lifelike," a phrase commonly used in the business. The mounted deer head sitting beside him is easier to spot as an example of his work. Goller practiced in Roosevelt, Wiscon-

9. A number of American companies specialized in the production of high-quality mounts sold to a national and international clientele. In addition to individuals who could afford the fees, museums and universities began using their services. In addition to Northwestern, the Jonas Brothers in Colorado served these audiences; the Jonas Company still provides these services (Asma 2001).

9.6. Zoology class, National University, 1927. Photo by Venus Studio. Jim Matthews Coll.

9.7. Graduate of Northwestern Taxidermy School, ca. 1914. Joel Wayne, Pop's Postcards Coll.

sin. Given the size of the bucks' racks in the image, that location must have been known for its trophy deer.

In our search for real photo postcards bearing on taxidermy, we found very few interior or exterior images of taxidermy shops. Perhaps most taxidermists were locals who practiced out of their homes and chose to feature their mounts, rather than their workplaces, in advertisements. Illustration 9.9 shows the interior of

what appears to be a large professional taxidermy business in Watsonville, California. Two taxidermists are at work with mounted deer heads dominating the scene.

TROPHY TAXIDERMY

In the early part of the twentieth century, wealthy hunters, or sportsmen as they liked to be called, amassed

9.8. Rudolph Goller, taxidermist, "Roosvelt," Wisconsin, ca. 1912. Private Coll.

9.9. Studio of Miller and Herring, expert taxidermists, Watsonville, California, ca. 1912. Bogdan Coll.

elaborate displays of taxidermy trophies in their own homes and vacation retreats. Big-game trophy hunters used mounted heads to acquire points in the Boone and Crockett trophy book for killing exceptional specimens of game (Bryant and Shoemaker 1988). A stellar example is the case of Edwin McAlpin, who did his shooting mainly in North America but occasionally took trips to other parts of the world. Illustration 9.10 shows only one of the many walls his collection adorned. Note the moose, caribou, elk, mountain goat, wolf, bear, cougar, tiger, and giraffe heads, as well as the fox on the mantel and the full-body mounts of the bear cubs by the fireplace. McAlpin's private menagerie filled his Adirondack retreat at Brandreth Lake, New York (Bogdan 2003).

Hunters of lesser means imitated the rich by having their locally shot game mounted for more modest trophy

9.10. Display of hunters' trophies, Brandreth Lake, New York, ca. 1908. Photo by Beach. Bogdan Coll.

9.11. Mule deer on porch, ca. 1910. Private Coll.

displays in their less extravagant abodes. For rural dwellers and town folks, mounting was reserved for a personal record of hunting accomplishments. Special catches—the deer or elk with the largest rack, the biggest bear—were singled out for these trophy displays. An example is the mule-deer mounts shown on the porch in illustration 9.11. These specimens were taken off the walls inside the building and brought outside so that a well-exposed photo postcard could be shot in the daylight.

Occasionally, people brought their taxidermy possessions to photography studios to have their portraits taken with their trophies. The man in illustration 9.12 is from a small town in Vermont. He brought his prize nine-point trophy white-tailed buck to a photographer's studio to pose with his rifle beside it. The well-dressed and manicured young sportsman in illustration 9.13 brought the pelican he shot to the photographer's studio along with the gun he used to kill it.

9.12. Hunter with large deer mount, Vermont, ca. 1908. Joel Wayne, Pop's Postcards Coll.

9.13. Boy with pelican, ca. 1910. Joel Wayne, Pop's Postcards Coll.

For the most part, mounting one's hunting trophies, whether for the rich or not so rich, was a male practice, a direct way of displaying masculine prowess, outdoor skills, man's power over nature, and his mastery over dangerous forces in the wilderness (Hummel 1994; Kalof and Fitzgerald 2003). Photo postcards of trophy animals captured the hunters' triumph, enabling them to preserve the memory and share the moment with friends and family who could not see firsthand the evidence of the hunter's virility or acknowledge his success in person. At another level, such symbolization of masculinity was connected to nationalism because obtaining hunting trophies resulted from contact with and conquering of the American frontier as well as distant continents and peoples (Herman 2001).

DÉCOR AND PRACTICAL TAXIDERMY

When taxidermy spread from museums to households, it provided everyday people with scientific curiosities, educational tools, and bragging rights. In addition, taxidermy acquired a decorative quality as a type of home furnishing. Members of the growing middle class, who took hunting holidays outside of, or back to, their areas of origin, had their hunting kills mounted and hung in their homes; others purchased taxidermy solely for decoration.

Illustration 9.14 shows a well-dressed gentleman displaying two of his mounted trophies inside his Victorian living room. Note the decorative wallpaper, the

9.14. Man with deer mounts, ca. 1914. Private Coll.

9.15. Women with small mounts, ca. 1911. Private Coll.

velvet stuffed couch, and the pictures on the wall. The deer appear to be huge. Judging from the size of their racks, they were large, but their size was enlarged by the way the picture was taken. We suspect the distortion was done intentionally. Placing an object in the foreground with a person in the background is an old sportsman's trick to increase the catch's dimensions.

There was another kind of household and public display of dead animals at the start of the twentieth century, a practice inherited from the British and not just favored by men. In the nineteenth century, during Victorian times, stuffed animals, especially birds and small mammals, became a decorating fad in England.[10] That practice was imported to the United States and continued during the postcard era. Illustration 9.15 shows an amateur taxidermist posing with several small mounted specimens she displayed in her home.

10. They also had anthropomorphic specimens: small animals, such as squirrels, dressed like people and presented as if they were engaged in human activity.

Small-animal taxidermy mounts, some in glass domes and cases in one's home or place of work, showed sophistication as well as an appreciation of nature. Affluent families sometimes purchased mounted specimens of animals and birds to display in their homes for the edification of family members and friends. Such displays in the home suggested intellectual enlightenment and became a status symbol (Bryant and Shoemaker 1988). Some of these decorating items were imported, but local taxidermists produced them as well. Such was the case with the fox pictured in illustration 9.16. The message on the back of the postcard identifies the man as a naturalist.

As a decorative art, taxidermy also developed a practical side. Useful articles made from dead animals served a number of household functions (Bryant and Shoemaker 1988). Deer-feet hat racks, elephant-feet umbrella stands, hide and feather lamp shades, and hoof inkwells are just a few examples of utilitarian

9.16. Man and mounted fox, ca. 1909. Joel Wayne, Pop's Postcards Coll.

9.17. Taxidermy chair, Morse Museum, ca. 1929. Arluke Coll.

taxidermy. The unusual chair in illustration 9.17 would have been a conversation piece in any home.

NOSTALGIA TAXIDERMY

Mougeole, a taxidermist who operated his business in Chicago, provides an example of yet another use of this craft—mounting of dead pets for owners who cannot bear to part with their companions and want keepsakes in their homes (illustration 9.18). The artist chose not to appear in the photograph, leaving the space for three of his mounts arranged as a still life. Note the formality and drawing-room quality of the arrangement. Mougeole appears to have wanted to appeal to a more genteel, urban clientele with Victorian pretensions. The white animal is a dog. Mounting one's pet was part of early taxidermy practice.[11]

Without a message on the back of illustration 9.19 or other sources of information about it, we do not know for whom it was produced or the identity or role of the man holding the cigar. The setting is a home, and

11. According to Irmscher, the first specimen Charles Willson Peale tried to preserve for his Philadelphia museum was Benjamin Franklin's Angora cat (1999, 84).

9.18. Taxidermist's advertisement, Chicago, ca. 1909. Jim Matthews Coll.

9.19. Man with mounted pets, ca. 1911. Joel Wayne, Pop's Postcards Coll.

the portrait is less formal than a professional photographer would have arranged. The man is either a pet owner who chose to have his companions preserved postmortem or a taxidermist showing off his skills with pets. A third guess is that he is an amateur taxidermist who worked with his own domestic animals.

Although we do not know what percentage of taxidermists' trade was the result of pet owners mourning the death of beloved companions, the small number of postcards showing mounted pets suggests that this practice was only a minor part of taxidermists' business (Desmond 2002). Currently, taxidermists do not mount pets. They refer such inquiries to specialists in freeze-drying.

NOVELTY TAXIDERMY

It was not always necessary for people to bring their own mounted trophies to photographers for studio portraits. Small-time professional photographers tried successfully to lure customers into their shops by offering them unusual taxidermy props to include in their portraits. Interesting mounted animals were often the come-on in shops that appealed to tourists. The animals chosen were species associated with the geographic location—sea lions in California, alligators in Florida, and bucking broncos in the West—so the picture could be part of tourists' documentation of their journey.

9.20. Tourists with alligators, St. Augustine, Florida, ca. 1909. Photo by Harris. Joel Wayne, Pop's Postcards Coll.

There are many outrageous examples of this use of taxidermy specimens. The two women in illustration 9.20 pose with constrained smiles among the alligators in a St. Augustine, Florida, photo studio. The person sitting on the largest of the beasts is holding a small cigar in one hand and an empty beer bottle in the other. They posed this way to jokingly show friends back home that they were enjoying themselves.

In addition to mounted animals, photo studios provided regionally appropriate costumes for patrons to adorn when being photographed. The two older gentlemen in illustration 9.21 wear stereotypical cowboy outfits—vests, chaps, bandannas, and hats. One is mounted on a bronco ingeniously created in a half-bucking position by a talented taxidermist.

Taxidermists produced other novelty specimens. Though typically they configured their products in natural poses accompanied by wilderness accessories, taxidermists popularized another form that created anthropomorphized sculptures. Some of them, such as bears holding trays and wearing glasses, were used as attention-getting advertising for restaurants and other commercial establishments. Others—groupings of small domesticated animals—were outfitted with sports gear and arranged in displays that were meant to be humorous conversation pieces, such as squirrels playing golf.

FASHION HIDES

Taxidermists were not the only occupational group that transformed animal skins into objects to be admired. At the same time that deer heads and other mounts were displayed in museums and decorated homes, garments made from animal fur were popular both as a fashion statement and as a practical way of keeping warm (Stirity 2001).[12] The man holding the furs in illustration 9.22 is a furrier proudly displaying recent purchases that he will skillfully turn into wearing apparel.

Although most furs worn by Americans came from animals subdued or grown in North America, exotic furs from distant continents were highly desirable to wealthy, status-conscious consumers. Studio photo postcard portraits show style-conscious women in fur

12. Some people include the processing of animal fur and hide into garments as part of taxidermy, but we are treating furriers and others related to garment production as a separate occupation requiring some of the same skills as taxidermy but also additional skills.

9.21. Studio prop of bronco-riding tourist, ca. 1916. Private Coll.

9.22. Furrier showing his recent purchases, ca. 1908. Joel Wayne, Pop's Postcards Coll.

coats (Doughty 1975). Illustration 9.23 provides an example of the use of fur in the pursuit of fashion. The woman is wearing a leopard-skin coat trimmed with another fur. As you can see, her small dog, standing on his back legs, is wearing matching apparel. A second dog's head is peeking out from under the woman's coat where it was tucked under her arm.

Women who could not afford to, or chose not to, have full fur coats trimmed their outfits with fur and wore hats, muffs, stoles, and other fuzzy accoutrements. Some fur garments adorning women's shoulders consisted of the outside remains of the whole animal, in most cases a fox, complete with head, glass eyes, and tail. The woman in illustration 9.24 either is a model for a furrier or just went to a photo studio to have her picture taken with her new finery. The heads and other parts of the animals that make up her fur accessories are in full view.

It was not just women who wore fur for fashion and used animal skins as protection against the elements (Joselit 2001). We found many studio portraits of men dressed in raccoon and other animal pelts showing off their garments.

The pursuit of fur-bearing animals to provide pelts to be made by furriers into garments is a part of European Americans' earliest commercial tradition (M. E. Jones 1998; P. Phillips 1961). Some of the first Europeans to travel into parts of the North American wilderness were traders who bartered with Native Americans for pelts in exchange for manufactured goods (Vaughan and Holm 1990). Fur-trading posts were often the first

9.24. Woman with fur stole and muff, ca. 1910. Arluke Coll.

9.23. Woman and dogs in leopard-skin coats, ca. 1920. B. Nelson Coll.

settlements that later became forts and legitimized territorial claims. The Hudson's Bay Company, incorporated in 1670, was the first commercial corporation in North America based on fur trade. Some animal furs were so sought after that supply could not keep up with demand. Through the mid-nineteenth century European buyers gobbled up beaver pelts that they sold to hat manufacturers. By 1900 trappers had depleted the population of beavers to the point of near extinction (Hine and Faragher 2000).

European Americans as well as Native Americans continued to trap and hunt fur-bearing animals well into the twentieth century (Baldwin 1999; Kersey

1975).[13] Photo postcards record early twentieth-century trappers displaying their catches. In the studio portrait in illustration 9.25, a proud old-timer is pictured draped with large fox and raccoon pelts. Note the small white pelt over his chest. It was probably a weasel wearing its winter coat; in northern regions weasels change color during the snowy months.

In the next illustration we see a Maine trapper, trap in hand, with an array of animal pelts hung on the wall of his house. The caption tells us that in twenty-one days the trapper caught seven skunks, twenty-eight

13. There are still trappers today, but very few make a living from trapping as an occupation.

foxes, eight mink, four cats, and one raccoon. The cats that are referred to were probably bobcats, animals not present in the display of pelts. Interestingly, the trapper dressed up for his portrait.

Illustration 9.27 shows a Minnesota fur trader bringing back pelts he purchased from various trappers who were his suppliers in the far northern headwaters of the Mississippi. The sign reads: "Henry H. Herreid, Largest Buyer of Raw Fur in Itasca County, a Return Trip from Upper Mississippi." (Itasca County is named after a source lake of the Mississippi River.) Herreid was a middleman who bought from trappers and sold either to another dealer down the supply line or to urban furriers, such as the one in illustration 9.27. Furriers turned the pelts into wearing apparel. Herreid used this photo postcard as an advertisement for his business.

With the depletion of natural fur-bearing stock by trappers, the increased use of land for agriculture, and a growing taste among American urbanites for fur, it became impossible to meet the people's demand for quality furs. Fur farms, locations where fur-bearing animals are raised in cages, had been around well before the turn of the century. During the first third of the twentieth century, as techniques for raising fur-bearing animals improved and taste for furs by urbanites grew, fur farms proliferated.

9.25. Fur trapper, ca. 1907. Joel Wayne, Pop's Postcards Coll.

9.26. Trapper with catch, Maine, ca. 1907. George C. Gibbs Coll.

9.27. Fur traders, Itasca County, Minnesota, ca. 1909. Joel Wayne, Pop's Postcards Coll.

Further accelerating fur-farm growth and improvement, wealthy buyers became more discerning about the types of furs that were desirable—with high-quality furs such as silver fox or later mink becoming status symbols to wear. Fur farming became a big and lucrative business in most northern states. A large fur farm in the early part of the century, such as the one in illustration 9.28, produced at first a few hundred pelts each year, but as demand increased the pelts numbered into the thousands. The postcard shows 175 silver-fox furs.

Some of these farms expanded and reorganized to meet the growing demand for superior furs. As fur farming became competitive and taste in furs became more sophisticated, fad-driven breeders developed animals with specific colors and richer and smoother coats.

New species were introduced and embraced. The advertising card in illustration 9.29 was for an upstate New York fur farm that opened in 1915. At first the farm raised silver fox exclusively, but as the caption claims, the owners began raising sable, "the first sables ever to be raised in captivity," in the 1920s.[14]

14. Russian sable was the most prized fur in the world because of its silky quality and rich color. The American sable is different from the Russian variety. It demanded a high price, but not as high as the Russian variety.

Given as gifts by men to their female partners, mink and sable coats became status symbols. Wearing one, or having your female partner wear one, gave the appearance that you had both money and taste. They were second to diamonds as love icons. Mink fur production peaked in 1966 and more recently has been the object of animal-rights protest.

Mink is the most common animal raised on fur farms, and fox is second. Mink raised for fur are killed within a year after birth, while those mink used for breeding are kept for as long as five years. In the wild mink occupy unlimited space, but on farms they live in the unnatural state of being packed into small cages. They are fed meat and fish by-products. Killing is accomplished by methods that emphasize preserving the pelt, so electrocution, gassing, poisoning, and lethal injection are preferred. Animal-rights activists point out that for every fur coat, dozens of animals endure intense suffering.

CHIC CORPSES

To some people, taxidermy and fur apparel represent the ultimate objectification of animals. Mounted creatures were displayed far from their natural habitats, and fur garments were dissociated from their origins. Further objectifying animals, many trophies were not the

9.28. Rest Island Silver Fox Farms, Lake City, Minnesota, 1921. Arluke Coll.

9.29. Alaska Silver Fox Farms, Ausable Chasm and Lake Placid, New York, ca. 1925. Don and Newly Preziosi Coll.

whole animal. They consisted of only parts of animal bodies—just their heads, their racks, or their hooves—parts that were important to the hunter. They became objects of conspicuous display (Brower 2005, 23).

The objectification critique of taxidermy and the fur trade may be too pat and simple; taxidermy has a more complex and contradictory social meaning. These dead mounts are still part animal. They are authentic in that they use real skin, feathers, and bones. What is

unusual is that some are re-creations of nature, domesticated by humans and posing no threat to them (Marvin 2004). In this fixed state they become objects that humans interact with and create stories about, stimulating their imaginations and enriching their lives (Patchett and Foster 2008).

Raising questions about the function of mounted animals is something that could happen only in current times. During the postcard era they were taken for granted. There were more taxidermists and products of their work on display in the United States than at any other time in the country's history. What people would now consider bizarre, politically incorrect, or distasteful were fad and fashion.

Hunters in rural areas and a few sportsmen still have trophies mounted. A small number of companies, such as Jonas's in Colorado, specialize in preparing high-quality mounts for sportsmen who can afford them. They employ a small staff of taxidermists. Taxidermists in private practice still can be found in rural areas throughout the United States, and although the number of hunters has diminished, some still go to these craftspersons to have their trophies mounted. A few exemplary practitioners offer courses in the art, but the number of trainees is minuscule compared to the numbers enrolled at Northwestern when it was in its prime.

Although a disappearing craft, mounted animals have not been eliminated from public display. Still the mainstay of natural history museums, these institutions employ a few taxidermists, but they are mainly involved in maintaining, not expanding, the collections. The remaining mounts that were so pervasive during the early part of the twentieth century can still be found in antique shops, inns, and bars that keep them to create an old-time rustic atmosphere. The sporting goods store Dick's sometimes uses mounted deer heads to decorate the walls above the gun display. These mounts are merely vestiges of an occupation that once flourished.[15]

Interest in mounted animals is, for the most part, a thing of the past. As a sign of this flagging interest, in the early 1990s the Morse family, heirs of the founder of the museum in New Hampshire discussed earlier, decided to put their collection up for public auction. They did so after they had offered it to the Smithsonian, to Dartmouth College, and to the Museum of Natural History, among others. There were no takers, not even as a gift. The auction drew five hundred bidders. Although some items went to antique dealers and restaurant decorators, most bidders were New Hampshire residents and others who had visited the museum in their childhood and wanted to bring home an object of remembrance.

Whereas taxidermy waned during the twentieth century, a different kind of display—the living wild animal—captured Americans' interest. The number, size, and complexity of zoos grew rapidly to meet this demand. Animals began appearing in movies and took their place in other forms of mass entertainment such as circuses. We examine the public's enthusiasm for these wild animal spectacles next.

15. In *Still Life: Adventures in Taxidermy* (2010), Melissa Milgrom writes about a subculture of taxidermists that she estimates to number one hundred thousand practitioners. She celebrates present-day taxidermy and suggests that the practice is alive and well even though it is hidden from most Americans.

10

Spectacles

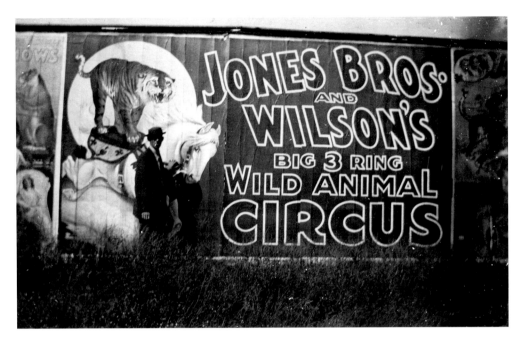

10.1. Wild Animal Circus, ca. 1920. Coll. of Leonard A. Lauder.

*T*he postcard era was a time of widespread and lavish public displays of animals for the purposes of human education, amusement, and profit. In no other period of American history were animals exhibited with such frequency or did they draw larger crowds. At the turn of the century the circus, an institution where animals were the major attraction, was at the height of its popularity (C. Fox and Parkinson 1969). Carnivals, another institution where animals played an important entertainment role, were on the rise (Bogdan 1989, 58–62). Public urban zoos had been established in the late 1800s as educational and recreational centers as well as sources of civic pride (Hanson 2002). The number and size of zoos greatly expanded in the first three decades of the twentieth century. Private roadside amusement displays popped up as Americans took to the road in their automobiles (Margolies 1998). Animals

were regularly on the vaudeville program (Stein 1985). But animals in vaudeville declined as motion pictures drew larger audiences and animals played roles on the silver screen (Bowers 1986).

This chapter's title has several meanings. In the simplest sense, animals are spectacles when displayed as objects of the human gaze. Whether dead and mounted or living and performing in circuses, zoos, or movies, animals provoke human curiosity and imagination (Berger 1980, 3–28). Animals are also spectacles in a congratulatory sense, as in spectacular, terrific, or elaborate. It is amazing to stand just inches away from exotic animals and watch them perform tricks involving uncanny intelligence, strength, and agility. Last, animals are spectacles when their display represents excess, goes to extremes, or tries to be novel. A circus might brag about having the most elephants, a zoo might advertise the only platypus in the Western hemisphere, and a traveling animal act might feature chimps dressed like humans at a tea party. Rather than animals making spectacles of themselves, humans make spectacles of animals.

THE CIRCUS

Urbanites appreciated traveling circuses;[1] rural and small-town Americans loved them. The day of the year that the circus came to town was a festive holiday where young and old, rich and poor, townsfolk and their farming neighbors from near and far turned out to view the spectacular display. The big circuses, such as Ringling, Barnum and Bailey, Sells-Floto, John Robinson, Miller Brothers, Hagenbeck-Wallace, Al Barnes, and Sparks, were extravagant three-ring affairs, with acrobats, jugglers, trapeze artists, clowns, and other human entertainers (Chindahl 1959). Human acts were exciting, but animals were the core of the show (C. Fox and Parkinson 1969). The circus could not have obtained its popularity without an array of animal performers and without a menagerie. An indication of animals' prominence is a montage postcard produced to promote the Ringling's hometown, Baraboo, Wisconsin. Of the seven inserts, six featured animals.

Circus day began when the company train pulled into town and animals were unloaded. Eager townsfolk were at the tracks to greet their arrival. In illustration 10.2 a young elephant with an advertising message painted on his side, "Pay to See the Elephant Act," is unloaded.

Although the main event of the day was the paid performance in the big top, the parade down Main Street—from the tracks to the where the huge tents were being erected—was quite a show. Citizens lined the streets to see the animals march past. Elephants, the largest land mammals in the world, were the stars.[2] Any respectable circus would have at least one elephant in the parade, and larger circuses competed with each other for who

had the most, occasionally topping twenty. In addition to their star billing, elephants played multiple roles in the circus. After the parade they were draft animals, pulling the heavy circus equipment and helping to erect the big top (C. Fox 1990). Then, they appeared in the menagerie before their performance under the big top.

Town photographers featured elephants in their parade coverage. A few even captioned their cards "Elephant Day." In illustration 10.3 we see the pachyderms leading the way through Winfield, Kansas. Trainers with pith helmets sit perched on their heads reminding us that the animal trade had a colonial legacy. The Kansas postcard photographer captioned his card of the parade down Main Street as "Show Day," as if to say, "Now the circus can begin because the elephants are here." You can count nine elephants in the photo of that parade. Circus days were common at the beginning of the century. On these occasions, circuses tried to outdo each other with more enjoyable and spectacular parades. These special days involved the entire community whose residents showed up in great numbers to see the free parade (Culhane 1990).

For most Americans, elephants and other large foreign mammals were extraordinary, almost beyond the range of what the typical citizen could fathom. Other animals joined elephants in the parade. Circuses typically included lions, tigers, polar bears, zebras, giraffes, camels, hippos, various primates, and more. The large giraffes and camels rivaled elephants in their strangeness. When the Ringling show's harnessed camels paraded though town, folks turned their heads (illustration 10.4). Common animals such as horses, dogs, and brown bears were included too, but they played second fiddle to the foreign beasts.

Caged animals were also present in the parade. Illustration 10.5 shows an imperially themed horse-drawn wagon with bars containing a rhinoceros. Whereas most animals were performers or draft animals (or both), large circuses also included animals like rhinos, whose only contribution was that they were on display in the menagerie.

The menagerie was located in a large tent immediately after the ticket stand and before the entrance to the big top. Citizens bought tickets to the main show and

1. For example, in the spring, the Ringling show played Madison Square Garden in New York City. This annual event was the country's marker of winter's end.

2. P. T. Barnum's purchase of the London Zoo's famed elephant Jumbo made headlines for weeks and became a nationwide sensation (Chambers 2008).

10.2. Unloading a circus elephant, ca. 1907. Private Coll.

10.3. Elephant parade on Main Street, Winfield, Kansas, ca. 1909. Private Coll.

then, as part of the admission fee, could gawk at the animals—caged, fenced, or chained to stakes—before proceeding to find their seats in the big tent. In addition to the animals that were there purely for display, the menagerie included select creatures that would later perform in the big top.

Before the big show began, the performing animals left the menagerie to get prepared for the show. Most animal acts consisted of the decorated creatures going through their show routines under the direction of flamboyant trainers who shouted, snapped their whips, and made other demonstrative gestures. Some of the acts consisted of synchronized, choreographed tricks with humans on board. Scantily clad women accomplished death-defying feats on the backs of white stallions. Men and women rode elephants and engaged in other activities with the beasts that appeared to be, and often were, dangerous (Culhane 1990).

10.4. Ringling camels, Baraboo, Wisconsin, 1908. Private Coll.

10.5. Caged rhinoceros, ca. 1907. Coll. of Leonard A. Lauder.

As illustration 10.6 shows, even saddled camels with spangled and fringed blankets performed cooperatively with humans. The camel's rider, who may have been a woman or a man in drag, is about to enter the main tent to perform.

There were many animal acts in which large decorated, exotic creatures went through their paces.

Although every act and each animal had a special contribution to the show, no type of animal elicited more fear than felines. Lions, tigers, and others locked in a cage with either a male or a female trainer equipped with only a whip stirred the imagination and anxiety of the audience. These animal performers were referred to as "wild animals," but, in the strict sense of the

10.6. Camel ready to appear in the big top, ca. 1908. Coll. of Leonard A. Lauder.

10.7. Trainer with head in lion's mouth, San Francisco, California, ca. 1910. Coll. of Leonard A. Lauder.

term, they were trained, not "wild." Calling them wild heightened their appeal.

The act's most thrilling moment happened when the trainer got close to the beast, even face-to-face. Performers from different circuses competed with each other to see who could have the most daring encounters. The ultimate, as shown in illustration 10.7, defied people's sense of the possible, the trainer putting his head in the lion's mouth.

The image in illustration 10.8 is a publicity photo postcard for the famous Hagenbeck-Wallace Circus. In this case, rather than heightening the fear element in the "wild animal," the danger is played down for the purpose of humor. The trainer sits nonchalantly at a table he is sharing not with a feline, but with a polar bear while they have a beer. The image's caption, "No Local Option for John and Bruno," is a reference to town Prohibition ordinances.

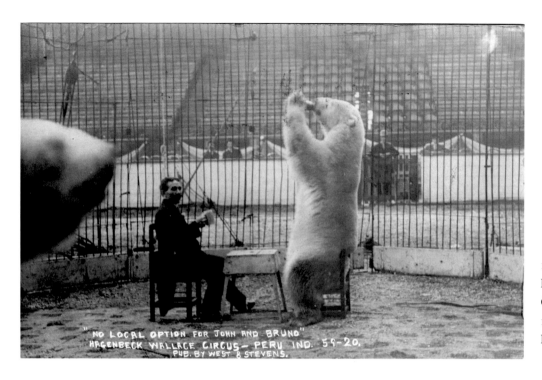

10.8. Polar bear with Hagenbeck-Wallace Circus, Peru, Indiana, ca. 1907. Coll. of Leonard A. Lauder.

There were many famous wild animal trainers, but the one who rose to the status of national celebrity during the postcard era was Clyde Beatty. Between 1925 and 1935 he was a big draw for the largest circuses in the country. Beatty's act was designed to highlight the conflict between humans and beasts. He entered the cage inhabited with lions, tigers, and other cats—as many as forty at one time—in a jungle hunter's outfit with a whip, pistol, and a chair. Outfits worn by Beatty and other wild animal performers were designed to suggest that they were just back from a safari. Beatty used the chair to direct the animals and to provoke them into showing their teeth and roaring. Beatty's diminutive five-foot-five stature enhanced his appeal as a courageous master of wild beasts, although he was not the wild animal safari hunter his persona suggested. So popular, Beatty became a film star in 1933. In the late 1930s he opened the Clyde Beatty Jungle Zoo, a tourist attraction in Fort Lauderdale, Florida. The photo postcard in illustration 10.9 was produced by that enterprise, but shows Beatty at work in 1933.

Although Beatty died in 1965, a circus with his name still puts on shows. That organization has been repeatedly charged with violating the Animal Welfare Act's guidelines for humane treatment of performing animals and has been a target for animal-rights advocates.

In addition to circuses, other traveling amusement displays with shows of performing animals existed. Wild West shows featured animal acts as well as Indian war enactments with pseudobands of Native Americans and cavalry soldiers reliving western battles (Moses 1996). The rodeo, another venue for animal displays, will be examined in the next chapter.

ANIMALS ON THE MIDWAY

As circus goers walked to the ticket sellers' booths, they had to walk down a thoroughfare that was lined with food stands, souvenir booths, freak shows, mini shows, and other exhibits. Vendors sold their wares, and show people charged a fee to enter these auxiliary exhibits. This assembly of concessions was called the midway.

Circuses were not the only entertainment venues with midways. In the late nineteenth and early twentieth centuries, carnivals came into being. These entertainment organizations were traveling bands of entrepreneurs who set up at local and state fairs and other locations (Bogdan 1989, 58–62). In addition to all that would be found

10.9. Clyde Beatty and his trained wild animals, ca. 1933. Private Coll.

on the circus midway, they had Ferris wheels, merry-go-rounds, and other mechanical rides, as well as games of chance. The carnival's offerings were lined up along a fair-goers' lane, also called a midway. In addition, there were midways at World's Fairs and other expositions (Rydell 1984). Amusement parks, such as Coney Island, had areas that were equivalent to midways (Kasson 1978). Animal exhibits appeared in all of these venues. Typically, "barkers" lured strollers into their tents with the call of "step right up." For the price of a small admission fee, they promised a view of sights never seen before. Such hype was part of the come-on for animal exhibits.

The fear and titillation snakes provoked were crucial for the success of one type of midway sideshow performer, snake handlers or charmers. Women dominated the role. The incongruity in the juxtaposition of the feminine with a horrendous snake had special audience appeal. The act involved little skill, just a willingness to be draped with one or a number of serpents. That alone combined with the hyperbole of the barker lured sideshow customers to pay the entrance fee. Snake performers attached to larger circuses and carnivals did not use domestic snakes. As shown in illustration 10.10, they preferred the larger imports, such as pythons and anacondas.

But smaller traveling midways often employed American rattlesnakes and featured people who were presented as having superpowers over the deadly serpents. The man with the cowboy hat in illustration 10.11 is an example. He has rattlers draped over his arms and poses outside a midway tent with two other performers.

In the chapter on veterinarians, we described how animals with physical anomalies—a two-headed calf, for example—were exhibited as freaks of nature. There were other attractions that were presented as freaks, but what made them special had more to do with how they were presented than any physical irregularity. On the midway and in other such venues, deceit was part of the entertainment culture. The father of the amusement world, P. T. Barnum, was considered the king of exaggeration and misrepresentation (Harris 1973). An example of animal misrepresentation is revealed in illustration 10.12. It shows an exhibition of a diminutive breed of ponies presented as "Equine Wonders," the "smallest horses in the world." Although breeds of miniature horses are fairly common and exist all over the world, exhibits such as this one suggest that the animals on display are unique and that the horses are "midgets" or genetic freaks.

10.10. Snake handler in a carnival sideshow, ca. 1910. Joel Wayne, Pop's Postcards Coll.

10.11. Snake handler, Hornbeak, Tennessee, 1913. Vaule Coll.

Another favorite, but misrepresented, attraction was the South American rodent, caviomorphs, a creature that resembles a rat; it was sometimes billed as weighing up to two hundred pounds. Calling it a giant urban rat, sideshow hucksters would claim that the one they had on exhibit was captured in an American city.

Some midway shows featured small performing animals such as dogs and monkeys. Illustration 10.13 shows a midway attraction for a traveling carnival that presented dog performers as well as a trained goat. In addition, a larger animal, a horse, was on the roster. This horse, like others on the midway, did not do physical tricks; it was presented as a psychological wonder, an "educated horse." Educated horses, ones that counted or talked, were common attractions during the postcard era. Illustration 10.14 shows "Ruby," who could, among other skills, answer the phone, tell time, and add a string of four-digit numbers. These feats were all

10.12. Equine wonders, world's smallest horses, 1915. C. Trenton Boyd Coll.

10.13. Midway-performing animals at carnival, ca. 1908. Lew Baer Coll.

accomplished with directions from her exhibitor whose cueing went undetected by the audience.[3]

3. Perhaps the most famous counting horse was Clever Hans, who, in 1907, was shown to be actually picking up cues from his trainer's body language, according to a study by psychologists.

"Diving horses" were another attraction. Although they were often included as an exhibition on the midway, they also performed as an act by themselves at fairs and town events. Dr. Carver's diving-horse act was one of the first, and in the finale the horse jumped from a forty-foot tower (Sarah Duzynski, personal

10.14. Ruby, an educated horse, Savin Rock, Connecticut, ca. 1915. Joel Wayne, Pop's Postcards Coll.

10.15. King and Queen, diving horses, White River Junction, Vermont, ca. 1908. Joel Wayne, Pop's Postcards Coll.

communication, 2009). His act was rivaled by Woodmen's diving horses, King and Queen, one of whom can be seen jumping in illustration 10.15.

Local postcard photographers would attend such displays and sell their images to people who witnessed the spectacle. As can be seen, the horse walked up a ramp to a high platform where it jumped into a tank of water. Witnesses testified that the horses were not coerced into jumping; rather, they willingly climbed the ramp and plunged. Woodmen also set up his ramp over lakes and other bodies of water. There were diving horses that jumped into saltwater at such resort areas as Atlantic City and Coney Island.

At nineteenth-century American World's Fairs and Expositions, the midway was entirely private and arranged outside the fairgrounds proper (Rydell 1984).

Starting in the twentieth century, officials, realizing the revenue-raising potential of such a line of concessions, incorporated them as a regular part of the exhibition. Often it was unclear which exhibits were sponsored by the exposition and which were private exhibitors. There were animal shows, such as Hagenback's concessions of animal displays at American international expositions, and freak shows that exhibited people and animals with physical anomalies (Bogdan 1989).

The animal exhibits varied considerably, but the emphasis was on entertainment rather than enlightenment. Illustration 10.16 is a picture of an orangutan named after the Rudyard Kipling character Mowgli in *The Jungle Book*. This Mowgli, dressed in human clothes, was featured at the Alaska-Yukon-Pacific Exposition in Seattle in 1909. He and his partner, Akela, were trained as part of Hagenback's menagerie and were booked as "wonders of the world."

Countries had areas along the midway where they showcased their own cultures and practices (Adams 2001). Ethnographic displays were features of early-twentieth-century World's Fairs and Expositions, too. These displays were not fashioned or initiated by the people being exhibited. Rather, they were the work of colonial governments and fair officials, with the help of anthropologists. People from third-world countries were brought to the United States and placed in what were poorly conceived simulated native villages where fair attendees could observe them. In some of these exhibits, animals indigenous to the culture accompanied the people on display. For example, Laplanders were shown with reindeer and Egyptians with camels.

The next two illustrations feature Filipinos. During the postcard era, in the aftermath of the Spanish-American War, the United States occupied the Philippines. Members of particular native tribes were brought to the United States and exhibited in many venues, including both the St. Louis World's Fair in 1904 and the Alaska-Yukon-Pacific Exposition in 1909 (Fermin 2004). Exhibitors erected imitation native villages to house the tribesmen. Organizers touted one tribal group, the Igorot, as savage and primitive.[4] One Igorot custom that was featured and presented as a normal part of their everyday life was dog eating. Dogs were featured in the exhibit, not as performers or as strange animals, but as pending meals. Illustration 10.17 is captioned "Dog Market" and shows four dead dogs with an Igorot standing in the background. We are not sure whether this picture was taken in the Philippines or in one of the American exhibition villages. It was printed on U.S. postcard stock and sold in the States, likely in conjunction with the Igorot's appearances. The second illustration (10.18) is a photo postcard that was an official souvenir of the 1909 Alaska-Yukon-Pacific Exposition in Seattle, showing Igorot eating dog at the expo.

10.16. Mowgli at Alaska-Yukon-Pacific Exposition, Seattle, 1909. Dan Kerlee Coll.

4. Their depiction gave credence to the notion that they were not quite human and therefore justified American colonization of the Philippines.

10.17. Dog market, ca. 1910. Private Coll.

10.18. Dog feast. Igorot at the Alaska-Yukon-Pacific Exposition, Seattle, Washington, 1909. Dan Kerlee Coll.

Postcards like illustrations 10.17 and 10.18 were not accurate depictions of normal life for the people photographed. The displays and postcard images of tribal peoples promoted the view that dog meat was an everyday item in their native diet, which was not the case (Fermin 2004, 17). Rather than serving a documentary purpose, they were produced to shock and disgust.

They were anti-Filipino propaganda that justified white Americans' discrimination and colonization.

By the start of the twentieth century, most animal exhibits had joined organizations such as circuses, carnivals, fairs, and expositions. But there were vestiges of an earlier form of exhibition—single, itinerant showmen with their animal performers. A common animal

10.19. Performing bear, Dexter, Michigan, ca. 1910. Private Coll.

10.20. Iola's poodles at the Bijou, ca. 1909. Joel Wayne, Pop's Postcards Coll.

species displayed this way was a large trained bear. Illustration 10.19 shows a performing bear entering a small town in Michigan. Some of the exhibitors were woodsmen with straggly beards who dressed in old clothes, while others were dressed as "Gypsies."

Circuses and midways were not the only organizational venues where arrays of performing and exhibited animals could be found. Vaudeville, circuits of variety acts that did one-night stands in thousands of theaters that spotted the country, had animal acts. Most were small-animal exhibits, such as dogs and monkeys, although educated horses appeared too and even an occasional elephant. Illustration 10.20 features the Easter attraction, "Iola's Troop of Italian Silk Poodles," at the Bijou theater. The poodles shared the bill with a contortionist, a "rubber man," and three thousand feet of new movie film. Short-subject moving pictures first appeared as part of the vaudeville program. Longer films with plots eventually competed with vaudeville stage shows and gradually replaced them.

ROADSIDE ATTRACTIONS AND ANIMAL FARMS

As automobile touring became popular in the United States, small-time entrepreneurs launched roadside animal displays to attract tourists (Margolies 1998). We have already seen some of this activity in the prior chapter's discussion of furs. In addition to their fur business, some northern fur farms welcomed tourists during the summer months. For a fee, they could see the caged animals and buy souvenir furs as well as photo postcards featuring the operation.

In addition to fur farms, hundreds of other tourist stops featured live animals. In rural areas, on the newly paved state highways, crude zoolike exhibits displayed local game in makeshift cages and fenced-in pens. They were accompanied by refreshment and souvenir stands. The down-home roadside exhibit in the "See 'Em Alive Zoo" in Red Lodge, Montana, confined local owls in a

crudely constructed cage (illustration 10.21). The card was sold at a stand in conjunction with the exhibit.

Most of these animal exhibits were established and managed by people with little experience in animal care and were grossly substandard in their treatment of animals. As with the owls pictured in illustration 10.21, animals were confined to small, overcrowded, and barren cages, deprived of any opportunity to exercise or take part in their natural behaviors.

Not all roadside attractions or privately run animal displays were small and in out-of-the-way places. One well-known tourist attraction that spanned the gap between vaudeville, roadside exhibits, and the movies was Gay's Lion Farm in El Monte, California. The Gays, a husband-and-wife team that at one time performed in the circus, started their farm in the early 1920s to breed and raise lions. It evolved into a tourist destination and served in that capacity from 1923 through 1942. Tourists paid an admission fee to see the beasts as well as to watch the Gays perform with the felines in an act that paralleled big-top performances. The Gays had a brisk business selling an extensive series of photo postcards of animals and their trainers. Illustration 10.22 shows Mr. Gay astride a so-called king of the beasts named Pluto. At the height of their success, the couple kept two hundred lions.

10.21. See 'Em Alive Zoo, Red Lodge, Montana, ca. 1924. Private Coll.

10.22. Mr. Gay riding Pluto. Gay's Lion Farm, El Monte, California, ca. 1931. Arluke Coll.

The Gays claimed that because of superior care the cats were larger and better looking than cats found in the wild. Part of the business of the farm was to supply their handsome lions to the booming movie industry, where they appeared in early jungle films, including *Tarzan*. In fact, the famous lion logo at the start of MGM films is said to have been one of the Gays' stars.[5] Although his current location is unknown, Numba, one of the Gays' lions that starred in Charlie Chaplin's 1929 Academy Award–winning film, *The Circus*, was mounted by a taxidermist.

5. There are many claims regarding the MGM lion. Volney Phifer, an early-twentieth-century New Jersey animal trainer, claimed to own Leo, the lion who roared at the start of MGM films.

By the 1920s roadside "animal farms" and other tourist sites that displayed exotic beasts could be found across the country. Down the road from Gay's Lion Farm was Cawston's Ostrich Farm, one of a number of such establishments in southern California where tourists not only viewed the huge birds but could go for a ride in a specially designed cart pulled by a harnessed bird. At some Ostrich farms, tourists could have pictures taken not only riding in a cart but also while mounted bareback on a bird.

Another popular West Coast tourist destination was the California Alligator Farm outside Los Angeles (1907–53). It claimed to be the largest farm of its kind in the world with more than a thousand reptiles on view, including trained alligators. Alligator bags decorated with genuine alligator heads and claws could be purchased in their souvenir shop.

However, California did not have a monopoly on alligator farms or other similar establishments. Florida probably led the nation in roadside alligator farms and parks. St. Augustine brags about having one of the first alligator displays, which is on the National Register of Historic Places. Arkansas, Louisiana, and other southern states had them, too. Some featured regular exhibitions of alligator wrestling. Musa Isle in Miami opened to tourists in 1922, allowed visitors to walk through a Seminole village and watch young Seminoles wrestle alligators (illustration 10.24).

Some of these animal exhibits were outrageous in what they displayed, how they displayed it, and how the display was sold to the public. One photo postcard taken near Baltimore, probably outside an amusement park, shows an exhibition of what was advertised as a "Monster Embalmed Whale, 70 tons, the Biggest Creature That Ever Lived on the Land or in the Sea." Pitching the exhibit as educational, the sign over the entrance read: "Biological Exhibition, Blue and Killer Whales." Following the pattern of these kinds of exhibits, what was shown was likely a lot less than what was promised.

All roadside and other private animal attractions, regardless of their size or location or whether they were called "farms," "zoos," or "exhibits," pitched themselves to the public as educational, even scientific, rather than as mere entertainment. By comparison,

10.23. Ostrich wagon with passenger. Cawston's Ostrich Farm, southern California, ca. 1926. Arluke Coll.

10.24. "Cowboy Billy. His Head in Jaw of Alligator." Musa Isle, Miami, Florida, ca. 1928. Photo by Doubleday. Private Coll.

public zoos, as we see next, took this educational claim somewhat more seriously.

ZOOS

At the start of the twentieth century, there were fourteen public urban zoos in the United States.[6] By 1940 there were more than a hundred. Naturalists and their sponsors who established the early zoos emphasized their educational, recreational, and conservational functions.[7] They attempted to distance themselves from what they thought were crude amusement displays in circuses and on midways (Hanson 2002). Although many zoos

6. We are referring to both municipal zoos and zoos established for the public by zoological societies.

7. In 1874 Philadelphia opened the first zoo in the United States as a matter of civic pride after visits to European zoos convinced its founders that America needed a proper zoological garden instead of menageries (Mullen and Marvin 1987).

10.25. Black bears, Point Defiance Zoo, Tacoma Washington, ca. 1908. Photo by Andrews. Private Coll.

billed themselves as "rational entertainment," the public still did not put them on a par with museums where visitors went for edification and enlightenment (Mullen and Marvin 1987).

One would expect that zoos would have been a favorite destination for snapshot amateurs and that commercial photographers would have done a vigorous business producing postcards for sale. Yet we came across relatively few. Illustration 10.25 is one. The animals are black bears, and the picture was taken at the Point Defiance Zoo in Tacoma, Washington, circa 1908. It is an unusual view in that the bars of the cage are prominent and the human visitors are shown from inside the cage.

Why were zoo real photo postcards so scarce? Making exceptions only to those photographers who produced official postcards for the facility, many early zoos banned cameras. Zoo officials cited safety as a factor in their decision, suggesting visitors, in their zeal to get close-ups, might put themselves in danger. There were other reasons behind the restriction. The parks created a monopoly and could do a brisk postcard business selling their own wares. In addition, a more philosophical or political factor came into play (Hancocks 2001). By controlling who could photograph zoo animals,

officials could create the kind of image they wanted the public to have of captive animals. As a reaction against circuses and other gaudy displays of animals, early zoo advocates wanted their parks to be places where visitors could enjoy nature and where animals could be viewed in natural settings. Although it is not always clear what they meant by "natural," zoo designers wanted to create environments that looked like the places where the animals normally lived. However, the limits imposed by climate and topography made such a goal unrealistic, and their zoos often fell short of this vision.

William Hornaday the first director of the New York Zoological Park, better known as the Bronx Zoo (Hanson 2002, 29), was an adamant supporter of the natural approach to presenting animals (H. Horowitz 1981).[8] At the turn of the century, when the park opened, he banned visitors' cameras (Hanson 2002, 137). The director did not trust picture takers to produce images that would present the zoo or the animals in a positive way. As he explained, outsiders' pictures might provoke pity rather than appreciation.

8. Hornaday was one of the most influential naturalists of his time. He was the head taxidermist at the Smithsonian's Natural Museum in the 1880s (Hancocks 2001).

To control the images made of animals, the Bronx Zoo produced its own postcards. As with most official zoo postcards, almost all were the printed variety. But in 1905 they produced a real photo series. Looking at these cards today, it seems that many of the images contradict the natural image officials advocated. One of these figures is illustration 10.26. It shows the display of bear cages with thick bars separating the spectators from the animals. Although this method of animal keeping might look unnatural to us, those officials that produced the image probably saw it another way. Because the cages were spacious and there was a rock formation in the rear of the setting, they considered it to be "natural." Note that the caption defines the display as "bear dens," not "bear cages." At best, "natural" within the context of the zoo meant that the animals were not displayed in barren boxlike cages made of cement and steel.

By protecting and breeding creatures in captivity, zoos have contributed to animal preservation, especially in the case of endangered species. The Lincoln Park Zoo was the first facility to breed American bison (commonly and incorrectly referred to as the buffalo) in captivity. Hornaday was also concerned about the preservation of endangered species, especially the bison (Kisling 2001). One of Hornaday's pet projects was to

establish a breeding herd in his zoo. He established what he referred to as a "free-range" buffalo enclosure at the Bronx Zoo that he hoped would create for visitors the illusion of being on the Great Plains. The photo postcard in illustration 10.27 is another image that was part of the official real photo postcard series. It shows one of the zoo's bison in the way Hornaday thought they should be presented, as if they were not in captivity. Ironically, the card's caption refers to the pictured bison as "Apache," a name that seems to contradict the goal of naturalism. Soon after Hornaday released the first group of bison on their twenty-acre home at the Bronx Zoo, they all developed intestinal disease and died (Hanson 2002, 134–36). Later bison inhabitants did better, but when they and others were on display, they often looked shabby, their grounds trampled and covered with scrawny vegetation. Although the display never lived up to Hornaday's vision, many credit him as instrumental in saving the American bison from extinction.

As much as zoo officials tried to distinguish themselves from circuses, midways, and other similar places, they were plagued with the razzmatazz of the amusement world. In order to attract people, they had to be fun in addition to being educational. After all, the number of people passing through the gate has always been

NO. 2010
SERIES C.

Bear Dens,
New York Zoological Park.

Copyright 1906
The New York Zoological Society

10.26. Bear dens. Official real photo postcard of the New York Zoological Society, Bronx, New York, 1906. Private Coll.

No. 1165
SERIES C.

American Bison,"Apache"
New York Zoological Park

Copyright 1905
The New York Zoological Society.

10.27. American bison,
Apache. Official photo
postcard of the New York
Zoological Society, Bronx,
New York, 1906. Private
Coll.

10.28. Elephant ride at a
zoo, ca. 1910. Semel Coll.

such public institutions' measure of success. Early in the century, urban public zoos began offering attractions that would lure children to the parks. Animal rides on camels and elephants, such as the one in illustration 10.28, were popular draws. So were seal performances during scheduled feeding times. These acts were the predecessors of Sea World shows (S. Davis 1997).

Even with its emphasis on naturalness the Bronx Zoo was not immune from spectacle. The zoo had animal rides and staged public orangutan teas with the primates sitting at a table, featuring them in their photo postcard series. As in illustration 10.29, animals were given names, in this case the orangutan was called Dohong. Naming contests were part of the zoo's

No. 2182.
SERIES C.

Dohong dining with a Friend.
New York Zoological Park.

Copyright 1906
The New York Zoological Society

10.29. Dohong dining with a friend. Official photo postcard of the New York Zoological Society, Bronx, New York, 1906. Private Coll.

publicity campaigns. Despite a desire to separate themselves from the rowdy amusements of circuses and to project a more professional image, many early American zoos struggled with balancing their entertainment and educational goals (Despain 2005). Although displaying animals as entertaining attractions was more subdued than in circuses and on midways, the line separating zoos from circuses was often hazy.

Zoos even used celebrities to attract attention. The postcard in illustration 10.30 is of James Jeffries, who once held the world heavyweight boxing crown. With great public attention, he came out of retirement in 1910 to fight the African American Jack Johnson. Jeffries and his promoters framed the fight as Jeffries proving that a white man was better than a Negro. Jeffries, known as "the great white hope," lost. The photo of Jeffries holding lion cubs was taken at Chicago's Lincoln Park Zoo and was used to publicize the facility.

There were other overlaps between early zoos and animal amusement organizations. Personnel from zoos were recruited from circuses, and circuses often retired their exotic animals to public zoos. Circus-animal celebrities were often boarded at zoos during the off-season. Both amusement organizations got their animals from the same sources (Flint 1996). Carl Hagenbeck was the major

supplier of exotic animals to both zoos and circuses, had his own zoo and circus, and organized traveling animal shows that appeared at American international expositions (Croke 1997). Many of the animals he trained appeared in early movies. Hagenback's ideas about animal training and zoo design were widely influential (Hancocks 2001). His approach to training emphasized positive reinforcement rather than fear, and he promoted showing animals in open settings surrounded by moats and ditches rather than in cages or behind bars.

"Bring 'em back alive" Frank Buck was an animal importer and a showman who walked a tightrope between the zoo and circus worlds (Croke 1997). He was important in the 1920s, bringing animals from abroad to the States. Capitalizing on Clyde Beatty's success, Buck's book *Bring 'Em Back Alive* embellished his escapades on third-world animal excursions and became a best-seller in the early 1930s. The book was followed by a series of movies, starting with one based on the book. The film was released in 1932, and in 1938 he joined the Ringling Bros. Barnum and Bailey Circus as the star attraction. In 1939 he was still drawing crowds at the New York City World's Fair with his huge Jungleland exhibit. Both Beatty and Buck rode "wild" animals to extremely successful careers and notoriety.

10.30. James Jeffries, former world champion boxer, holding lion cubs at Chicago's Lincoln Park Zoo, ca. 1921. Photo by Osborn. B. Nelson Coll.

Most exotic species that were part of the animal trade came from Africa, Asia, and South America. Thus, zoos and other organizations wanting these animals were intimately tied to colonialism. Indigenous people in these countries were controlled by their colonizers, and besides, although their share of the profit was minimal, natives were often willing participants in the animal trade. In illustration 10.31 we can see a young tiger aboard a ship on its way to the States where it would be sold for a hefty profit to a zoo, a circus, or another amusement organization.

In the early part of the twentieth century a number of zoos launched their own animal-collecting expe-

ditions.[9] In 1915 William Mann, the director of the National Zoological Park in Washington, D.C., went collecting in East Africa. The Smithsonian mounted its expedition in the same year. Just as zoos were expanding, the gap between professional and amateur naturalists was widening. Zoo keeping became a profession with the help of the American Association of Zoological Parks and Aquariums, established in 1924 (Hanson 2002, 32).

During the postcard era, humane societies did not mount campaigns opposing zoos or even publicly criticize them. The primary humane focus was on horses and other working animals, and later on companion animals (see chapter 6). However, there were particular occasions when citizens raised questions about the conditions and training of circus animals. These rare complaints neither stopped new zoos from opening nor deterred the ever-increasing numbers of visitors.

MOVIES

As the century progressed motion pictures gradually improved both technically and artistically, evolving from a novelty to a dominant form of entertainment and an important industry (Stewart 2005). Early venues for showing motion pictures were midways and vaudeville theaters. At first, they were mainly demonstrations of the new medium; the thrill of seeing moving images on screen was enough to satisfy audiences. Quickly, they evolved into short subjects and then to feature films with plots and movie stars. During the first decades of the twentieth century, as the industry evolved, distributors made it possible for films to be shown in the thousands of movie houses that had opened across the country (R. Lewis 2003).

From their origins, movies included animals both as featured attractions and as background characters. One 1910 documentary entitled *Roosevelt in Africa*

9. To enhance their collections, U.S. secretaries of state and war asked U.S. representatives overseas to arrange for the transport of exotic specimens to American zoos, and foreign dignitaries often gave exotic animals to zoos as gifts to the U.S. government (Mullen and Marvin 1987).

10.31. Tiger aboard a ship headed for a life of being displayed, ca. 1913. Tom Gates Coll.

featured footage of the former president's safari with scenes of animals in their natural environments as well as trophies shot by the hunting party. The film was shot while Roosevelt was on a collecting trip sponsored by the Smithsonian and the New York Museum of Natural History.[10] Another documentary short that drew crowds was footage of the Hagenbeck-Wallace Circus, featuring wild animal displays and performances.

As mentioned in our earlier discussion of Gay's Lion Farm, trainers and breeders got into the business of supplying animals to appear in or "act" in feature films. Lions were regularly featured in various jungle movies, such as *Tarzan*. The first Tarzan movie was a silent film entitled *Tarzan of the Apes* (1918). There were eight other Tarzan silent movies, the last being *Tarzan and the Golden Lion* (1927). The first Tarzan talkie was *Tarzan the Tiger* (1929). In 1932 Johnny Weissmuller appeared in his first Tarzan role in *Tarzan the Ape Man* (1932).[11] He went on to do eleven other Tarzan movies, accompanied by his chimpanzee, Cheeta (illustration 10.32).

10. Prior to the release of the film, trying to cash in on interest in Roosevelt's safari, the Selig Company released a fake documentary shot at a California game farm using a look-alike stand-in for Roosevelt (Bowers 1986, 99).

11. The spelling of his name is incorrect in the caption on illustration 10.32.

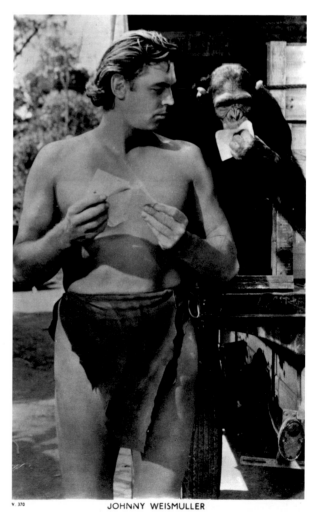

JOHNNY WEISMULLER

10.32. Johnny Weissmuller and Cheeta, ca. 1932. Bogdan Coll.

Jungle movies were not the only ones that featured animals. Early westerns highlighted cowboys and their horses. In illustration 10.33 a movie theater in a small Wisconsin town shows *The U. P. Trail* (Union Pacific), a silent cowboy film released in 1921, based on a novel by Zane Grey. Out front is a covered wagon with a sign advertising the movie and theater. Oxen pull the rig, while a young cowboy rides beside on a white stallion. The wagon, accompanied by horse and rider, toured the town and surrounding area to publicize the show.

The Lone Ranger's horse, Silver, did not appear in a movie serial until the midthirties. However, another prominent western star and cowboy movie hero, Tom Mix, appeared in films as early as 1910 and, after appearing in 336 films, ended his film career in 1935 (Reddin 1999). Tom Mix defined the role of cowboy that all actors after him followed. Mix's horse Tony (he actually had a series of horses that all looked similar and had the same name) was part and parcel of his image. Other horses became movie partners with their human stars. Roy Rogers's horse Trigger was an essential part of the star's persona. Trigger joined Rogers soon after he launched his cowboy career in the mid-1930s. After Trigger died Rogers had him mounted, and he could be

seen in his taxidermy state at the Roy and Dale Rogers Museum in Broson, Missouri, until the museum closed in 2009.

The history of film is marked with a number of dog stars who won fame and bolstered the reputation of specific breeds of dogs as well as the species itself. Rin Tin Tin, a German shepherd, was the nation's first canine movie star (illustration 10.35). The real Rin Tin Tin was rescued from the trenches during World War I and went on to make his first movie in 1925. He, and look-alikes, went on to make twenty-four additional movies. He was the forerunner of stars such as Lassie.

Dogs and other animals played minor roles, too. Toto, Judy Garland's dog that traveled with her in *The Wizard of Oz* (1939), was actually Terry, a cairn terrier. The *Our Gang* comedy series was innovative at this time because it used a more naturalist style than previous movies. The series started in 1922 and featured children involved in various play activities, including pranks and excursions. A veteran film animal, a pit bull named Petey, accompanied the group. Petey appeared as a cast member through 1938, the longest-running character of the series. Careful examination of the animal in the films reveals that the same dog did not play Petey for the whole run of the series. Also, the distinctive

10.33. Movie theater with advertisement for *The U. P. Trail*, Rice Lake, Wisconsin, ca. 1921. Joel Wayne, Pop's Postcards Coll.

10.34. Tom Mix on his horse Tony, ca. 1915. Private Coll.

10.35. Rin Tin Tin, ca. 1926. Private Coll.

10.36. Our Gang with their dog, Petey, ca. 1922. Private Coll.

ring around his eye that was applied with paint did not always appear on the same side of his face.

THE HUMAN LANDSCAPE

The animal spectacles examined in this chapter are riddled with ambiguities. As photo postcards demonstrated, circuses, zoos, and other animal attractions were located between civilization and wilderness, popular culture and science, entertainment and education (Hanson 2002). During the photo postcard era and later, the displays were taken for granted as existing merely to educate and entertain visitors with wildlife.

Zoos, circuses, and other displays may have less to do with appreciating animals than with disrupting their natural existence (Montgomery 1995). These displays remove animals from the wild and transport them to strange habitats that require them to adapt to humans who put them on a feeding schedule and basically control all aspects of their lives (Berger 1980; Malamud 2003).

Whether benign or destructive, these alterations and transformations, like the fairy tale of this book's title, blur the line separating humans from other animals. As paying spectators gawk at, are in awe of, or otherwise contemplate the similarities or dissimilarities of humans and other animals, these beasts gradually become beauties as they are watched behind glass cage barriers or across moats of water. They become familiar, knowable, maybe even like friends. They even change their natural behavior to respond to us (Hosey and Druck 1987). By altering animals' behavior and manufacturing their environment, people make them more akin to our tastes and whims than to their natural world. In the final analysis, we have made zoo animals into utopian dwellers of a human-imagined "wildlife" paradise (Sax 1997) and have made circus animals and other performers into stage stars, even celebrities, on national tour with adoring fans.

The defining characteristic of these spectacles is that humans get to see wild or exotic animals up close and personal, whether these animals sit passively in cages or jump through hoops of fire. They are on display for us to enjoy. However, as we see next, there can be spectacles that join humans and animals together as teams, or pit humans against animals in a competitive struggle for control.

11

Sports

Copyright 1914
C Moore.

38x Roy Hunter Bulldoggig Time 24⅘ Seconds.
Round Up Pendleton Ore "Electric Studio."

11.1. Roy Hunter, bulldog-ging champion, Pendleton, Oregon, ca. 1911. Photo by Electric Studio. Susan Nichols Coll.

𝒞ircuses and zoos were not the only early-twenti-eth-century venues where people exhibited animals and made them perform for viewers. Certain sporting events did so too, albeit with a competitive twist.[1] Some sports pitted animals against one another, such as dog- or cockfighting. Others pitted humans against animals, as happened in bullfights. Finally, some sports involved humans cooperating with animals, forming teams to compete against one another such as dogsled racing

(McFadden 2007). Whatever form they took, there were winners and losers.

We focus on the rodeo in this chapter. Rodeos are gatherings in which humans both teamed with animals (horses in races, trick riding, and other competitions) and competed against them (bronc busting, steer wres-tling, and calf roping) to the delight of spectators.[2] In addition to rodeos, we briefly look at horse track and dogsled racing, along with the more controversial blood sports of dog- and cockfighting.

During the first third of the twentieth century, the rodeo was immensely popular, becoming an American

---

1. Not everyone viewed these events the same way. With rodeo, for example, participants considered it to be a sporting event, but urban spectators likely saw it as a display. Today, many people concerned with humane treatment of animals see it as abuse rather than sport.

2. Although *bronco* is the given term in standard dictionar-ies (a wild or semiwild horse), *bronc* is favored among rodeo participants.

sport of national importance.[3] Enthusiasm for rodeo extended beyond western states to major cities in the Midwest and East. As cowboys and cowgirls competed with each other in large stadiums, upwards of seventy thousand fans per show paid to cheer and watch their heroics. When the rodeo came to New York City in 1922, Madison Square Garden turned away thousands. *Billboard* proclaimed, "New York is rodeo mad" (LeCompte 1993, 83).

Rodeo cowboys and cowgirls were national celebrities. Newspapers carried reports describing their feats. Certain animals achieved notoriety for their skills and partnership with rodeo participants or for their unwillingness to fold under the power of the humans who tried to conquer them. Adults and children had favorite rodeo stars and collected rodeo photo postcards much like baseball fans today seek cards of their favorite players. Both humans and animals were pictured. Owning a real photo postcard of the champion bulldogger Roy Hunter and the steer he upended in record time would have delighted any rodeo fan (illustration 11.1). Images like this one did not just capture the drama of man versus beast; they also depicted the qualities of legendary range cowboys—toughness, courage, hard work, strength, rugged individualism, competitive spirit, and pride—with a dose of showmanship thrown in. Making this connection to America's frontier past was no accident, given how rodeo started.

THE DEVELOPMENT OF THE RODEO

The American rodeo evolved into a sport and folk festival whose development reflected the history of the West (M. Allen 1998). Since the rodeo emerged from ranching and the cattle industry, some events were actual activities range cowboys engaged in during horse and cattle roundups and on cattle drives (Porter 1971; also see chapter 2). Activities that made up the mainstay of rodeos were proficiencies that a good cowhand had to have. Other rodeo events embellished cowboy tasks or

were invented to add glamour and excitement to the enterprise.

On regular roundup and cattle drives, some of the work that cowboys did evolved into competitive sport. Who had the most control over their horse, who was the fastest rider, and who was the best roper or bronc rider were tested by staging contests. At first these "Sunday rodeos" were informal and free. But as more and more people gathered, ranchers began collecting modest admission fees. Cowboy Roy Robbins rides his bronc at one such ranch-based, small-scale rodeo in illustration 11.2.

Although the rodeo emerged from the real experiences of working cowboys, its development is linked to the Wild West show. As rodeo organizers aggressively sought to attract more customers, they copied many aspects of these shows (LeCompte 1990). Wild West shows were elaborate amusement businesses resembling circuses in the range of colorful entertainment they offered (Reddin 1999). Some even had midways. Like circuses, they varied in size from small versions that traveled regionally to huge extravaganzas that moved on a national and even international circuit.

Similar to the rodeo, Wild West shows were rooted in nostalgia for America's mythic and rapidly changing West. They made links to the past by featuring trick roping and riding, horse races, and other rancher-related displays (Boatright 1964). A few of these events were staged as competitions, but others were purely performances or demonstrations. Wild West shows also featured appearances by frontier icons such as Sitting Bull and Geronimo, the "greatest chiefs." Buffalo Bill, Pawnee Bill, Wild Bill Hickock, Annie Oakley, Kit Carson, Calamity Jane, and other Wild West–show owners and performers manufactured personae for themselves that made them frontier legends and national celebrities. Horses were an important part of their presentation. They pranced around arenas fully costumed on handsome steeds (J. Schwartz 1970). The largest Wild West shows included embellished reenactments of horseback battles between Native Americans and the U.S. Cavalry. Stagecoach robberies and other acts of crime and violence with villains on horseback were also staged. Wild West shows also sometimes exhibited animals

3. Other countries such as Canada and Australia had rodeos. American and Canadian cowboys and cowgirls regularly participated in each other's competitions.

11.2. Roy Robbins on Tom Horn, Rawlins, Wyoming, 1908. Susan Nichols Coll.

11.3. "Let-Er." Famous buffalo roundup, 1920. "Only One Ever Tamed and Trained." Photo by C. Moore. The Schlesinger Library, Radcliffe Institute, Harvard University.

that were part of our national past (Mellis 2003). One show claimed to have the only "tamed and trained" buffalo (illustration 11.3). Even today rodeos traditionally include a buffalo exhibition.

Some rodeos were annual affairs held in particular locations; others had home bases where they staged events but also toured. Still others were traveling enterprises. Two of the largest and best-known American locations linked to rodeos were the Pendleton, Oregon, "Roundup" and the Cheyenne, Wyoming,

"Frontier Days." Alberta Province in Canada had the famous Calgary "Stampede." (We include that rodeo in our discussion because it attracted many participants from the United States.) All featured rodeo events were accompanied by a heavy dose of Wild West–show-like entertainment. They were a complex mix of pageantry, amusements, and sporting competition.

The influence of Wild West shows on early rodeos can be seen in the elaborate and celebratory opening-day ceremonies. Rodeo parades on Main Street and on

11.4. Indian parade, Pendleton Roundup, ca. 1920. Susan Nichols Coll.

stadium grounds incorporated and flaunted frontier imagery and icons. Horses, covered wagons, Native Americans, cavalry, people dressed as western characters like mountain men or Pony Express riders, and rodeo stars decked out in their best cowboy attire all participated. As illustration 11.4 documents, the first day of the Pendleton Roundup featured both an Indian parade and a grand march of cowboys and cowgirls, all on horseback.

RODEO'S MAIN EVENTS

Almost all rodeo events involved humans and animals. In some cases, such as horse races, the person and the horse worked together to win. In others, like bronc busting, the person and the animal fought each other for victory. And in yet other events—calf roping, for example—humans teamed with horses to overpower cattle. This array of relationships falls on a continuum; one end is defined by human-animal cooperation, harmony, tameness, and control, while the other end is marked by conflict, violence, wildness, and unruliness (Lawrence 1982). Those individuals who scheduled rodeo events took into account the continuum, often building the program starting from the tame and moving to the wild.

A rodeo event at the wild extreme, usually reserved for the grand finale, was the "wild horse race." It was inspired by the task of breaking (taming to ride) "wild" or free-range horses on the plains. In the early days of rodeos, the event featured horses that had never been saddled or ridden, horses that were not disposed to cooperate. Three people formed each team. Two restrained one of the horses and tried to saddle it, while the third attempted to mount and ride the resisting creature around a track. The first cowboy to cross the finish line won. Horses struggled fiercely to keep from being saddled and then ridden, making for a violent and confusing scene. It was a "melee of plunging hooves and rearing bodies, dust, and the sounds of shouts and whinnying" (Lawrence 1982, 42).

Riding bucking broncos was only slightly tamer than wild horse racing, clearly at the conflict end of the continuum. The event involved a contestant mounting a bronc contained in a bucking chute. Once let loose, the horse burst into furious bucking to toss the rider. Using only one hand to hold on, the competitor attempted to stay on for a fixed amount of time. In early rodeos the horse was ridden until it was too exhausted to buck or until the rider was thrown off. The event gradually evolved to where the rider had to stay on the horse only

11.5. Wild horse race, Calgary Stampede, ca. 1925. Susan Nichols Coll.

11.6. "Bare Back *Riding?*" ca. 1924. Photo by Doubleday. Susan Nichols Coll.

for a set amount of time—eight seconds became the standard.[4]

There were two rodeo adaptations of bronc riding. The one closest to the wildness end of the continuum was bareback riding—no saddle, halter, or reins. Without these restrictions, horses had their heads free to

maneuver. They had a better chance against the rider, a more direct clash between human and beast. Illustration 11.6 confirms the raw drama of the event. The photographer, Doubleday, added a question mark in the photo's caption, indicating that there was an issue about who was in charge, as the rider holds on for dear life.

Saddle bronc riding was the other event. It was similar to the bareback event, but it was much tamer. The saddle and other gear allowed the rider to impose more

4. In addition to having stayed on the horse, the winner was determined by a score arrived at by judges who studied and ranked the details of the horse and the rider's performance.

control, thus favoring his or her chances. Both events were grueling for both human and horse.

Although we have been discussing broncs as "wild," this label is a misnomer. Participants using "wild" to describe participating horses cast this event as a contest between man and beast, tame and wild. In the early years of the rodeo, some broncs really did have limited contact with humans before they appeared in rodeos and were, therefore, to some degree "wild." In the twentieth century most broncs were either horses that were naturally ornery and resisted being broken, were encouraged to be that way, or had been specially bred to buck. The horses' unruly behavior was also a function of the use of spurs, prodding, noise, and tightening of the flank strap around their bodies.

Some of the most difficult broncs to ride developed the reputation of being "outlaws" or "criminals" who were bad by nature, unpredictable, mean, and tough. From the rider's outlook, these brutes enjoyed tossing cowboys off their backs. If fast enough, rodeo photographers could capture these "wild" horses in the act of throwing the contestants. Bad, even fatal, injuries that resulted from the contests reinforced the idea that some rodeo events really were battles between man and beast. Illustration 11.7 is a photo postcard that captures the horse Buzzar's conquest over, and injury to, the contestant McDonald.

Brahma bull riding was similar to bareback bronc riding. Brahma is a breed of cattle that was imported from India in the early part of the twentieth century and crossbred with other varieties of cattle. Brahma bull riding, instituted as a rodeo event in the early 1930s, has no direct link to the working lives of cowhands. The unusual-looking, furious, huge, but surprisingly limber humped animal made it one of the most dangerous and popular events among rodeo spectators. It clearly fitted at the wild and unruly end of the continuum.

Timed rodeo events, including calf roping, steer roping, and steer wrestling, were, in some aspects, tamer contests. All these events involved a person working with a cooperative, trained horse against a resistant bovine. With calf roping, the young animal was given a running head start before a contestant galloping on horseback pursued it, lasso in hand. The goal of the event was to rope the running calf, dismount from the horse, throw the calf on its side, and tie three of its legs with a rope in the shortest time possible (Groves 2006). Steer roping was similar to calf roping, except that the roped animal was a full-grown steer. The process of throwing or tripping the animal was more difficult and complex, requiring even more coordination between horse and contestant.[5] Although these events were based on subduing the unwilling calf or steer, winning depended on a harmonious relationship between rider and mount.

Although calf and steer roping had some connection to the practical world of ranching, steer wrestling, also known as bulldogging, was created for the rodeo. The participant dropped from a running horse onto the galloping steer's neck, grabbed him by his horns and, if successful, wrestled him to the ground by twisting his neck. The contestant with the best time won (Groves 2006). The horse had to be skilled and trained enough to gallop next to the running steer and position the rider so he or she could descend at the right moment and hit the right spot.[6] Illustration 11.8 shows a bulldogger who has just left his horse and is about to slow down the bull before wrestling it to the ground. (The illustration that started this chapter, 11.1, shows a successful bulldogger.)

In addition to the raw pitting of humans against animals, rodeos provided a venue for the public display of their working together as cooperative couples. Most of these events involved skilled riding and racing. One competition, Roman racing, was a novelty event that originated in the American Wild West show. Contestants stood straddling a pair of horses, one leg on each horse, and riding at full gallop (illustration 11.9). The tandem horses had to be trained and trusted to run at full speed side by side.

5. There was a form of steer roping, team roping, that involved two mounted cowboys or cowgirls (Groves 2006). Team roping was the only rodeo event where men and women competed together on the same team.

6. Steer wrestling is one of the most dangerous rodeo events because participants risk missing the steer and having it land on top of them, sometimes horns first.

11.7. Buzzar breaking McDonald's shoulder, ca. 1918. Photo by Doubleday. Arluke Coll.

11.8. Slats Jacobs bulldogging, ca. 1920. Photo by Doubleday. Susan Nichols Coll.

Standard at most rodeos was a variety of lighthearted competition that took place immediately following opening ceremonies. One such event was the wild-cow milking race. The competitors chased and roped one of the many cows fenced in a corral and attempted to milk it. The first to complete the task by producing the specified amount of milk won. Such events often included a rodeo clown on the sidelines. One favorite frolic was mockingly trying to milk a bull.

Another novelty rodeo race was the "rangeland derby," or what some called the chuck-wagon race.

Rodeos also featured horse and rider performances that were not formal competitions. These events fell clearly at the tame end of the continuum in that the horse and rider were partners with a long-standing and close relationship. These special exhibitions served as counterpoints to rodeo's focus on human domination of wild animals. In contrast to bulldogging's violent con-

ROMAN RACE DOUGLAS, WYO, "P.F.P.CO,INC,"

11.9. Roman race, Douglas, Wyoming, ca. 1922. Photo by D. F. P. Company. Susan Nichols Coll.

CHAMPION TRICK RIDER, (COPYRIGHT 1923. DOUBLEDAY)

11.10. Trick rider, 1923. Photo by Doubleday. Susan Nichols Coll.

flict, trick riding personified human-animal harmony (illustration 11.10).

Clown acts often featured humanized animals and relied on the tamest equines (illustration 11.11). Rodeo clowns began to appear in Wild West shows and rodeos around 1914 and quickly became standard features. When clowns entertained spectators using horses, they reversed the typical human-animal relationship. Clowns with baggy pants and painted faces played the role of inept human, while the horses were the smart ones. For example, in one routine a horse would outwit a dumb clown as he tried unsuccessfully to saddle the mount. Not only was the horse portrayed as smarter than the human, but the horse was also depicted as having the upper hand by refusing to accept a symbol of human dominance, the saddle. These acts required long training, mastery over the horse, and much human prompting, but they were made to appear as if the horse were in charge.

11.11. "School Days." Charlie Shultz and Danger, ca. 1920. Photo by Doubleday. Susan Nichols Coll.

Another aspect of clown rodeo humor involved dressing horses with hats, skirts, or pants, or having them smoke a pipe and wear glasses. In illustration 11.12, Charlie Shultz, one of the most famous rodeo clowns, "dances" with his skirt-wearing equine partner (Sheffield 2006). Clowns also dressed their horses in human garments to march in the opening-day rodeo parades.

Clowns also played an important role as a safety valve in bull-riding events. Bulls are unpredictable and would often attack a fallen rider. Skilled rodeo clowns manipulated bulls away from competitors to help reduce injury. Playing to the enthralled crowd, clowns also made the bull look foolish by tricking it in humorous ways to obstruct potential violence.

WOMEN IN THE RODEO

Women played a major role in the rodeo. They were frequently photographed both in action and in glamour poses. Like cowboys, women's relationships with animals ranged from cooperative to combative ones, although they leaned more toward cooperating with their charges.

Women excelled in trick riding and equestrian displays, events that required close relationships between human and animal. These performances straddled the Wild West show and the rodeo as well as the roles of the

strong woman and the glamour queen. Many women crossed back and forth between these two institutions and roles.

11.12. "Dance of the May." Charlie Shultz and Danger, ca. 1919. Photo by Doubleday. Arluke Coll.

11.13. Mamie Francis and Napoleon, ca. 1919. Photo by Doubleday. Sarah Duzynski Coll.

11.14. Bonnie Gray jumping King Tut over auto, ca. 1921. Photo by Doubleday. Arluke Coll.

In the realm of performance riding, cowgirls partnered with particular horses, displaying harmonious relations and long-term friendships. Cowgirls like Mamie Francis and her horses were national celebrities. In illustration 11.13 she is shown atop Napoleon performing in a style reminiscent of animal acts in the circus.

Many other women rose to national prominence as equestrian rodeo stars. Bonnie Gray became nationally known for her trick riding. In illustration 11.14 she is shown performing a novelty trick by jumping her horse, King Tut, over an automobile with rodeo officials as passengers. Bonnie Gray was voted Queen of the Rodeo in 1926.

11.15. Prairie Rose, ca. 1920. Photo by Doubleday. The Schlesinger Library, Radcliffe Institute, Harvard University.

Women's role in the rodeo was not limited to trick riding and noncompetitive events performed in partnership with horses.[7] Women competed against women in gender-segregated rodeo competitions where they battled unruly animals and raced against each other in contests that required exceptional skill. One of the most crowd-pleasing contests was the relay race, an event where women riders passed batons to team members as they completed each leg of the race around the stadium track. In addition, when allowed, women challenged men in their events.

At the Pendleton rodeo, the popular cowgirl Prairie Rose Henderson completed the saddle bronc competition with a score close to the total of the winning cowboy (Wooden and Ehringer 1996). In illustration 11.15 Henderson stands head-to-head with her horse, revealing an affectionate relationship. Although Henderson was an aggressive competitor in bronc riding, she, like many cowgirls, proudly held on to her feminine identity by the clothes she wore and the way she treated and decorated her show horse. In addition to wearing a split skirt that was customary, she added a glamorous touch

to her appearances by wearing spangles and a fancy embroidered vest as well as a fashionable western hat. As was the custom, she also outfitted her steed with a special individually designed saddle and bridle, in this case crafted with a heart pattern. Protective gear was not part of their outfits.

The most famous female steer roper and wrestler, Mabel Strickland, was also the most photographed cowgirl. In illustration 11.16 she strikes a flamboyant pose next to a conquered bovine. Strickland walked the line between cowgirl beauty, equestrian performer, and rodeo competitor. She appeared twice on the cover of the Cheyenne Frontier Days souvenir program, the only cowgirl to do so, and, in a more traditional female role, once served as the queen of the Pendleton Roundup (Bernstein 2007). In Strickland's twenty-five-year rodeo career, she competed in horse racing, trick riding, and steer roping, winning championships in all three events (LeCompte 1993). The combination of great riding skills and beauty made Francis a stunt actress in several Hollywood movies.

When it came to female bulldoggers, Eloise Fox Hastings was one of the best during the 1920s (illustration 11.17). Hastings's record of seventeen seconds in 1924 helped to establish her as a nationally known rodeo cowgirl star. Her career was marked by many

7. Some trick riding was competitive, and Bonnie Gray earned as much as four hundred dollars for winning a single trick-riding championship.

11.16. Mabel Strickland roping steer, ca. 1921. Photo by Doubleday. Susan Nichols Coll.

11.17. Fox Hastings bulldogging, ca. 1923. Photo by Doubleday. The Schlesinger Library, Radcliffe Institute, Harvard University.

spectacular performances, some done after she sustained injuries, including broken ribs, while competing. With a grin on her face and one arm raised to signal a properly downed steer, Hastings showed off her bravery, strength, and skill while the photographer took the classic shot in illustration 11.17.

Prior to the 1930s women regularly and successfully competed against men in many regular rodeo competitions (Laegreid 2006). At first, most cowboys welcomed women in both gender-segregated and integrated competitions, appearing to fully accept them as coparticipants (LeCompte 1993). However, debate over the propriety of women competing with men in the rodeo began long before the 1930s. Injuries and deaths of cowgirls became an accepted reason for preventing them from competing not only against men but also against other women in dangerous events, such as bronc and bull riding. These became "for cowboys only," as

MRS. ED. WRIGHT, WINNER
WORLD CHAMPIONSHIP
LADY BRONCO BUSTING
CONTEST, CHEYENNE, WYO,
JULY 28-1917,
KILLED AT UNION PARK
DENVER, COLO. AUG.11,
JUST AFTER THIS PICTURE
WAS TAKEN,

*12, © 1917, P.F. PHOTO. CO. INC."

11.18. Mrs. Ed Wright, winner of the World Championship Lady Bronco Busting Contest, Cheyenne, Wyoming, July 28, 1917. Photo by Doubleday. B. Nelson Coll.

men asserted that only they could face the challenge of wild animals and that women needed protecting from dangerous rodeo animals.

Illustration 11.18 captures the victorious face of Mrs. Ed Wright after winning the World Champion Lady Bronco Busting Contest in Cheyenne, Wyoming. The image is particularly poignant knowing that soon after the win she was killed by a scared horse during a bronco demonstration. She became a cause célèbre for the movement to get women out of dangerous rodeo events.

Nevertheless, between 1890 and 1943, more than 450 women competed in rodeos for cash prizes and fame, with some earning incomes equal to or greater than celebrity cowboys (LeCompte 1990). Such participation by women in contests with and against animals was significant because at the start of the twentieth century few worked outside the home, let alone as professional athletes. Long before the public accepted women in that capacity, rodeo cowgirls were earning a living and making names for themselves (Bernstein 2007).[8]

RODEO PHOTOGRAPHY

The rodeo emerged on the American scene at the same time the photo postcard rage swept the country. Some photographers specialized in taking rodeo photo postcards. Ralph R. Doubleday (1881–1958) was a pioneer, becoming the best-known, most prolific, and skilled. He, more than anyone else, captured the range of human-animal relations—the drama of the wild, the control of the tame.

Doubleday earned a living by taking, developing, and retailing photo postcards at rodeos to fans, cowboys, and collectors as well as wholesaling to stores and vendors (M. Allen 1998). Two hundred Woolworth stores carried his work, and estimates are that Doubleday sold more than thirty million postcards (Dickinson Research Center n.d.). Most of his images are of humans subduing and controlling animals. Many of the illustrations in this chapter are his work.

Doubleday realized when he started shooting rodeos that few action shots existed of the sport. With the help of faster film, he set out to produce them. Without a

8. Today, at "men's" rodeos, the only event women participate in is barrel racing, where horses and riders race to complete a course around barrels. Unlike the old days when women competed in the full range of rodeo events, barrel racing does not pit the participants against animals, nor is the activity directly tied to rodeo's ranching past (Lawrence 1982). All-women rodeos have gained some popularity, but none of the contemporary cowgirls comes close to the recognition given to the female rodeo pioneers of the early days.

11.19. Tex Crockett on South Dakota, Cheyenne, Wyoming, 1919. Photo by Doubleday. Susan Nichols Coll.

telephoto lens to get great close-up action shots, he risked his life by positioning himself close to the action. He sustained injuries, but his daring led to many great shots that capture the rodeo's thrill.

At the Cheyenne rodeo, Doubleday caught Tex Crockett riding the bronc South Dakota (illustration 11.19). This shot became an iconic image of the rodeo and the West. It personified the contest between man and beast. Although the Tex Crockett card was one of Doubleday's most popular, America loved all his work.[9]

RACING

Rodeos were a marker of the postcard period, a signature institution of a time when Americans were trying to hold on to the old while embracing the new. The prominence of the rodeo was not long-lived. Although rodeos are still a part of some Americans' lives, their popularity falls far short of what it was. Another form of human-animal competition, horse racing, took a slump during the postcard era but has fared better in the long run.

Organized racing did not develop until after the Civil War. The kind of racing that enjoyed the greatest public support involved young thoroughbreds racing on oval dirt tracks (Cassidy 2007).[10] By 1890 there were 314 tracks in the United States. The sport's growth was linked to gambling, betting money on the horses. Gambling also led to its decline. In the early 1900s racing was almost wiped out by antigambling sentiments. Many states banned betting on horses at the track as well as bookmaking or off-track betting available from bookies in local neighborhoods (Miner 2005). By 1908 only 25 tracks were operating. As state legislatures legalized certain forms of betting and the nation prospered after World War I, racing made a comeback, enjoying its golden age during the 1930s and 1940s. Events such as the Kentucky Derby grew in prominence. Thoroughbred and, perhaps more important, harness racing attracted millions of onlookers, rivaling baseball as the most widely watched sport.

The postcard record of racing at major racetracks is scant. What is available is far less interesting and documentary than what we came across for rodeos. Local photographers left a better record of state and local fairs, where harness racing was a popular event, and of

9. Walking with a cane and nearly blind, Doubleday last attended a rodeo in 1953. In recognition of his vast body of photographic work and promotion of the rodeo, Doubleday was inducted into the Rodeo Hall of Fame in 1988.

10. Thoroughbred is a breed of horse.

11.20. Young man with racehorse, ca. 1918. B. Nelson Coll.

individual racehorses. Photographers also took pictures of exceptional steeds (illustration 11.20), especially in regions of the country known for the horses they produced, such as Kentucky, where lean breeds, well suited for racing, were bred and raised.

Central to the history of horse racing during the photo postcard era and beyond was the quest to breed faster and faster horses, regardless of the health implication for the equines. Horses lying on the track with legs broken from the stress put on slender bones resulted from the lengths people went to produce muscular horses that could run the fastest.

Although less popular and common than horse racing, dogsled racing was well documented on photo postcards. Teams of harnessed dogs pulled a specially designed sled with a rider in tow. During the sport's early days, malamutes and large mixed-breed dogs were the power at the front of the sleigh. Siberian huskies, smaller but faster pullers, later became the favorites. The most common use of canines in the United States in this capacity was in the northern regions, where the cold and snow made travel difficult and teams of dogs regularly pulled sleds carrying goods and people. This utilitarian function evolved into a competitive sport.

Serious dogsled racing began early in the twentieth century, when Alaskan gold-mining towns shut down during the winter and miners took up the sport in earnest. The first major competition, a 408-mile run, was the popular All-Alaska Sweepstakes in 1908 (Mozee 1984). In 1917 the first race in the Lower 48 was held in Idaho. Other competitions became annual events in various towns across the Northwest, Midwest, East, and New England.

Many towns across the northern forty-eight states sponsored dogsled races (illustration 11.21). One such race that was well documented on postcards was the Laconia, New Hampshire, World Championship Sled Dog Derby. It started in 1929 as part of a series of weekend winter carnival events and went on to be a major winter sporting event. The race continued to be held annually until 1938 when it was suspended because of the threat of war. It was later reinstituted and still runs today.

The sport achieved its greatest recognition in 1932, when the Winter Olympics at Lake Placid, New York, included dogsled racing as a demonstration sport.

FIGHTING

Cockfighting had a large and enthusiastic following, especially in the South during the postcard era, even though many states barred it or were trying to do so.

11.21. Dogsled derby, ca. 1932. Bogdan Coll.

After the Civil War the popularity of cockfighting declined, along with other animal-based blood sports such as bear baiting, bull baiting, and gander pulling (Cobb 2003).[11] Even so, large events, sometimes lasting two weeks, attracted cock breeders throughout the southeastern and southwestern states. When breeders from different towns developed rivalries, as happened between St. Louis and Dallas in the late 1800s, their competition would be widely publicized, including information about the cocks' weight, record, and reputation as well as the odds and amount wagered on a particular day's main (Jebsen 1979). Illustration 11.22 shows fighting-cock owners at a regional gathering.

Cockfights often took place in refurbished warehouses or in crude buildings, sometimes called "clubs." Handlers placed their roosters in a "pit" where, while still holding them, they would allow the birds to take a quick peck at each other. The cocks would struggle to be set free so they could attack each other. At the referee's signal, the handlers released the birds who,

in a flurry of flying feathers and flapping wings, rapidly began their assault, slashing each other with sharp metal spurs attached to their legs (Del Sesto 1975). In less than two minutes, the intense fighting ended as one bird's razor-sharp spur penetrated the chest of its wounded opponent, who soon fell dead on the sand. Fans, in the all-male audience, then settled their bets, lit up cigars, and talked about the fight that just happened. Despite the bloody and violent nature of cockfighting—scores of roosters killed or severely injured each other—opposition to this sport focused on the immorality of gambling or on the sport's corrupting effects on its participants rather than on the cruelty of the combat (Maunula 2007).

Dogfighting also existed during this period, but with less publicity and fanfare than cockfighting. It flourished with broad fan support and was condoned by the United States Kennel Club. The sport was driven underground after that same organization withdrew its support in the 1930s. Dogfighting continued in some areas and was informally sanctioned by police who, by ignoring it, allowed the blood sport to continue.

Fighting dogs were imported with the hope of crossbreeding an even fiercer animal that would become the American pit bull terrier. They were bred to be small, compact, but very agile, strong, and athletic dogs whose

11. Bear baiting and bull baiting both pitted dogs against these respective animals in fights to the death. Gander pulling was a mostly southern sport where a gander whose head had been greased was hung upside down, and riders attempted to pull its head off while riding by on horseback.

11.22. Fighting cocks and their owners, ca. 1921. Joel Wayne, Pop's Postcards Coll.

11.23. "We Challenge the World." McFall Livery Company and their fighting dog, Jack, ca. 1909. Joel Wayne, Pop's Postcards Coll.

bite would inflict maximum muscle and tissue damage by clamping down and shaking vigorously; they were also bred to not be aggressive toward humans. As seen in illustration 11.23, owners trained their fighting dogs to bite violently by encouraging them to attack suspended pieces of meat. Perhaps the most important trait was "gameness," or a willingness of a dog to continue fighting despite injury and suffering.

"Dogmen" bred, trained, and fought their dogs in scheduled matches that often involved large bets. Although dogmen liked to gamble, the fights were about more than just winning money. Dogfighters attained the dogman status through their animal's ferocity, competitiveness, and strength. Such gameness was regarded as

a masculine dog trait that brought status and prestige in this subculture along with a perception of the owners as tough and masculine (Evans, Gauthier, and Forsyth 2004). In illustration 11.24, men display their fighting dogs at a photographer's studio.

THE COMPETITIVE ANIMAL

Men and women jumping from horses onto bulls to wrestle them to the ground, cowboys and cowgirls attempting to ride bucking broncs, dogs being turned against dogs and roosters against roosters in a fight to the death—even though these competitions are still played out today, they seem surreal. Why would people put themselves and animals in harm's way in such events, and why would people flock to watch?

11.24. Dogmen with pit bulls, ca. 1915. Joel Wayne, Pop's Postcards Coll.

The answer is more complex than merely that these events are thrilling to participate in or watch; it has to do with what they symbolize to us. Rodeos and other animal sports are rituals whose meaning and appeal can be experienced only by regular festival participants. Rich in symbolism and steeped in tradition, they articulate the range of human-animal relations and the human struggle to define people's place in nature (Lawrence 1982). Participants display their partnership with some animals and struggle to control others deemed wild, while never fully mastering the latter's wildness. In the rodeo, for example, the bronc is never fully broken, and the downed steer gets up and walks away; besides, there are many more broncs and steers to take their place. The rodeo is a metaphor for our attempt to tame the wild with all the inherent contradiction that such a struggle entails. Those individuals who participate, both competitors and spectators, are there to see this struggle acted out.

The symbolic value of animals is not limited to amusement and sporting events. As we see in the next chapter, all kinds of animals in very different situations can spark our imagination and enable us to articulate broad themes about what it means to be human and how we relate to other forms of life.

12

Symbols

12.1. Elephant carrying candidate for state office, ca. 1920. Photo by Nelson. Arluke Coll.

*W*e live in a symbolic zoo. Everywhere we look, wherever we go, whenever we think and speak, animals appear not just as flesh-and-blood objects but also as codes for something else. Our products and their packaging are adorned with animal symbols that attract consumer attention by associating the item being sold with the virtues of particular animals. Consider the vehicles that we use. A horse's strength describes the power of a car engine, and a greyhound's stamina suggests fast bus service. Mustangs and jaguars are car names, and bulldogs serve as ornaments on Mack trucks. Also think about how particular animals stand for states, countries, and all kinds of organizations. The grizzly bear appears on the California state flag, the lion represents England on its coat of arms, and the Chihuahua stands for Taco Bell. Even our vocabulary is loaded with animal references that describe human feelings and behavior—"monkey see, monkey do," "going ape," "take the

bull by the horns," "talking turkey," "greedy as a pig," "snake in the grass," or "being chicken" (Beck and Katcher 1996). In addition, we have bull and bear markets, carry rabbits' feet, avoid black cats, and wear the dove image as a peace symbol.

We are not the first society to rely heavily on animal symbolism to identify our products and groups or to talk about our dreams, conflicts, traumas, motivations, and ideals. All societies have long employed animals as figurative players in human thinking. The claim by anthropologist Claude Levi-Strauss (1963) that "animals are good to think" acknowledges their remarkable metaphoric ability to vividly depict human ideas and feelings not only in everyday conversation but also in folklore, myth, ritual, politics, art, and advertising.

Converting animals into tools to think with and symbols to manipulate transforms their biology. "Real" animals have their own physiology, behavior,

230

and psychology, but, through symbolism, our culture reconstructs animal nature to suit our ends. These symbolic interactions with animals have, for many people, replaced actual human-animal relationships (Lawrence 1997a). We may not get to the zoo often to see real tigers, but every morning millions of people interact with friendly and talkative "Tony the Tiger" who tells us that Frosted Flakes are delicious and nutritious. Marketers have even changed Tony's feline physique to a creature that walks upright and has a build resembling a muscular man.

Once converted into symbols, animals have enormous power to communicate our likes, dislikes, hopes, fears, aspirations, beliefs, and unity. Ideas can be expressed quickly and effortlessly when the symbolic meanings of animals become standardized. Their communicative power means that animal symbols can be used to persuade people to think or act a certain way. As with Tony the Tiger, businesses often use animal symbols to get us to buy their products. But animal symbols are more useful than merely getting consumers to buy. They can also be used to further the public's identification with and commitment to a group or organization. Sports fans cheer their "Bears," "Cubs," "Eagles," "Cardinals," "Timberwolves," or "Panthers" and proudly wear shirts and caps with their team's animal symbol prominently displayed. Animal symbols can even be used to convince people about the correctness of political ideas. Posters calling for America to "support its troops" in our "war on terror" sometimes feature a large bald eagle.

POLITICS

Animals are valuable as political symbols because they galvanize support and crystallize identity. The Republicans' elephant and the Democrats' donkey were part of American political symbolism long before the postcard era. Although the political cartoonist Thomas Nast popularized these images in *Harper's Weekly* during the 1870s, he was not the first to link these animals to our major parties (Batchelor 1996). After Andrew Jackson's critics called him a jackass, he used the symbol of the strong-willed donkey on his campaign posters.

Political cartoons were fashionable, and the parties were in search of easily recognizable identifiers, so Nast's jackass and elephant stuck.

Today, each party extols the great qualities of its symbol, while belittling the emblem of the other party. Republicans regard their elephant as strong, patient, wise, and dignified, while Democrats consider it to be dumb, slow, and conservative. Democrats view their donkey as reliable, strong, and brave, while Republicans think it is stubborn, awkward, and silly.

A century ago these animal symbols played a more important role in political campaigning than they do now. Everyone knew what the symbols stood for. Politicians distributed these animal images on photo postcards and the recipients easily identified their party affiliations at a glance (see illustration 12.1).

Citizens used these political symbols playfully. In illustration 12.2 we see a GOP (Grand Old Party, another name for the Republican Party) elephant used as a posing facade for portrait seekers at a photographer's studio. Patrons could show their party affiliation by inserting their heads onto the animal figure of their choice.

The moose was the next addition to America's "political zoo" (Kimble 1912). In 1912 the Republican Party split after Theodore Roosevelt lost the nomination to William Taft (Link and Link 1993). Roosevelt took his convention delegates, but not the elephant, and formed the Progressive Party, or what became known as the Bull Moose Party. The bull moose became the party's emblem when Roosevelt was on the campaign trail and was asked if he was fit to be president. He boasted that he was "as strong as a bull moose." The party's platform advocated women's suffrage, welfare assistance for children and women, and worker's compensation.

Despite this symbol's immense popularity, not everyone liked its political use. The members of the Loyal Order of the Moose (LOOM), a national fraternal organization of more than 250 lodges and 250,000 members, regarded the Bull Moose symbol as theirs and used it on posters, print ads, and postcards to promote the organization (illustration 12.3). LOOM charged that the Progressive Party was making "political capital"

12.2. Riding the GOP elephant, ca. 1913. B. Nelson Coll.

out of their organization (*New York Times*, October 18, 1912, 22).

But journalists and others helped to keep the name alive by routinely referring to the Progressive Party as the Bull Moose Party. The party insignia thrilled taxidermists in Maine because they expected a brisk business in mounted moose heads (*New York Times*, August 12, 1912, X2). Roosevelt featured the huge animal on posters and buttons and even used a mounted moose head while campaigning. For Roosevelt, the Bull Moose was a powerful identifier of the Progressive Party's strong agenda. It also enhanced his image as a rugged and hardy outdoorsman. In illustration 12.4 he stands in the middle of an excited crowd and behind a bull moose mount during a typical campaign oration. Although the Bull Moose Party lost at the national level in 1912, it continued to put forward candidates at the state and local levels over the next few years (Batchelor 1996).

Local politicians used animals as emblems to catch the public's eye and to associate the positive characteristics of the chosen creature with the group it represented. Sometimes the imagery backfired when used by others to discredit and undermine the group. The use of the tiger by the famous Tammany Hall, an organization that controlled New York City politics from the 1790s

12.3. "My Papa's a Moose." Danville, Illinois, 1912. Joel Wayne, Pop's Postcards Coll.

12.4. Theodore Roosevelt on campaign, Morrisville, Vermont, 1912. Bogdan Coll.

12.5. The Tammany Tiger, 1915. B. Nelson Coll.

to the 1960s, is a good example. The symbol first came into use in the mid-1800s, when a New York City fire department sought a mascot to emblazon on its wagons. The company adopted the image that personified speed, strength, and decisiveness, a ferocious Bengal tiger (O. Allen 1993). Tammany politicians appropriated the symbol by wearing pins and emblazoning posters with the same tiger image. Cartoonist Thomas Nast is usually credited with popularizing the association of the tiger with Tammany Hall, but, in his depiction, the animal portrays a bloodthirsty, predatory beast mauling democracy. Despite the Nast characterization, Tammany's leaders officially adopted the symbol. Illustration 12.5 shows a person using the Tammany Tiger symbol in a campaign to fight against Tammany politicians' attempt to control upstate New York.

The seeds of the modern practice of humanizing our presidents and other leaders by pairing them with animals can be traced to the postcard period (Kehl 1980). All presidents since Washington have kept favorite animals at the White House, but images of these relationships became apparent only with the advent of modern photography and the widespread use of photo postcards. Photographs of presidents with their pets make our powerful leaders appear warm and kind, as well as communicate to voters that "family values" will be upheld in our highest office. When Barack Obama ran for president, he reassured voters that, if he were elected, in addition to a wife and two daughters, there would be a dog in the White House (R. Rowan and Brooke 2009). Bush's Barney, Clinton's Socks, and, most famously, Nixon's Checkers were frequently photographed as important members of White House families.

During the postcard era, Calvin Coolidge had many presidential pets. Despite his reticence to interact with humans, Coolidge was at ease with animals (Booraem 1994). He and his wife, Grace, kept a menagerie around the White House, including canaries, mockingbirds, wombats, raccoons, an antelope, a hippopotamus, a bobcat, a goose, a donkey, a wallaby, a bobcat, two lion cubs, and of course cats and dogs. The couple was particularly fond of dogs. Calvin put it this way, "Any man that does not like dogs and want them about does not deserve to be in the White House." During their White House years, Calvin and Grace kept many dogs, including two chows. These dogs often appeared in public with the president and were frequently captured by photographers.

The president returned to Plymouth Notch, Vermont, often to counter the idea that his lofty position was pulling him away from his farm boy roots (Pietrusca 2008). As a graphic way to remind the public of this connection, he readily allowed himself to be photographed with farm animals. In illustration 12.6 we see him dressed like a farmer and milking a cow posing for a photo postcard opportunity.

Anyone who witnessed the ceremonies surrounding the death of President John F. Kennedy experienced the power of animal symbolism to solidify authority and embody noble sentiment toward the holder of the highest office in the land. A team of handsome horses pulled the caisson carrying the president's coffin to the cemetery. A prancing saddled stallion, riderless and held by its reins, followed the body, in keeping with the military symbol of a fallen leader.

Animals have also been used in grassroots lobbying campaigns, such as citizens in the early 1930s uniting around the Townsend Plan when Washington politicians were against it. In illustration 12.7 we see a rally in which a goat is used to make a political point. The banner on the animal reads: "The Townsend Plan Has Got the Politicians Goat."

The Townsend Plan was a proposal before Congress guaranteeing a pension to retirees over the age of fifty-

12.6. Calvin Coolidge milking a cow, ca. 1926. Private Coll.

12.7. "Townsend Plan Has Got the Politicians Goat," ca. 1934. Lew Baer Coll.

nine. The majority of people supported it, seeing the plan as a way to end poverty among the aged and fight the Great Depression by boosting consumer spending. Politicians in Washington strongly opposed the plan because of its immense cost. Public demonstrations to support passage of the plan occurred throughout the United States. The clever sign on the goat refers to the mean-spirited attitude congressmen had toward the plan's provisions. The general expression "someone's got your goat" was derived from the practice of having a goat stay with a horse the night before a race as a method of keeping the animal calm. Competing horse owners would often steal or "get" such goats, upsetting the horse and weakening its chances of winning. Hence, the goat's banner in the above illustration suggests that, in the face of widespread citizen support for the Townsend Plan, it was believed that politicians had become riled, speechless, and unable to defend their opposition to it.

PATRIOTISM

Animal symbols are linked to more abstract ideas and institutions than just to political party membership and campaigning. They can embody national spirit and ideals, patriotism, and love of country. This is especially poignant in time of war. It is then that morale is tested by the call for personal and group sacrifice. Animal symbols are enlisted to motivate fighting men and women and to mobilize popular support for the war effort. As we shall see, these symbols rally citizens for all kinds of action, including donating money, blood, food, blankets, and other material for the troops. Photo postcards captured this patriotic use of animal symbolism during the First World War.

As part of the war effort, the Red Cross enlisted "liberty animals" to symbolize and publicize various campaigns to raise funds, collect goods, and recruit human volunteers. Postcards, posters, and print advertisements often featured a variety of liberty animals to attract attention to and create warm feelings toward the Red Cross. The liberty duck was one of the most effectively and extensively used symbols. The caption on the photo card in illustration 12.8 urges citizens to "help the Red Cross liberty duck."

On the local level, other animals came to stand for the war effort. Some even became famous for raising funds. One rooster, Jack, rose to celebrity status via a series of Iowa and South Dakota auctions that were held to raise money for the Red Cross Nursing Corps in 1917 (illustration 12.9).

In his first public appearance, the rooster was put up for auction in the town of Fontanelle, Iowa.

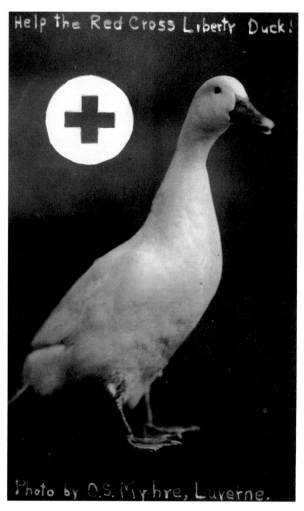

12.8. "Help the Red Cross Liberty Duck," ca. 1918. Photo by O. S. Myhre, Luverne. Semel Coll.

12.9. D. R. Jones, auctioneer, and famous Red Cross rooster, ca. 1917. Private Coll.

After the bidding for the rooster was over, the winner decided that he did not want the bird and returned him to the auctioneer. To the amusement of the onlookers, the auctioneer seized the moment and immediately auctioned the bird again. In the spirit of fund-raising and one-upmanship, the bird was repeatedly sold and returned, raising $217 for the war effort that night. At the end of the event the auctioneer, David Jones, took the bird home. A showman at heart, Jones named the rooster General Jack Pershing and took him and his reputation as a fund-raiser on the road to other auctions. As shown in the illustration, Jack would perch on Jones's shoulder and loudly crow as the bidding proceeded. Jones started the auctions telling of the rooster's money-raising achievements in other towns. This

evoked civic pride as well as a desire to outdo neighbors. Together, Jack and Jones solicited more than $40,000 by the end of the war. The rooster came to symbolize the war effort. His success inspired other repeating animal auctions, including a pig named Neptune who carried on the tradition during World War II. General Jack Pershing was allowed to live out his retirement in peace and quiet, but after he died he was mounted by a taxidermist and put on public display in the Iowa State Historical Museum. In 2001, in the wake of the World Trade Center and Pentagon terrorist attacks, he was taken out of storage and used to raise funds for the Red Cross again.

These ducks and roosters were only minor players in the menagerie of animal symbols used during wartime. Of all animals, the bald eagle stands supreme as a patriotic symbol. The bird has been our national symbol since 1782 (Doherty 1982). During World War I the bald eagle became a prominent symbol of national unity and strength. Since then American presidents have embraced the eagle's symbolic importance with the exception of Franklin Roosevelt, who preferred turkeys because they were less bellicose. Most recently, President Obama's inauguration festivities displayed a live American bald eagle.

The eagle's eligibility as a national symbol was enhanced by its habitat, physiology, and behavior. Its natural range in North America makes it uniquely American. Its appearance is striking, with a wingspan of more than six feet and a snow-white head. It was easy to attribute noble human attributes to the magnificent creature (Lawrence 1990a). Its powerful brow and intense eyes imply alertness and valor, its soaring flight suggests independence and freedom, and its strong body and razor-sharp talons promise a deadly response if provoked. Americans embraced the eagle, placing its likeness on the official seal of the country, buttons, flags, hats, medals, and tombstones. During the war, eagles sprouted everywhere. The most used representation, the one on the dollar bill, shows the eagle clutching an olive branch in its right talon to symbolize the power to make

peace and holding arrows in its left talon to represent the power to wage war.

Illustration 12.10 shows a dramatic World War I patriotic photo of the eagle. Look closely; it is not the real bird. The image was constructed by arranging 12,500 officers, nurses, and soldiers in a pattern resembling an eagle. The photographer who created the formation and the resulting photo postcard was Arthur Mole. After supervising the arrangement of military personnel into an eagle formation, Mole climbed up an eighty-foot tower, equipment in hand, to get a bird's-eye view of the crowd he ingeniously assembled. He called images, such as the one here, "living photographs," because they were brought to life by actual military people who, when positioned live in front of the lens, embodied the spirit of patriotism.

In addition to the eagle, Mole did many patriotic living photographs during World War I that he sold on postcards, larger prints, and posters. His work functioned as nationalistic propaganda to rally support for U.S. involvement in the war. He believed, probably correctly, that these photos would marshal energy and stimulate morale as part of the war effort.

Mole was not the only photographer who used the bald eagle in World War I picture taking. Soldiers going off to war typically visited photo studios to have

12.10. "The Human American Eagle." Camp Gordon, Atlanta, Georgia, 1918. Photo by Mole and Thomas. Vaule Coll.

12.11. Soldier with national symbols, ca. 1917. Arluke Coll.

PRODUCTS

The first quarter of the twentieth century saw phenomenal growth in the retail industry, corresponding to a vast increase in the availability of mass-produced consumer goods. Although modern advertising started in the middle of the nineteenth century, manufacturers and retailers began to invest huge sums in advertising to stimulate consumer buying during the postcard era. Trademarks, logos, and sales slogans emerged as nationally known symbols of products.

Companies using animals as pitchmen to hawk their products to the public is not new, but in the early 1900s advertisers escalated the use of animals as an effective way to help consumers identify their brands and encourage them to buy their products. Having a symbolic spokesperson, whether a live or imaginary animal, enabled companies to capitalize on desirable and memorable animal traits (Jackall and Hirota 2000).

One of the most famous associations of an animal with a product from this period is the dog Nipper's connection to the music industry. The use of this dog, and look-alikes, as an advertising symbol can be traced to an oil painting depicting a small white terrier-type dog with black markings standing on a table and focused intensely on the sound emanating from the horn of a cylinder phonograph machine. The title of the painting was *His Master's Voice*. Around 1900 the newly formed Gramophone Company purchased the painting, had the artist change the machine to a gramophone, and began using the image in its advertising (Kenney 1999). Soon after, Victor Talking Machine Company, a major producer of phonographs and records, bought the U.S. rights to the picture. In 1902 Victor began using the Nipper image in all of its ads, catalogs, stationery, and records. In 1929 RCA bought Victor and stuck with "his master's voice" and Nipper as its record logo.

Victor and RCA were huge companies that did not use real photo postcards in their advertising, but small retail stores borrowed the symbol of "his master's voice" and created their own Nipper look-alike postcard images. Nipper in many versions was, and still is, a marketing celebrity. In illustration 12.12 a local

portraits taken to share with relatives, friends, and lovers. The American flag was the most common symbol used as a backdrop, but it was often embellished by the presence of a stylized bald eagle. Standing at attention and bursting with pride, flag and eagle in the background, the soldier in illustration 12.11 had no idea what he was about to confront in the trenches.

Despite the growing importance of the bald eagle as our national symbol, hunters continued to shoot them, causing their numbers to dwindle. Efforts to protect the national symbol gained momentum during the early decades of the twentieth century. To preserve this living symbol, Americans passed the National Emblem Act, also known as the Bald Eagle Protection Act of 1940.

PLATT HOUSE
HORSEHEADS, N. Y.

12.12. "His Master's Voice." Platt House, Horseheads, New York, 1913. Semel Coll.

merchant captured the symbol, in modified form. A puppy resembling the original model sits in the speaker horn of a hand-crank phonograph machine.

The image of Nipper was hugely popular and continued to be used throughout the twentieth century, albeit in other forms, including several iterations of Chipper, supposedly Nipper's puppy. As testament to his adoration, a four-ton statue of Nipper still sits on top of a former RCA building in Albany, New York, and a street named Nipper Way exists in the dog's hometown of Baltimore, Maryland.

Some product associations featured real animals as pets. In 1902 the Brown Shoe Company developed

brand recognition after it bought the rights to a cartoon starring a mischievous rich boy, Buster, and his pet American pit bull terrier, Tige. Buster Brown shoes were introduced at the 1904 World's Fair. By 1912 the company published national ads in magazines such as the *Saturday Evening Post*, featuring Buster and Tige (K. Smith 2005). In a publicity stunt that appalls current disability rights advocates, the company hired dwarfs to play the part of Buster Brown. They trained dogs to be Tige and then sent the pairs across the country to visit shoe outlets in order to promote sales. Real photo postcard photographers captured Buster and Tige who were on the road in a number of towns visiting department stores, theaters, and shoe stores where they encouraged parents to buy Buster Brown shoes. The various Tiges were lively and friendly dogs that interacted with their human companions when making appearances.

Tige and Buster symbolized the prototypical adolescent-dog relationship. In the cartoon strip Tige played many roles for Buster, including his conscience and his guard. Although the cartoon version of Tige had him speaking to Buster, photographs and real-life appearances obviously could not do so. Yet there were other ways that Tige could be made almost human. In illustration 12.13 Buster seems to be lecturing to an attentive, top hat–wearing Tige, who listens to every word. As a product character, Tige's personality fulfilled two functions necessary to effectively promote a product: he gave meaning to the Buster Brown brand by symbolizing friendship and fidelity, and he lent emotional appeal to the brand by personifying the product (B. Phillips 1996).

Pairing a sweet young child with a cute and cuddly small dog could enhance the appeal of almost any product. The little white dog in illustration 12.14, resembling the widely popular Nipper, eagerly awaits his bite of the smiling boy's treasured biscuit cookie. The dog with the boy was used extensively by the National Biscuit Company (Nabisco Foods) during the postcard era to promote its products. An aside: that company started manufacturing "Barnum's Animal Crackers" in 1902.

In some cases, rather than using animals to represent a company in general, a company used them in

12.13. The original Buster Brown and Tige. Cherokee, Iowa, ca. 1912. Photo by Sternhaus. Joel Wayne, Pop's Postcards Coll.

12.14. Child, dog, and biscuit, ca. 1909. Joel Wayne, Pop's Postcards Coll.

specific campaigns for particular products. Illustration 12.15 provides an example. The Rexall Drug Company used the image of a dog to promote Cherry Juice Cough Syrup, a new Rexall product at the time. The pun, "Don't Bark," adds levity to the campaign and links the product to the animal. Having a live dog decked out with a company pennant containing the slogan and the bulldog image was probably a local merchant's touch to the national campaign.

The belief that black cats signaled danger and misfortune provided a marketing hook for an insurance company that made the advertising card in illustration 12.16. Such cats have long been viewed as a symbol of evil omens in many modern societies, especially if one crosses your path. To get this point across, the postcard

reminds us that Friday the 13th is a day of bad luck, another superstition that might also encourage a viewer of the postcard to consider a little extra protection.

Rather than using animals to make product associations, some businesses simply used animals in their advertising to grab the attention of potential customers. Williams' Studio in Haverhill, Massachusetts, posed a Boston terrier dressed in a vest, wearing a hat, and having pipe in its mouth for promotional purposes (illustration 12.17).

Many large companies and the establishments that retailed their products did not use real photo postcards to advertise products. They relied mainly on printed materials. Nonetheless, photo postcards document early-

12.15. "Don't Bark. Use Rexall Cherry Juice," ca. 1919. Semel Coll.

12.16. "Beware! Friday, the 13th," ca. 1932. Arluke Coll.

twentieth-century marketing's use of animal symbols because signs and product window displays unintentionally appear in town views and in images of storefronts.

By 1900 the artist-rendered bull logo of the Bull Durham Tobacco Company was one of the most recognizable trademarks in the world. Over time, the portrayal of the bull in advertisements became more spirited and was eventually trademarked by W. T. Blackwell. It was reported that one advertising company painted sixty-six thousand feet of Bull Durham outdoor signs in seven states. The signs contained 315 bulls, each supposedly unique (Roberts and Roberts 2002). In a number of cards we reviewed, the icon, in large form, appears painted on buildings and billboards. Illustration 12.18, taken in Texas, provides another. Behind the water cart, the large and distinctive Bull Durham symbol adorns a good part of the barn's side.

In some cases, animals were used opportunistically to promote products just because they could capture the interest of potential customers and make the right point. Exotic animals like elephants were good attention getters. Illustration 12.19, produced by the Kissel Kar Company of Hartford, Wisconsin, promoted the idea that its trucks (five-ton capacity) were strong and powerful enough to carry an elephant. Actually, the company supplied vehicles for various circuses,

12.17. Ad for Williams' Studio, Haverhill, Massachusetts, ca. 1907. Semel Coll.

including the Campbell Brothers Shows. The vehicle company used the visit of that circus to their town to produce this advertising photo.

When circuses came to town and the animals paraded down Main Street, businesspeople typically paid to have the elephants decked out with advertising banners promoting products available in their stores. Unlike the other examples we have provided, the relationship between products and animals was irrelevant; there was no real symbolism involved. The important thing was to get the crowd's attention and direct it to whatever was being promoted.

PLAYTHINGS

Photo postcards captured another symbolic use of animals. From the postcard era to the present time, animals have had a special meaning and importance in children's lives. Stuffed animals, animal toys, animal stories, and make-believe animals all figure prominently in children's everyday activities as well as in their imaginations (Melson 2001). Some fabricated animal playthings have come to symbolize love, comfort, and childhood itself to both children and adults.

No other stuffed animal or toy has rivaled the popularity or symbolic meaning of the teddy bear. Although its number-one position is sometimes eclipsed by short-lived toy fads, the teddy bear endures as an

12.18. Mexican water cart in front of Bull Durham logo, ca. 1917. B. Nelson Coll.

12.19. Elephant ad for Kissel Kar Truck, ca. 1916. Photo by Montgomery. Private Coll.

12.20. "You Know My Name. I'm from Barre, Vt.," ca. 1909. Semel Coll.

icon of childhood and a steadfast symbolic friend to millions of children and adults (see illustrations 12.20 and 12.21).

The potent and enduring role of the teddy bear had its origin at the start of the photo postcard era. In 1902 President Teddy Roosevelt was on a bear hunt in Mississippi. After three days without success, his guide captured an old live bear for Roosevelt to shoot. The pathetic, beaten-down bear had been tracked and attacked by dogs, hit on the head with a rifle, and tied to a tree. According to the tale, Roosevelt, the sportsman, refused to shoot the animal, although he did eventually have it killed for humane reasons (Ambrose and Brinkley 2003). A political cartoonist heard this story and produced a published drawing in which Roosevelt was shown turning his back to the bear and holding his arms outstretched to indicate his unwillingness to shoot.

As the cartoon was redrawn and reprinted, the bear's size and personality changed. In the original version, the bear was a realistic-looking, defiant adult animal. Eventually, the animal was transformed into a cute cub, quaking with fear. A shopkeeper capitalized on the story by making and selling stuffed toy bears named Teddy (Kehl 1980). As demand escalated, the bear maker formed the Ideal Toy Company. What started as a national fad matured into an American icon. Along the way, the teddy bear's link to Roosevelt faded, and its use grew, both symbolically and tangibly as a comforter. Its popularity was so great, some feared that the teddy bear would eventually cause the "extinction" of baby dolls in general.

The toy bear is often the first toy for infants and children and their earliest and closest companions. The bear is also appealing to adults, whether adolescent or aged. The teddy bear's appeal to children as well as to adults seems to stem from the stuffed animal's ability to console people while also eliciting their nurturance. To meet this considerable interest, there are books and magazines about teddy bears as well as stores and companies that specialize in their production and sale.

The teddy bear tale illustrates how human culture appropriates wild animals into human objects (Lawrence 1990b). As with the teddy bear, the form this often takes is neoteny, or our cultural tendency to view animals as infantlike, with big heads, big eyes, and chubby cheeks (Lawrence 1989b). Makers of teddy bears exaggerate infant qualities, as well as human features like longer arms and legs, in order to make the animal appear upright. Although the teddy bear is obviously an inanimate object, it is now often treated as a pet. "Teddy bears are animals that nearly, but not quite, become people" (Lawrence 1989b, 151).

HOLIDAYS

In the early part of the twentieth century, and today, animals played a special symbolic role in many American holidays. In addition to the Thanksgiving turkey, there are the Easter bunny and chicks and Christmas reindeer. Although one might argue that these holiday animals are frills to the main celebration and mainly for children's amusement, starting in the postcard era, animal symbols have become central to defining what these holidays mean for people of all ages (Clark 1995).

The symbolic use of the rabbit predates the postcard and Easter by thousands of years. The prolific

12.21. Children with teddy bears, ca. 1912. Coll. of Leonard A. Lauder.

rabbit was once a pagan fertility symbol. With the birth of new life that is associated with spring, the rabbit came to represent that season and later Easter. Chicks and eggs are also linked to the fertility season. German immigrants brought Easter-bunny folklore to America in the 1700s, and the first edible sweet Easter bunnies, made of pastry and sugar, were introduced in Germany during the 1800s and brought to the States by the end of that century. The holiday was not generally celebrated in the United States until after the Civil War.

During the postcard era photographic studios created many novel backdrops and scenes to draw people to their establishments during the Easter season. The photo postcard format made it possible to share these seasonal photo opportunities with relatives and to add

12.22. Chick pulls girl in egg cart, 1911. Arluke Coll.

pictures to family albums. The photographers appealed to parents who wanted special holiday portraits of their children by offering cute holiday props and backdrops that included animals. Illustration 12.22 is an example of these holiday cards. This particular prop, the chicken pulling the egg-shaped wagon, also appears in other images taken in studios across the country, suggesting that a company that marketed them nationally probably manufactured them.

Animals were and continue to be used to represent other major holidays. The turkey is one of America's most important national icons. Each year, cardboard turkeys adorn homes, schools, and other establishments in November (A. Smith 2006). With turkeys and Thanksgiving, the connection between the beast and the holiday seems direct—we eat turkeys at Thanksgiving.[1] Reindeer and Christmas are linked by virtue of Santa Claus. During the postcard era photo studios, as well as

fledgling department stores that offered photographic services, not only used Santa as a holiday photo prop but also used reindeer. Some of these reindeer were fabricated from wood and other products, but others were real deer in taxidermy form. Because reindeer were not readily available, they used stuffed local white-tailed deer (illustration 12.23).

One photographer used the stuffed American eagle accompanied with American flags to make a patriotic image that could have been used to celebrate Independence Day or Memorial Day. Studio photographers were prepared with a variety of these props to satisfy the desires of both walk-ins and regular customers who wanted to express their love of country. Although most of the eagle images were fabricated, a few were once live birds that had been brought to taxidermists. Such was the case with the studio in illustration 12.24 where women draped in American flags stand holding onto the wings of the stuffed eagle in the foreground.[2]

1. An interesting exception is the recent presidential tradition of "pardoning a turkey." After a turkey is sent to the president as a gift it is not killed, helping to portray the president as a kindly leader who cannot eat a turkey he met or received as a present. However, an anonymous turkey is eaten later.

2. The eagle in the picture is probably a golden eagle. Clearly, the intent was to link the bird to patriotism.

12.23. Santa and his reindeer, ca. 1925. Arluke Coll.

12.24. Photographer's American-eagle studio prop, ca. 1918. Bogdan Coll.

BETWEEN THE SYMBOLIC SPECIES

This chapter's photo postcards showed animals being used for many symbolic purposes, but images throughout this book remind us that animals play this role, albeit not always so deliberately, in every kind of relationship we have with them. In earlier chapters we saw that working animals symbolized power and achievement, produce animals were regarded as commodities, pets and mascots filled in as surrogate friends and family, prey embodied abundance and frontier spirit, vermin represented threat and danger, trophies reflected achievement and masculinity, circus and zoo animals signified dominance over nature, and rodeo animals illustrated the ambiguous status of animals as either wild or tame.

Why do people inevitably turn to the animal kingdom to symbolically express many aspects of life, to advertise our products, represent our teams, characterize our organizations, articulate our dreams, color our language, and convey our very identities? One reason is that animals are easy to use for this purpose because they are widely available, well recognized by most people, and varied enough to create many different symbols. Also, some animals are similar enough to us that we see ourselves in their behavior and appearance. But at a deeper and perhaps simpler level, we often resort to using animals as symbols because of the power of human affinity with animal life (Lawrence 1997a; Wilson 1986). We are drawn to animals, desire to be in their presence, and often choose to watch, think, and talk about other creatures. So it should not surprise us that we turn so readily to animals to satisfy our species' symbolic needs, including the story of the *Beauty and the Beast* and the images on real photo postcards.

13
Living with Inconsistencies, Past and Present

13.1. Woman with chicks, Midwest, ca. 1911. Private Coll.

We started this book discussing the centuries-old fairy tale *Beauty and the Beast* and pointing to themes we would address in the chapters that followed. Central to our discussion were the inconsistencies, dualisms, ambiguities, and paradoxes of the story and their parallels in early-twentieth-century human-animal relationships. The beast, as well as the animals we have discussed and shown in illustrations, were both loved and hated, wild and tame, caressed and abused, commoditized and anthropomorphized, distanced and embraced, both builders and destroyers of relationships.

The illustration that starts this chapter (13.1) reminds us of the contradictory ways we treated and represented animals. The starry eyed-woman who

appears with her sweet chicks will eventually consume them. Paradoxically, people adored some creatures, such as rabbits, thinking they were cute and cuddly, while others of the same species were hated and killed as vermin. Humans produced lovable stuffed teddy bears, while relentlessly tracking and killing bears in the wild. Parents read the *Three Little Pigs* to their children and served them bacon and eggs for breakfast. Sportsmen killed exotic and trophy animals in order to preserve them as taxidermy specimens. Zookeepers took rare and unusual animals out of the wild to display them in fabricated "natural" displays for the general public to gawk at. Citizens made elk and moose the symbols of fraternal organizations because they were "noble creatures," while stalking them as prey. The apparent contradictions were endless.

Animals acquired never-ending roles in human society. In these pages we saw that animals became whatever people needed and wanted, producing a broad array of associations. We saw them as coworkers on many different jobs and as sources of human nourishment and clothing. We saw them as sick and needy patients cared for by veterinarians and humane workers. We saw them as domestic pets and as comrades aboard ships. We saw them as vermin to be exterminated through wholesale killing. We saw them as game to be hunted for sport, with the results sometimes mounted and hung in museums and living rooms. We saw them as spectacles for human amusement and education. We saw them as competitors pitted against one another, in some cases to their death. We saw them as symbols to sell products, win support for war, and represent our political parties and nation. We saw all these things and more.

The result of our looking was a complex picture of human-animal relationships, filled with contradictions. However, most people in the early part of the twentieth century did not see these inconsistencies as such and were not troubled by them if they did. This is in spite of the fact that during the postcard era people had more direct contact with animals—ones they ate, working animals, game in the wild—than we have today. People witnessed what many people today would call animal abuse and death up close and regularly. They saw animals kept in conditions that now would be considered inhumane. Why this silence, why this lack of awareness?

Although there were rumblings of a humane movement, animal welfare was not as widespread or strongly felt as it is today. Now there are scores of scholars and many national and international organizations that advocate for the humane treatment of animals, if not for granting them legal rights to ensure their protection and autonomy. Also, during the postcard era, sensitivity to and awareness of animal intelligence and emotion paled by comparison to the attention given to it today. Now, there is a growing body of scientific literature that suggests we are more similar to other animals than we thought. Animal advocates, researchers, philosophers, and scholars call attention to the ways we dismiss animal cognition and ask us to rethink the premise that animals do not think and feel (Bekoff 2000, 2006; Darwin 1872; Dawkins 1993). But how different today are things in the human-animal realm from a century ago? Do the old contradictions remain? Have new ones emerged?

THEN AND NOW

A century ago people depended on animals in a different way than we now do. Photo postcards showed the essential role animals played as objects to exploit by American institutions and industries. Animals' contribution helped make possible America's enormous economic growth and its international dominance as a political power. Images documented the many ways that animals contributed to the development, productivity, and effectiveness of agriculture, business, politics, and the military. The illustrations also document how, for the most part, working animals were treated as machines, not as individual creatures, to carry out every imaginable labor needed by individuals, families, small business, city services, the government, and large corporations. In short, early-twentieth-century America came to depend heavily on animals for just about everything.

We no longer need animals to pull wagons or to do other things they did in the past, but in another way we seem immeasurably more dependent on them, although not as objects or commodities. In our highly urbanized, impersonal, and modern lives, many people rely on pets, or animal companions, for support, friendship, affection—indeed, for general psychological well-being. As we have shown in many illustrations, pet owners appeared to treat their pets as genuine family members or very good friends, almost as if they were persons (Gosse and Barnes 1994; Katcher 1989). This love of companion animals continues today in a more intense and pervasive form. The vast majority of contemporary pet owners view their animals as friends and members of the family (Cain 1983; Stallones et al. 1988; Voith 1985). Many owners buy Christmas and birthday gifts for their pets, allow them to sleep on their beds, turn to them for emotional support, carry photos of them in their wallets or cell phones, provide day care for them when at work, and experience significant grief when they die.

And we still depend upon animals as commodities. The exploitation of produce animals we witnessed in postcard images, whether views of meatpacking plants or cattle being confined to feedlots, increased substantially as we moved into the twentieth century. This practice continues today. As our population grew, became more urban, and saw its standard of living improve, we developed a growing appetite for processed meat and other animal products. As farming became increasingly mechanized and industrialized, Americans slaughtered and processed more and more animals. The distance between the production of produce and its consumption grew, leaving the majority of Americans disconnected from the source of their food and other animal products. Not only did farms become distant production sites, but slaughterhouses and meatpacking plants moved to interstitial neighborhoods or industrial centers far from consumers.

Ironically, at the same time that Americans consumed more meat, they became less likely to think of what they ate as animal produce. It is not just children who, like the boy we referred to in the food and goods chapter, fail to link the Chicken McNuggets with the clucking barnyard bird. With the exception of the small minority of Americans who live on or near farms, most Americans are completely out of touch with the source of their food. And it is not just restaurant food that is distant from its origins. The association between packaged, uncooked, as well as precooked meats sold in supermarkets and animal flesh is obscure (Nelson 1998).

Our need for animals, whether as commodities or companions, is not one-sided. Legions of animals are now dependent on us, more so than a century ago: they would die without being given food, shelter, and care. This fact is as true of the great majority of pets as it is for produce animals such as cattle, sheep, and fowl. Domestication has robbed them of the physiology and behaviors required to survive alone. If we did not need them for food and companionship, many animals would disappear from the face of this earth. They live because we consume or are attached to them (Pollan 2006).

Another difference a century ago was that human interaction with animals was direct and sustained, involving a variety of wild as well as domesticated animals in people's everyday lives. This era saw the beginning of a growing trend in the twentieth century to reduce the frequency and variety of our contacts with real animals. Photo postcards remind us that humans have physically transformed animals, altering their biology for various purposes. Growing interest in purebred dogs, competition at state fairs for the largest cattle, and breeding horse stock to accentuate certain features were all methods of manipulating animal biology that were accelerated and regularized during the postcard era. At the extreme, manufactured facsimile animals, like teddy bears, only vaguely resembled their natural forebears, increasingly becoming stand-ins for the real things.

Now, we have few encounters with real animals, and the ones we do meet are mostly tame or the product of our creation. We take artificial insemination and other human-made breeding practices for granted. Cloning has become the next step in human production of produce animals. And it is not just produce animals. Dead dogs are cloned so grieving owners can continue to play with a virtual version of their companion. Pigs are bred to create heart valves that can be harvested to keep ailing humans alive, hybrid dog breeds like cockapoos are widely popular, and entire strains of mice are bred to be born with diabetes to aid biomedical research.

We also have fewer direct experiences with wild animals in their natural settings and many more in zoos where their "natural state" is fabricated. By the end of the twentieth century a different and more critical perspective emerged toward zoo animals (Sax 1997). Some saw captive animals as creatures that were forced into a state of unnatural leisure, given food rather than hunting and gathering food themselves, forced to live in a human-constructed world that shrinks entire continents into acres and often combines different species in the same exhibit, even though they may live far apart in their normal climatic zone.

In the later decades of the twentieth century the conversion of wild animals into creatures considered tame increased. Think about our evolving conception of primates. Apes have gradually moved from being considered exotic and wild to being seen as almost human (Sperling 1988). Post–World War II anthropologists and archaeologists began emphasizing how nonhuman primates were our ancestors. Observational studies of primates showing them using tools and engaging in other activities that suggested they had a culture and their intellectual skills were disseminated to the public first in magazines such as *National Geographic,* and then on television nature shows such as *Wild Kingdom,* and eventually in movies like *Gorillas in the Mist.* These depictions, like the earlier fictionalized *Tarzan* portrayals of Cheeta, suggested that primates were smart, so smart that they were closer to human beings than previously thought. Compounding the humanizing effect of these studies and media presentations were field studies like Jane Goodall's, in which chimpanzees were given human names with personalities described in human terms. Further, researchers who studied ape language acquisition often lived with the animals, treating them like foster children who could talk and adapt to life in the suburbs. The consequence was the reconstruction, if not the lifting, of the border between humans and other primates.

Primates are not the only wild creatures that we have humanized. Many captive wild animals are regarded as humans in animal skins. A good example is the giant panda. Many of the panda's physical features—the round head, large eyes, upright posture—facilitate or lend themselves to anthropomorphizing the species. Through press coverage and zoo promotional schemes, such as holding naming contests, the animal becomes a cuddly friend endowed with a human personality.

Even aquariums blur the line between wild and tame by naming popular marine mammal attractions, holding parties for them, and allowing children to touch them in petting tanks. Visitors even regard the killer whale "Shamu" as a quasi pet (S. Davis 1997). At such times, the distinction between wild and tame evaporates.

Our relationships with animals a century ago differed from modern ones in yet another way. At the beginning of the postcard era, little or no anxiety existed about losing the wilderness or seeing the extinction of species. Yet people did apparently have an affinity for being in the presence of animals and experiencing nature. Postcards captured some of this positive feeling toward all living creatures and life forms, known as biophilia (Wilson 1986). We saw that many images of hunting focused on trophies and weapons, yet part of hunting's appeal, albeit more difficult to capture, was the enjoyment of being in the woods and observing its many creatures away from the noise and congestion of cities. Some people even "hunted" only with their cameras, eager to track down evasive forest dwellers and capture their exciting encounter on film (Brower 2005).

This lackadaisical attitude toward the conservation of nature and wildlife started to change during the postcard period as concern mounted for animals, particularly wild animals such as the American bald eagle and the buffalo, and for the natural environment. Teddy Roosevelt's effort to protect natural open spaces from human encroachment was part of the beginning of that movement. Further fueling this interest in wildlife were advances in automobiles and improvements to highway infrastructure that made natural areas more accessible to the general public. In the 1930s the public grew increasingly concerned about the harmful effects of exploiting natural resources (Kellert 1985).

During the postcard era wildlife tourism often consisted of wealthy people going off to countries that were colonial enclaves, such as taking hunting safaris to the African continent. We saw the results of some of these outings in postcards of the Morse Museum. By the close of the twentieth century, wildlife tourism had become big business, attracting tens of thousands of people willing to pay high prices just to see and photograph wild animals. Their destinations were far and wide: the jungles of Central and South Americas were and still are popular as is East Africa for game watching. People of lesser means accomplish their wildlife tourism closer to home. Whale watches and swim-with-dolphin programs grew into tourist staples in many coastal vacation spots. The growing number of visitors to our national parks spend days riding around in their cars spotting wildlife. Attendance at zoos and aquariums continues to grow, exceeding the gate at all sporting events combined. Viewing media programs about wild animals has sharply risen, and volunteer efforts to save and protect endangered species draw increasing support.

A century ago there was another twist in human-animal relationships when compared to contemporary ones. We saw that Americans divided animals into two broad categories for unequal treatment. Throughout our book images showed certain animals were beloved, while others were hated; some provided important services, while others were nuisances and even threats. In the early decades of the century the systematic destruction of vermin was largely confined to rural America. Despised and feared animals like wolves, coyotes, rabbits, and snakes were tortured and slaughtered with abandon.

During the twentieth century Americans still saw animals as either good or bad, but classified different animals as vermin. In later decades, with the growth of cities and urban populations, wild creatures in our backyards, streets, and parks became the living pests. Rats have always been the urban vermin, but more recently officials in New York City, hoping to get rid of their unsightly and unsanitary droppings, declared "war" on pigeons. White-tailed deer have become the scoundrels of many suburban gardeners and an increasing danger to motorists.

Many photo postcards showed pit bulls as adored pets or popular celebrities, but in the last decades of the twentieth century they were transformed into demons. Americans were bombarded with newspaper reports of assaults by pit bulls on humans, some even referring to their attacks as a "national epidemic." Pit bulls became cause for widespread alarm, with the breed branded as "dangerous" or "killers." A few cities even banned ownership or placed restrictions on owning this breed. Although some pit bulls can become extremely dangerous if trained to fight or if mistreated, evidence shows that pit bull bites were just as common as bites by Saint Bernards, huskies, malamutes, and Great Danes (Rowan 1986).[1]

1. The statistics are highly unreliable because many are collected secondhand, the definition of a dog bite is ambiguous, and the attacking dog's breed is often not clearly specified (V. Hearne and Hollander 1991).

How different, then, are human-animal relationships today compared to what we saw in photo postcards a century ago? Our relationships with animals remain complex long after the end of the postcard era. Some things seem to have hardly changed. Many people today are as oblivious to inconsistencies as people living at the start of the twentieth century. And we continue to dominate animals in almost all domains (Tuan 1984). We control them through breeding and castrating, training, herding, hunting, exterminating, raising them for produce, confining them in zoos and in our homes, and subjecting them to circuses and other performances.

Yet citizens' attitudes have changed dramatically. Increasingly, people actively point out contradictions as a way of demanding that we change our relationships with animals. One example is the legal definition of animals as mere property. Although most people believe that animals should be protected, most laws still define animals as property that people own, much like a car or boat (Francione 1995). But there are indications of change, especially in regard to companion animals (Wise 2001). For example, take two court rulings in the 1990s. In a Florida divorce case in which the parties were contesting custody of their pet rottweiler, the judge awarded the dog to the husband and ruled that, because the animal was legally an item of personal property, the wife was not allowed the visitation rights she requested (*Hartford Courant*, January 26, 1995, A2). However, in another case heard at about the same time, a New York judge ruled that the plaintiff's dog was "somewhere between a person and personal property" and that he was eligible to receive more than the "fair market value" from the owners of the veterinary clinic in which the dog had died as the result of surgery (*Erwin v. The Animal Medical Center, New York Law Journal*, August 29, 1996). The legal definition of animals as property will likely be successfully challenged and overturned in court in the near future as animal-rights lawyers wait for the right case to contest this significant issue.

On a different legal front, many states have seen legislative action to further the humane treatment of animals. Recently, California citizens voted two to one on a ballot initiative to ban factory farms from keeping

produce animals in tiny cages where they cannot move or stretch. In Massachusetts citizens voted to ban greyhound racing. Such steps further the legal protection of animals in the United States.

Much has changed since the postcard era in terms of organized efforts to improve the lot of animals in America. Since World War II, the humane movement has mounted continued efforts to protect the welfare of animals. And since the publication in 1975 of Peter Singer's *Animal Liberation* (and, later, of Tom Regan's 1983 book, *The Case for Animal Rights*), there has been significant growth in what has come to be called the animal-rights movement (Jasper and Nelkin 1991). These movements are by no means unified or coherent, and the activities in which their constituent groups engage vary from lobbying and protest marches to attacks on laboratories and biomedical scientists. In addition, these movements have almost as many critics as they have advocates, as reflected in the proliferation of publications deliberating the philosophical pros and cons of animal rights (Sunstein and Nussbaum 2005). Nevertheless, the animal protection and rights movements have become part of the contemporary landscape (Sperling 1988).

Movement supporters tend to see more similarity than difference between humans and animals, while opponents see a significant gap between the species. Moreover, the gap acknowledged by supporters is a difference of degree, whereas the gap for opponents is a difference in kind. The question then becomes: are these differences significant enough to exclude animals' interest and welfare when there is a conflict between their interests and our own? Debate ensues as to whether animals possess intrinsic value regardless of their contribution to human life, or whether their value is primarily instrumental because they are useful to humans.

The animal protection and rights movements have influenced many institutions that used and sometimes exploited animals in the early 1900s. For example, the use of laboratory animals by scientists is now far more scrutinized and controlled than it was in the past (Carbone 2004). Fewer animals are used in experiments, and more concern exists that we experiment humanely by reducing pain and suffering when possible. Other examples of successful activism include pressuring school systems to provide alternatives to dissection, the fishing industry to use dolphin-safe nets, circuses to eliminate harmful practices, slaughterhouses to use more humane methods, and zoos to improve animal housing, to name just a few.

Nevertheless, these movements have had only slight influence on the everyday choices of many Americans. Whereas some people no longer want to wear fur coats, most continue to eat chicken and meat. And, of course, many of the movements' gains are incremental; more absolutist-minded activists will be satisfied only if these practices, regardless of how humane they become, simply end. However, there is growing interest in "free-range" and "cruelty-free" consumption.

In the final analysis, in certain respects, contemporary human-animal relationships in the United States still resemble the ones depicted in photo postcards from the beginning of the last century. This fact should not surprise us; how we think about and act toward animals is built into our culture, and cultures usually change very slowly, sometimes imperceptibly. But they can and do change. Instead of photo postcards, we now send digital images of animals on our cell phones and on our computers to friends and family members or even to the anonymous public at large on photo sharing Web sites. Doing so represents more than a mere technological change in image making and sending. Modern versions of "postcards" tell a new story about the nature and significance of animals in human society that is a far cry from the images we have seen in our book, *Beauty and the Beast*.

References

Index

References

Adams, Rachel. 2001. *Sideshow U.S.A.: Freaks and the American Cultural Imagination*. Chicago: Univ. of Chicago Press.

Allen, James. 2000. *Without Sanctuary: Lynching Photography in America*. Santa Fe, N.Mex.: Twin Palms.

Allen, Michael. 1998. *Rodeo Cowboys in the North American Imagination*. Reno: Univ. of Nevada Press.

Allen, Oliver. 1993. *The Tiger: The Rise and Fall of Tammany Hall*. Reading, Mass.: Addison-Wesley.

All Hands, ed. n.d. "U.S.S. *Seattle*: During the War." Brooklyn: Brooklyn Daily Eagle.

Ambrose, Stephen, and Douglas Brinkley. 2003. "The Centennial of the Teddy Bear: The Most Celebrated Bear in American History." *Theodore Roosevelt Association Journal* 25, no. 3: 17–20.

Antle, Jay. 1997. "Against Kansas's Top Dog: Coyote, Politics, and Ecology, 1877–1970." *Kansas History* 20, no. 3: 160–75.

Arluke, Arnold, and Clinton Sanders. 1996. *Regarding Animals*. Philadelphia: Temple Univ. Press.

———. 2008. *Between the Species: Readings in Human-Animal Relations*. Boston: Pearson.

Asma, Stephen T. 2001. *Stuffed Animals and Pickled Heads: The Culture and Evolution of Natural History Museums*. New York: Oxford Univ. Press.

Atherton, Lewis. 1961. *The Cattle Kings*. Bloomington: Indiana Univ. Press.

Baker, Steve. 1993. *Picturing the Beast: Animals, Identity, and Representation*. Manchester: Manchester Univ. Press.

Baldwin, Elisa. 1999. *Where the Wild Animals Is Plentiful: Diary of an Alabama Fur Trader's Daughter, 1912–1914*. Tuscaloosa: Univ. of Alabama Press.

Barrett, James. 2002. *Work and Community in the Jungle: Chicago's Packinghouse Workers, 1894–1922*. Urbana: Univ. of Illinois Press.

Barrow, Mark. 2002. "Science, Sentiment, and the Specter of Extinction: Reconsidering Birds of Prey During America's Interwar Years." *Environmental History* 7: 69–98.

Batchelor, John. 1996. *"Ain't You Glad You Joined the Republicans?": A Short History of the GOP*. New York: Henry Holt.

Bateman, Fred. 1968. "Improvement in American Dairy Farming, 1850–1910: A Qualitative Analysis." *Journal of Economic History* 28: 255–73.

Beck, Alan, and Aaron Katcher. 1996. *Between Pets and People: The Importance of Animal Companionship*. West Lafayette, Ind.: Purdue Univ. Press.

Becker, Howard. 1986. *Doing Things Together*. Evanston: Northwestern Univ. Press.

Beers, Diane. 2006. *For the Prevention of Cruelty: The History and Legacy of Animal Rights Activism in the United States*. Athens: Swallow Press, Ohio Univ. Press.

Bekoff, Marc. 2000. *Strolling with Our Kin: Speaking for and Respecting Voiceless Animals*. New York: Lantern/ Booklight.

———. 2006. *Animal Passions and Beastly Virtues*. Philadelphia: Temple Univ. Press.

———. 2007. "Human Anthropogenic Effects on Animals." In *The Encyclopedia of Human-Animal Relationships*, edited by Marc Bekoff, 909–19. Westport, Conn.: Greenwood Press.

Berger, John. 1980. *About Looking*. New York: Pantheon Books.

———. 1991. *Ways of Seeing*. New York: Penguin.

Bernstein, Joel. 2007. *Wild Ride: The History and Lore of Rodeo*. Salt Lake City: Gibbs-Smith.

Bettelheim, Bruno. 1977. *The Uses of Enchantment*. New York: Alfred A. Knopf.

Boatright, Mody. 1964. "The American Rodeo." *American Quarterly* 16: 195–202.

Bogdan, Robert. 1989. *Freak Show: Exhibiting Human Oddities for Amusement and Profit*. Chicago: Univ. of Chicago Press.

———. 1999. *Exposing the Wilderness: Early-Twentieth-Century Adirondack Postcard Photographers*. Syracuse: Syracuse Univ. Press.

———. 2003. *Adirondack Vernacular: The Photography of Henry M. Beach.* Syracuse: Syracuse Univ. Press.

Bogdan, Robert, and Todd Weseloh. 2006. *Real Photo Postcard Guide: The People's Photography.* Syracuse: Syracuse Univ. Press.

Booraem, Hendrick. 1994. *The Provincial: Calvin Coolidge and His World, 1885–1895.* Lewisburg, Pa.: Bucknell Univ. Press.

Bowers, Q. David. 1986. *Nickelodeon Theatres and Their Music.* Vestal, N.Y.: Vestal Press.

Brahm, Rebecca. 2003. "The Changing Face of Veterinary Medicine: Women in the Profession." *Veterinary Heritage* 26, no. 2: 36–39.

Brandt, Keri. 2004. "Human-Horse Communications." *Society and Animals* 12: 299–316.

Brower, Matthew. 2005. "Trophy Shots: Early North American Photographs of Nonhuman Animals and the Display of Masculine Prowess." *Society and Animals* 13: 13–32.

Bryant, Clifton. 1985. "Animal Doctors: Careers, Clientele, and Practice Modes of Veterinarians." In *Rural Work Force: Non-agricultural Occupations in America,* edited by C. Bryant, D. Shoemaker, J. Skipper Jr., and W. Snizek, 199–217. South Hadley, Mass.: Bergin and Garvey.

Bryant, Clifton, and Donald Shoemaker. 1988. "Dead Zoo Chic: Some Conceptual Notes on Taxidermy in American Social Life." *Free Inquiry in Creative Sociology* 16:195–202.

Buckendorf, Madeline. 1993. "The Poultry Frontier: Family Farm Roles and Turkey Raising in Southwest Idaho, 1910–1940." *Idaho Yesterdays* 37, no. 2: 2–8.

Burnett, Jeremiah. 2007. "Past, Present, and Future Responses by the Veterinary Medical Profession to Socioeconomic Change." *Veterinary Heritage* 30, no. 2: 33–38.

Burt, Jonathan. 2006. "Conflicts Around Slaughter in Modernity." In *Killing Animals,* edited by the Animal Studies Group, 120–44. Urbana: Univ. of Illinois Press.

Byerly, T. C. 1976. "Changes in Animal Science." *Agricultural History* 50: 258–74.

Cain, A. 1983. "A Study of Pets in the Family System." In *New Perspectives on Our Lives with Companion Animals,* edited by A. Katcher and A. Beck. Philadelphia: Univ. of Pennsylvania Press.

Carbone, Larry. 2004. *What Animals Want: Expertise and Advocacy in Animal Laboratory Welfare Policy.* New York: Oxford Univ. Press.

Carson, Gerald. 1968. "He Brought Mercy to Massachusetts." *New England Galaxy* 9: 3–11.

Cartmill, Matt. 1991. *A View to a Death in the Morning: Hunting and Nature in History.* Cambridge: Harvard Univ. Press.

Cassidy, Rebecca. 2007. *Horse People: Thoroughbred Culture in Lexington and New Market.* Baltimore: Johns Hopkins Univ. Press.

Casto, Stanley. 2006. "Texas Sportsmen and the Conservation of Bird Life, 1890–1915." *East Texas Historical Journal* 44, no. 1: 7–22.

Chambers, Paul. 2008. *Jumbo: The Greatest Elephant in the World.* Hanover, N.H.: Steerforth Press.

Chindahl, George. 1959. *A History of the Circus in America.* Caldwell, Idaho: Caxton Printers.

Clark, Cindy. 1995. *Flights of Fancy, Leaps of Faith: Children's Myths in Contemporary America.* Chicago: Univ. of Chicago Press.

Clements, Kendrick. 2007. "Managing a National Crisis: The 1924 Foot-and-Mouth Disease Outbreak in California." *California History* 84: 23–27.

Cobb, Russell. 2003. "Chickenfighting for the Soul of the Heartland." *Text, Practice, Performance* 4: 69–83.

Cohn, Priscilla. 2007. "Hunting Beliefs." In *Encyclopedia of Human-Animal Relationships,* edited by Marc Bekoff, 973–75. Westport, Conn.: Greenwood.

Coleman, Jon. 2004. *Vicious: Wolves and Men in America.* New Haven: Yale Univ. Press.

Collins, Howard. 1969. "North America's Whooping Crane." *Canadian Geographical Journal* 78, no. 1: 18–23.

Cooper, Jilly. 1983. *Animals in War: Valiant Horses, Courageous Dogs, and Other Unsung Animal Heroes.* Guilford, Conn.: Globe Pequot Press.

Crisman, Kevin, and Arthur Cohn. 1998. *When Horses Walked on Water: Horse-Powered Ferries in Nineteenth Century America.* Washington, D.C.: Smithsonian Institution Press.

Croke, Vicki. 1997. *The Modern Ark: The Story of Zoos.* New York: Scribner.

Culhane, John. 1990. *The American Circus: An Illustrated History.* New York: Henry Holt.

Dale, Edward. 1960. *The Range Cattle Industry: Ranching the Great Plains from 1865 to 1925.* Norman: Univ. of Oklahoma Press.

Darwin, C. 1872. *The Expression of Emotions in Man and Animals.* Chicago: Univ. of Chicago Press, 1965.

Daston, Lorriane, and Gregg Mitman, eds. 2008. *Thinking with Animals: New Perspectives on Anthropomorphism.* New York: Columbia Univ. Press.

Davis, Lance, Robert Gallman, and Karen Gleiter. 1997. *In Pursuit of Leviathan: Technology, Institutions, Productivity, and Profits in American Whaling, 1816–1906*. Chicago: Univ. of Chicago Press.

Davis, Susan. 1997. *Spectacular Nature: Corporate Culture and the Sea World Experience*. Berkeley and Los Angeles: Univ. of California Press.

Dawkins, M. 1993. *Through Our Eyes Only: The Search for Animal Consciousness*. Chicago: Univ. of Chicago Press.

Del Sesto, Steven. 1975. "Roles, Rules, and Organization: A Descriptive Account of Cockfighting in Rural Louisiana." *Southern Folklore Quarterly* 39, no. 1: 1–14.

Derr, Mark. 2004. *A Dog's History of America: How Our Best Friend Explored, Conquered, and Settled a Continent*. New York: North Point Press.

Desmond, Jane. 2002. "Displaying Death, Animating Life: Changing Fictions of 'Liveness' from Taxidermy to Animatronics." In *Representing Animals*, edited by Nigel Rothfels, 159–79. Bloomington: Indiana Univ. Press.

Despain, Matthew. 2005. "From Menagerie to Modern Zoo: Nature, Society and the Beginning of the Oklahoma City Zoo." *Chronicles of Oklahoma* 83: 284–307.

Dessommes, Nancy. 1999. "Hollywood in Hoods: The Portrayal of the Ku Klux Klan in Popular Film." *Journal of Popular Culture* 32: 13–22.

Dethloff, Henry, and Donald Dyal. 1991. *A Special Kind of Doctor: A History of Veterinary Medicine in Texas*. College Station: Texas A&M Press.

Dickinson Research Center. n.d. *Ralph R. Doubleday Rodeo Photographs*. Oklahoma City: National Cowboy and Western Heritage Museum.

Dimitri, Carolyn, Anne Effland, and Neilson Conklin. 2005. *The 20th Century Transformation of American Agriculture and Farm Policy*. Electronic Information Bulletin no. 3. Washington, D.C.: U.S. Department of Agriculture, June 2005.

Dinsmore, R. J. 1940. *"Hoss" Doctor*. Boston: Waverly House.

Dizard, Jan. 1994. *Going Wild*. Amherst: Univ. of Massachusetts Press.

———. 2003. *Mortal Stakes: Hunters and Hunting in Contemporary America*. Amherst: Univ. of Massachusetts Press.

Doherty, Jim. 1982. "Bald Eagle Thrives as Our Symbol, Survives in the Wild." *Smithsonian* 13, no. 1: 104–23.

Dolan, Eric. 2007. *Leviathan: The History of Whaling in America*. New York: W. W. Norton.

Donnelly, Peter. 1994. "Take My Word for It: Trust in the Context of Birding and Mountaineering." *Qualitative Sociology* 17: 215–41.

Doughty, Robin. 1975. *Feather Fashions and Bird Preservation: A Study in Nature Protection*. Berkeley and Los Angeles: Univ. of California Press.

Drum, Susan, and Ellen Whiteley. 1991. *Women in Veterinary Medicine: Profiles of Success*. Ames: Iowa State Univ. Press.

Duncan, Joyce, ed. 2004. "Women and Fishing." In *Sport in American Culture*, 393. Santa Barbara: ABC-CLIO.

Dunlap, Thomas. 1984. "Value for Varmints: Predator Control and Environmental Ideas, 1920–1939." *Pacific Historical Review* 53, no. 2: 141–61.

———. 1988. "Sport Hunting and Conservation, 1880–1920." *Environmental Review* 12, no. 1: 51–60.

———. 1991. "Organization and Wildlife Preservation: The Case of the Whooping Crane in North America." *Social Studies of Science* 21: 197–221.

Dunlop, Robert, and David Williams. 1996. *Veterinary Medicine: An Illustrated History*. St. Louis: Mosby.

Ellis, Richard. 1991. *Men and Whales*. New York: Alfred A. Knopf.

Emel, J. 1998. "Are You Man Enough, Big and Bad Enough? Wolf Eradication in the U.S." In *Animal Geographies: Place, Politics, and Identity in the Nature-Culture Borderlands*, edited by J. Wolch and J. Emel, 91–118. London: Verso.

Evans, Rhonda, DeAnn Gauthier, and Craig Forsyth. 2004. "Dogfighting: Symbolic Expression and Validation of Masculinity." *Sex Roles* 39: 825–38.

Fermin, Jose. 2004. *1904 World's Fair: The Filipino Experience*. West Conshohocken, Pa.: Infinity Press.

Fletcher, Robert. 1960. *Free Grass to Fences: The Montana Cattle Range Story*. New York: Univ. Publishers.

Flint, Richard. 1996. "American Showmen and European Dealers: Commerce in Wild Animals in Nineteenth-Century America." In *New Worlds, New Animals: From Menagerie to Zoological Park in the Nineteenth Century*, edited by R. J. Hoage and William Deiss. Baltimore: Johns Hopkins Univ. Press.

Fox, Charles. 1990. "The Golden Age of the Railroad Circus." *American History Illustrated* 25, no. 3: 38–53.

Fox, Charles, and Thomas Parkinson. 1969. *The Circus in America*. Waukesha, Wis.: Country Beautiful.

Fox, James G. 1998. *Biology and Diseases of the Ferret*. Baltimore: Lippincott, Williams, and Wilkins.

Fox, Philip Charles. 1990. *Working Horses: Looking Back 100 Years to America's Horse Drawn-Days*. Whitewater, Wis.: Heart Prairie.

Francione, Gary. 1995. *Animals, Property, and the Law*. Philadelphia: Temple Univ. Press.

Franke, Mary Ann. 2005. *To Save the Wild Bison: Life on the Edge in Yellowstone*. Norman: Univ. of Oklahoma Press.

Frazer, David, Joy Mench, and Suzanne Millman. 2001. "Farm Animals and Their Welfare in 2000." In *The State of the Animals, 2001*, edited by D. Salem and A. Rowan, 87–99. Washington, D.C.: Humane Society Press.

Gardiner, David. 2006. "The Age of Veterinary Specialization." *Veterinary Heritage* 29, no. 2: 44–52.

Gillespie, Robert. 2005. "A Streetcar Named Grand Rapids." *Michigan History Magazine* 89, no. 3: 34–40.

Glaser, Barney, and Anslem Strauss. 1967. *The Discovery of Grounded Theory: Strategies for Qualitative Research*. Chicago: Aldine.

Glenn, Cathy. 2007. "Factory Farm Animal Discourse." In *Encyclopedia of Human-Animal Relationships*, edited by Marc Bekoff, 734–41. Westport, Conn.: Greenwood Press.

Gosse, G., and M. Barnes. 1994. "Human Grief Resulting from the Death of a Pet." *Anthrozoos* 7: 103–12.

Greene, Ann Norton. 2008. *Horses at Work: Harnessing Power in Industrial America*. Cambridge: Harvard Univ. Press.

Grier, Katherine. 2006. *Pets in America: A History*. New York: Harcourt.

Griswold, Jerry. 2004. *The Meanings of "Beauty and the Beast": A Handbook*. Peterborough, Ont.: Broadview Press.

Groves, Melody. 2006. *Roses, Reins, and Rawhide: All About the Rodeo*. Albuquerque: Univ. of New Mexico Press.

Haines, Francis. 1970. *The Buffalo*. New York: Thomas Y. Crowell.

Hampton, Bruce. 1997. *The Great American Wolf*. New York: Henry Holt.

Hancocks, David. 2001. *A Different Nature: The Paradoxical World of Zoos and Their Uncertain Future*. Berkeley and Los Angeles: Univ. of California Press.

Hanson, Elizabeth. 2002. *Animal Attractions*. Princeton: Princeton Univ. Press.

Haraway, Donna. 1985. "Teddy Bear Patriarchy: Taxidermy in the Garden of Eden, New York City, 1906–1936." *Social Text* 11 (Winter): 20–64.

Harper, Douglas. 1994. "On the Authority of the Image." In *Handbook of Qualitative Research*, edited by N. Denzin and Y. Lincoln, 403–12. Thousand Oaks, Calif.: Sage.

Harris, Neil. 1973. *Humbug*. Chicago: Univ. of Chicago Press.

Hearne, Betsy. 1989. *Beauty and the Beast: Visions and Revisions of an Old Tale*. Chicago: Univ. of Chicago Press.

Hearne, Vicki, and John Hollander. 1991. *Bandit*. New York: Harper Collins.

Herman, Daniel. 2001. *Hunting and the American Imagination*. Washington, D.C.: Smithsonian Institution.

Herzog, Hal. 1993. "Human Morality and Animal Research." *American Scholar* 62: 337–49.

Hine, Robert, and John Faragher. 2000. *The American West: A New Interpretive History*. New Haven: Yale Univ. Press.

Hoage, R. J., ed. 1989. *Perceptions of Animals in American Culture*. Washington, D.C.: Smithsonian Institution Press.

Hornaday, William. 1891. *Taxidermy and Zoological Collecting: A Complete Handbook for the Amateur Taxidermist, Collector, Osteologist, Museum-Builder, Sportsman, and Traveler*. New York: Scribner's.

Horowitz, Helen. 1981. "Seeing Ourselves Through the Bars: A Historical Tour of American Zoos." *Landscape* 25, no. 2: 12–19.

Horowitz, Roger. 2006. *Putting Meat on the American Table: Taste, Technology, Transformation*. Baltimore: Johns Hopkins Univ. Press.

Hosey, Geoffrey, and Patricia Druck. 1987. "The Influence of Zoo Visitors on the Behavior of Captive Primates." *Applied Animal Behaviour Science* 18: 19–29.

Hughes, Everett. 1958. *Men and Their Work*. Glencoe, Ill.: Free Press.

Hummel, Richard. 1994. *Hunting and Fishing for Sport: Commerce, Controversy, Popular Culture*. Bowling Green: Bowling Green State Univ. Popular Press.

Hutson, Cecil. 1994. "Texas Fever in Kansas, 1866–1930." *Agricultural History* 68: 74–104.

Irmscher, Cristoph. 1999. *The Poetics of Natural History: From John Bartram to William James*. New Brunswick: Rutgers Univ. Press.

Irvine, Leslie. 2004. *If You Tame Me: Understanding Our Connection with Animals*. Philadelphia: Temple Univ. Press.

Jackall, Robert, and Janice Hirota. 2000. *Image Makers: Advertising, Public Relations, and the Ethos of Advocacy*. Chicago: Univ. of Chicago Press.

Jasper, J., and D. Nelkin. 1991. *The Animal Rights Crusade.* New York: Free Press.

Jebsen, Harry, Jr. 1979. "The Public Acceptance of Sports in Dallas, 1880–1930." *Journal of Sport History* 6: 5–19.

Jerolmack, Colin. 2008. "How Pigeons Became Rats: The Cultural-Spatial Logic of Problem Animals." *Social Problems* 55: 72–94.

Johnson, Paul. 1975. *Farm Animals in the Making of America.* Des Moines: Wallace Homestead Book Company.

Johnson, W. B. 1922. "A Kansas Wolf Hunt." *Hunter-Trader-Trapper Magazine.*

Jones, Karen. 2002. *Wolf Mountains: A History of Wolves Along the Great Divide.* Calgary: Univ. of Calgary Press.

Jones, Mary Ellen. 1998. *Daily Life on the 19th-Century American Frontier.* Westport, Conn.: Greenwood.

Jones, Susan. 2002. *Valuing Animals: Veterinarians and Their Patients in Modern America.* Baltimore: Johns Hopkins Univ. Press.

Jordan, Terry. 1972. "The Origin and Distribution of Open Range Cattle Ranching." *Social Science Quarterly* 53: 105–21.

Joselit, Jenna Weissman. 2001. *A Perfect Fit: Clothes, Character, and the Promise of America.* New York: Henry Holt.

Kalof, Linda, and Amy Fitzgerald. 2003. "Reading the Trophy: Exploring the Display of Dead Animals in Hunting Magazines." *Visual Studies* 18: 112–22.

Kasson, John. 1978. *Amusing the Million.* New York: Farrar, Straus, and Giroux.

Katcher, Aaron. 1989. "How Companion Animals Make Us Feel." In *Perceptions of Animals in American Culture,* edited by R. J. Hoage. Washington, D.C.: Smithsonian Press.

Katcher, Aaron, and Alan Beck. 1983. "Safety and Intimacy: Physiological and Behavioral Responses to Interaction with Companion Animals." *Proceedings from "The Human-Pet Relationship" International Symposium.* Institute for Interdisciplinary Research on the Human-Pet Relationship, Vienna, Oct. 27–28.

Kauffman and Liebowitz. 1997. "Draft Animals on the United States Frontier." *Overland Journal* 15: 13–26.

Keeney, L. Douglas. 2001. *Buddies: Men, Dogs, and World War II.* Osceola, Wis.: Zenith Press.

Kehl, James. 1980. "White House or Animal House?" *South Atlantic Quarterly* 79: 343–54.

Kellert, Stephen. 1985. "Historical Trends in Perceptions and Uses of Animals in 20th Century America." *Environmental Review* 9: 19–33.

Kendall, Charles. 1973. "Arizona's War Against the Foot and Mouth Epidemic of 1924." *Journal of Arizona History* 14, no. 1: 47–61.

Kenney, William. 1999. *Recorded Music in American Life: The Phonograph and Popular Memory, 1890–1945.* New York: Oxford Univ. Press.

Kersey, Harry, Jr. 1975. *Pelts, Plumes, and Hides: White Traders Among the Seminole Indians, 1870–1930.* Gainesville: Univ. Press of Florida.

Kete, Kathleen. 1995. *The Beast in the Boudoir: Petkeeping in Nineteenth-Century Paris.* Berkeley and Los Angeles: Univ. of California Press.

Kimble, Edward. 1912. "The Latest Arrival at the Political Zoo." *Harper's Weekly,* July 20.

Kimmel, Michael. 1996. *Manhood in America: A Cultural History.* New York: Free Press.

Kisling, Vernon. 2001. "Zoological Gardens of the United States." In *Zoo and Aquarium History: Ancient Animal Collections to Zoological Gardens,* edited by V. Kisling. Boca Raton: CRC Press.

Kohler, Robert. 2008. "From Farm and Family to Career Naturalist: The Apprenticeship of Vernon Bailey." *Isis* 99: 28–56.

Kramer, J. J. 1981. *Animal Heroes: Military Mascots and Pets.* Novato, Calif.: Presidio Press.

Laegreid, Renee. 2006. *Riding Pretty: Rodeo Royalty in the American West.* Lincoln: Univ. of Nebraska Press.

Lang, Gerald, and Lee Marks. 1991. *The Horse: Photographic Images, 1839 to the Present.* New York: Harry N. Abrams.

Lawrence, Elizabeth. 1982. *Rodeo: An Anthropologist Looks at the Wild and the Tame.* Chicago: Univ. of Chicago Press.

———. 1985. *Hoofbeats and Society: Studies in Human-Horse Interaction.* Bloomington: Indiana Univ. Press.

———. 1989a. *His Very Silence Speaks: Comanche, the Horse Who Survived Custer's Last Stand.* Detroit: Wayne State Univ. Press.

———. 1989b. "Neoteny in American Perceptions of Animals." In *Perceptions of Animals in American Culture,* edited by R. J. Hoage, 57–76. Washington, D.C.: Smithsonian Institution Press.

———. 1990a. "The Symbol of a Nation: The Bald Eagle in American Culture." *Journal of American Culture* 13: 63–69.

———. 1990b. "The Tamed Wild: Symbolic Bears in American Culture." In *Dominant Symbols in Popular Culture,* edited by Ray Browne et al., 140–53. Bowling Green: Bowling Green Univ. Press.

———. 1997a. *Hunting the Wren: Transformation of Bird to Symbol.* Knoxville: Univ. of Tennessee Press.

———. 1997b. "A Woman Veterinary Student in the Fifties: The View from the Approaching Millennium." *Anthrozoos* 10: 160–69.

Leckie, William. 1999. *The Buffalo Soldiers: A Narrative of the Negro Cavalry in the West.* Norman: Univ. of Oklahoma Press.

LeCompte, Mary Lou. 1990. "Home on the Range: Women in Professional Rodeo, 1929–1947." *Journal of Sport History* 17: 318–46.

———. 1993. *Cowgirls of the Rodeo.* Urbana: Univ. of Illinois Press.

Lester, J. C., and D. L. Wilson. 1971. *Ku Klux Klan: Its Origins, Growth, and Disbandment.* Saint Clair Shores, Mich.: Scholarly Press.

Levenstein, Harry. 2003. *Revolution at the Table: The Transformation of the American Diet.* Berkeley and Los Angeles: Univ. of California Press.

Levin, Leslie. 2001. "One Man's Meat Is Another Man's Poison: Imagery of Wholesomeness in the Discourse of Meatpacking from 1900–1910." *Journal of American and Comparative Cultures* 24, no. 2: 1–14.

Lewis, Robert. 2003. *From Traveling Show to Vaudeville: Theatrical Spectacle in America, 1830–1910.* Baltimore: Johns Hopkins Univ. Press.

Lewis, Val. 2002. *Ships' Cats in War and Peace.* Shepperton, Middlesex: Nauticalia.

Licht, Walter. 1995. *Industrializing America: The Nineteenth Century.* Baltimore: Johns Hopkins Univ. Press.

Link, William, and Arthur Link. 1993. *American Epoch: A History of the United States Since 1900.* Vol. 1, *War, Reform, and Society, 1900–1945.* New York: McGraw-Hill.

Lockwood, Jeffrey. 2004. *The Devastating Rise and Mysterious Disappearance of the Insect That Shaped the American Frontier.* New York: Basic Books.

Loo, Tina. 2001. "Of Moose and Men: Hunting for Masculinities in British Columbia, 1880–1939." *Western Historical Quarterly* 32: 296–319.

Lopez, Barry. 1978. *Of Wolves and Men.* New York: Charles Scribner's Sons.

Lovin, Hugh. 1979. "Sage, Jacks, and Snake Plain Pioneers." *Idaho Yesterdays* 22, no. 4: 13–24.

Lynn, Morrow. 2002. "St. Louis Tourist Sportmen: Urban Clubs in the Wetlands." *Missouri Historical Review* 97, no. 1: 20–42.

Malamud, Randy. 2003. "How People and Animals Coexist." *Chronicle Review,* Jan. 24.

Margolies, John. 1998. *Fun Along the Road: American Tourist Attractions.* New York: Bullfinch.

Marks, Stuart. 1992. *Southern Hunting in Black and White.* Princeton: Princeton Univ. Press.

Marvin, Garry. 2004. *Transforming the Beast: The Cultural Life of Dead Animals.* Warren, N.H.: Morse Museum.

Mason, Jim, and Mary Finelli. 2006. "Brave New Farm?" In *In Defense of Animals: The Second Wave,* edited by P. Singer, 104–22. Oxford: Blackwell.

Maunula, Marko. 2007. "Of Chickens and Men: Cockfighting and Equality in the South." *Southern Cultures* 13: 76–85.

Maybury-Lewis, David. 1967. *Akwe-Shavante Society.* Oxford: Clarendon Press.

Mayda, Chris. 2004. "Pig Pens, Hog Houses, and Manure Pits: A Century of Change in Hog Production." *Material Culture* 36: 18–42.

McFadden, Cynthia. 2007. "Sport and Animals." In *Encyclopedia of Human-Animal Relationships,* edited by Marc Bekoff, 1321–25. Westport, Conn.: Greenwood Press.

McIntyre, Rick. 1993. *A Society of Wolves: National Parks and the Battle over the Wolf.* Osceola, Wis.: Voyageur.

———, ed. 1995. *War Against Wolf: America's Campaign to Exterminate the Wolf.* Osceola, Wis.: Voyageur.

McMillen, Wheeler. 1992. "The Horse and the Buggy." *Timeline* 9, no. 3: 44–54.

McShane, Clay. 2001. "Gelded Age Boston." *New England Quarterly* 74: 274–302.

McShane, Clay, and Joel Tarr. 2007. *The Horse in the City: Living Machines in the Nineteenth Century.* Baltimore: Johns Hopkins Univ. Press.

Mechling, Jay. 2004. "Picturing Hunting." *Western Folklore* 63.

Mellis, Allison. 2003. *Riding Buffalos and Broncos: Rodeo and Native Traditions in the Northern Great Plains.* Norman: Univ. of Oklahoma Press.

Melson, Gail. 2001. *Why the Wild Things Are: Animals in the Lives of Children.* Cambridge: Harvard Univ. Press.

Merillat, Lovisk, and Delwin Campbell. 1935. *Veterinary Military History of the U.S.* Chicago: Veterinary Magazine.

Michalko, Rod. 1999. *The Two in One: Walking with Smokie, Walking with Blindness*. Philadelphia: Temple Univ. Press.

Mighetto, Lisa. 1995. "Sport Fishing on the Columbia River." *Pacific Northwest Quarterly* 87, no. 1: 5–15.

Milgrom, Melissa. 2010. *Still Life: Adventures in Taxidermy*. New York: Houghton Mifflin Harcourt.

Miner, Curtis. 2001. "Hardhat Hunters: The Democratization of Recreational Hunting in Twentieth Century Pennsylvania." *Journal of Sport History* 28, no. 1: 41–62.

———. 2005. "And They're Off! Pennsylvania's Horse Racing Tradition." *Pennsylvania Heritage* 31, no. 2: 26–35.

Mom, Gijs, and David Kirsh. 2001. "Technologies in Tension: Horses, Electric Trucks, and the Motorization of American Cities, 1900–1925." *Technology and Culture* 42: 489–518.

Montgomery, Scott. 1995. "The Zoo: Theatre of the Animals." *Science as Culture* 21: 565–602.

Morgan, Hal, and Andreas Brown. 1981. *Prairie Fires and Paper Moons*. Boston: David Godine.

Morse, Robert, and Philip Morse Jr. 2003. *The Morse Museum Story*. Warren, N.H.: Morse Museum.

Moses, Lester. 1996. *Wild West Shows and the Images of American Indians, 1883–1933*. Albuquerque: Univ. of New Mexico Press.

Mozee, Yvonne. 1984. "Dog Racing Capital of the World." *Alaska Journal* 14, no. 2: 40–47.

Mullen, Bob, and Garry Marvin. 1987. *Zoo Culture*. London: Weidenfeld and Nicolson.

Nelson, Richard. 1998. *Heart and Blood: Living with Deer in America*. New York: Vintage.

Nickell, Joe. 2005. *Secrets of the Sideshows*. Lexington: Univ. Press of Kentucky.

Nyhart, Lynn. 2004. "Science, Art, and Authenticity in Natural History Displays." In *Models: The Third Dimension of Science*, edited by S. Chadarevian and N. Hopwood. Palo Alto: Stanford Univ. Press.

Palmer, Thomas. 1992. *Landscape with Reptile: Rattlesnakes in an Urban World*. New York: Ticknor and Fields.

Palmquist, Peter. 1981. "Westerners and Their Pets." *American West* 18, no. 1: 48–51.

Patchett, Merle, and Kate Foster. 2008. "Repair Work: Surfacing the Geographies of Dead Animals." *Museum and Society* 6: 98–122.

Pate, J'Nell. 2005. *America's Historic Stockyards*. Fort Worth: Texas Christian Press.

Pew Commission on Industrial Farm Animal Production. 2008. *Putting Meat on the Table: Industrial Farm Animal Production in America*. Available at http://www.ncifap.org/_images/PCIFAP_FINAL_REPORT.pdf.

Phillips, Barbara. 1996. "Defining Trade Characters and Their Role in American Popular Culture." *Journal of Popular Culture* 29: 143–58.

Phillips, Paul. 1961. *The Fur Trade*. Vol. 1–2. Norman: Univ. of Oklahoma Press.

Phineas, Charles. 1974. "Household Pets and Urban Alienation." *Journal of Social History* 7: 338–43.

Pietrusca, David. 2008. *Silent Cal's Almanack: The Homespun Wit and Wisdom of Vermont's Calvin Coolidge*. N.p.: Amazon Digital Services.

Plumb, Glenn, and Rosemary Sucec. 2006. "A Bison Conservation History in the U.S. National Parks." *Journal of the West* 45, no. 2: 22–28.

Pollan, Michael. 2006. *Omnivore's Dilemma: A Natural History of Four Meals*. New York: Penguin Books.

Porter, Willard. 1971. "The American Rodeo: Sport and Spectacle." *American West* 8, no. 4: 40–49.

Proctor, Nicholas. 2002. *Bathed in Blood: Hunting and Mastery in the Old South*. Charlottesville: Univ. Press of Virginia.

Reagan, Tom. 1983. *The Case for Animal Rights*. Berkeley and Los Angeles: Univ. of California Press.

Reck, Franklin. 1951. *The 4-H Story: A History of 4-H Club Work*. Ames: Iowa State Univ. Press.

Reddin, Paul. 1999. *Wild West Shows*. Urbana: Univ. of Illinois Press.

Reiger, John. 2001. *American Sportsman and the Origins of Conservation*. Corvallis: Oregon State Univ. Press.

Renner, G. K. 1980. "The Mule in Missouri Agriculture, 1821–1950." *Missouri Historical Review* 74: 433–57.

Ritvo, Harriet. 1988. "The Emergence of Modern Pet-Keeping." In *Animals and People Sharing the World*, edited by Andrew Rowan, 13–32. Hanover, N.H.: Univ. Press of New England.

Rivers, Jacob, III. 2002. *Cultural Values in the Southern Sporting Narrative*. Chapel Hill: Univ. of North Carolina Press.

Roberts, B., and Snow Roberts. 2002. *Bull Durham Business Bonanza 1866–1940: The Extraordinary Story of the Development of "Bull Durham Smoking Tobacco" and the Companies That Manufactured It*. Durham: Genuine Durham Press.

Robinson, Michael. 2005. *Predatory Bureaucracy: The Extermination of Wolves and the Transformation of the West*. Boulder: Univ. Press of Colorado.

Rotundo, Anthony. 1993. *American Manhood: Transformation in Masculinity from the Revolution to the Modern Era*. New York: Basic Books.

Rowan, Andrew. 1986. *Dog Aggression and the Pit Bull Terrier*. North Grafton, Mass.: Tufts School of Veterinary Medicine, Workshop Proceedings, July.

Rowan, Roy, and Janis Brooke. 2009. *First Dogs: American Presidents and Their Best Friends*. Chapel Hill: Algonquin Books of Chapel Hill.

Rubin, Cynthia Elyce, and Morgan Williams. 1990. *Larger than Life: The American Tall-Tale Postcard, 1905–1915*. New York: Abbeville.

Rydell, Robert. 1984. *All the World's a Fair: Visions of Empire at American International Expositions, 1876–1916*. Chicago: Univ. of Chicago Press.

Sanders, Clinton. 1994. "Biting the Hand That Heals You: Encounters with Problematic Patients in a General Veterinary Practice." *Society and Animals* 2: 17–66.

———. 1999. *Understanding Dogs: Living and Working with Canine Companions*. Philadelphia: Temple Univ. Press.

Sawers, Larry. 2004. "The Mule, the South, and Economic Progress." *Social Science History* 28: 667–90.

Sax, Boria. 1997. "The Zoo: Prison or Paradise?" *Terra Nova* 2, no. 1: 59–68.

Schlebecker, John. 1963. *Cattle Raising on the Plains, 1900–1961*. Lincoln: Univ. of Nebraska Press.

Schlosser, Eric. 2001. *Fast Food Nation: The Dark Side of the All-American Meal*. New York: Houghton Mifflin.

Schubert, Paul. 1999. "Mascot of the Texas." In *Old Dogs Remembered*, edited by Bud Johns, 154–57. San Francisco: Synergistic Publications.

Schwartz, Joseph. 1970. "The Wild West Show: Everything Genuine." *Journal of Popular Culture* 3: 656–66.

Schwartz, Marion. 1998. *A History of Dogs in the Early Americas*. New Haven: Yale Univ. Press.

Seguin, Marilyn. 1998. *Dogs of War: And Stories of Other Beasts of Battle in the Civil War*. Boston: Branden.

Serpell, James. 1986. *In the Company of Animals*. New York: Basil Blackwell.

Sheffield, Tommy. 2006. *Best Supporting Actors: Rodeo Clowns*. Walnut Springs, Tex.: Wild Horse Press.

Shelton, Deborah. 2001. "Pioneer Pets: The Dogs of Territorial Tucson: A Photo Essay." *Journal of Arizona History* 42, no. 4: 445–49.

Shepard, Paul. 1997. *How Animals Made Us Human*. Washington, D.C.: Island Press.

Shoemaker, Nancy. 1996. "Whale Meat in American History." *Environmental History* 10: 269–94.

Sinclair, Upton. 1906. *The Jungle*. New York: Doubleday, Page.

Singer, Peter. 1975. *Animal Liberation: A New Ethics for Our Treatment of Animals*. New York: New York Review/Random House.

Sitton, Thad. 1995. *Backwoodsmen: Stockmen and Hunters Along a Big Thicket River Valley*. Norman: Univ. of Oklahoma Press.

Skaggs, Jimmy. 1986. *Prime Cut: Livestock Raising and Meatpacking in the United States, 1607–1983*. College Station: Texas A&M Univ. Press.

Slater, Margaret, and Miriam Slater. 2000. "Women in Veterinary Medicine." *Journal of the American Veterinary Medical Association* 217: 472–76.

Smalley, Andrea. 2005. "Our Lady Sportsman: Gender, Class, and Conservation in Sport Hunting." *Journal of the Guilded Age and Progressive Era* 4: 355–80.

Smith, Andrew. 2006. *The Turkey: An American Story*. Urbana: Univ. of Illinois Press.

Smith, Kristine. 2005. "Following Buster Brown's Footsteps: Leading Families into Middle-Class Consumer Society." Ph.D. diss., St. Louis Univ.

Smithcors, J. F. 1957. "The Early Use of Anaesthesia in Veterinary Practice." *British Veterinary Journal* 113: 284–91.

———. 1975. *The Veterinarian in America, 1625–1975*. Goleta, Calif.: American Veterinary Publications.

Spear, Donald. 1982. "California Besieged: The Foot-and-Mouth Epidemic of 1924." *Agricultural History* 56: 528–41.

Sperling, Susan. 1988. *Animal Liberators*. Berkeley and Los Angeles: Univ. of California Press.

Spiegel, Marjorie. 1997. *The Dreaded Comparison: Human and Animal Slavery*. New York: Mirror Books/I.D.E.A.

Stalheim, Ole. 1988. "The Hog Cholera Battle and Veterinary Professionalism." *Agricultural History* 62: 116–21.

———. 1994. *The Winning of Animal Health: 100 Years of Veterinary Medicine*. Ames: Iowa State Univ. Press.

———. 2003. "From Local to Global: Agriculture, Veterinary Medicine, and Rural Society in South Dakota, 1859–2001." *Veterinary Heritage* 26, no. 1: 14–16.

Stallones, L., M. Marx, T. Garrity, and T. Johnson. 1988. "Attachment to Companion Animals Among Older Pet Owners." *Anthrozoös* 2: 118–24.

Starr, Paul. 1984. *The Social Transformation of American Medicine*. New York: Basic Books.

Stein, Charles. 1985. *American Vaudeville as Seen by Its Contemporaries*. New York: DaCapo Press.

Stewart, D. Travis. 2005. *No Applause—Just Throw Money*. New York: Faber and Faber.

Stillwell, Paul. 1991. *Battleship Arizona: An Illustrated History*. Annapolis: Naval Institute Press.

Stirity, Mimi. 2001. "The Romance of Alaska Seakskin: The Fur Trade in Twentieth Century St. Louis." *Gateway Heritage* 21, no. 4: 30–40.

Stith, Matthew. 2007. "'Women Locked the Doors, Children Screamed, and Men Trembled in Their Boots': Black Bears and People in Arkansas." *Arkansas Historical Quarterly* 64, no. 1: 1–17.

Stout, Joseph. 1986. "United Sates Army Remount Depots: The Oklahoma Experience, 1908–1947." *Military Affairs* (July): 121–26.

Strange, Mary. 1997. *Woman the Hunter*. Boston: Beacon Press.

Strauss, Claude Levi. 1963. *Totemism*. Boston: Beacon Press.

Striffer, Steve. 2005. *Chicken: The Dangerous Transformation of America's Favorite Food*. New Haven: Yale Univ. Press.

Strom, Claire. 2000. "Texas Fever and the Dispossession of the Southern Yeoman Farmer." *Journal of Southern History* 66: 49–74.

———. 2004. "Editorials and Explosions: Insights into Grassroots Opposition to Tick Eradication in Georgia, 1915–1920." *Georgia Historical Quarterly* 88: 197–214.

Sullivan, Robert. 2004. *Observations on the History and Habitat of the City's Most Unwanted Inhabitants*. New York: Bloomsbury.

Sunstein, Cass, and Martha Nussbaum. 2005. *Animal Rights: Current Debates and New Directions*. New York: Oxford Univ. Press.

Sweet, John. 2002. "Men and Varmints in the Gila Wilderness, 1909–1936." *New Mexico Historical Review* 77: 369–97.

Tardona, Daniel. 2007. "Wildlife and Humans in the U.S. National Park." In *Encyclopedia of Human-Animal Relationships*, edited by Marc Bekoff, 1184–90. Westport, Conn.: Greenwood Press.

Tarr, Joel. 1999. "A Note on the Horse as an Urban Power Source." *Journal of Urban History* 25: 434–48.

Tenner, Edward. 1998. "Citizen Canine." *Wilson Quarterly* 22, no. 3: 71.

Thiel, Richard. 1993. *The Timber Wolf in Wisconsin*. Madison: Univ. of Wisconsin Press.

Thompson, Ray. 1984. *The Feisty Veterinarians of New Jersey*. Rockaway: New Jersey Veterinary Medical Association.

Tuan, Yi-Fu. 1984. *Dominance and Affection: The Making of Pets*. New Haven: Yale Univ. Press.

Unti, Bernard. 2002. "The Quality of Mercy: Organized Animal Protection in the United States, 1866–1930." Ph.D. diss., American Univ.

Unti, Bernard, and Bill DeRosa. 2003. "Humane Education: Past, Present, and Future." In *State of the Animals, 2003*, edited by Andrew Rowan, 1–23. Washington, D.C.: Humane Society of the United States.

Vaughan, Thomas, and Bill Holm. 1990. *Soft Gold: The Fur Trade and Cultural Exchange on the Northwest Coast of America*. Portland: Oregon Historical Society Press.

Vialles, N. 1994. *Animal to Edible*. Cambridge: Cambridge Univ. Press.

Voith, V. 1985. "Attachment of People to Companion Animals." *Veterinary Clinics of North America: Small Animal Practice* 15: 289–96.

Wade, Louise. 1987. *Chicago's Pride: The Stockyards, Packingtown, and Environs in the Nineteenth Century*. Urbana: Univ. of Illinois Press.

Wallace, Scott, and Brian Gisborne. 2006. *Basking Sharks: The Slaughter of BC's Gentle Giants*. Vancouver: New Star Books.

White, John. 1986. *The Great Yellow Fleet: A History of American Railroad Refrigerator Cars*. San Marino, Calif.: Golden West Books.

Williams, J. 1997. "The Inhumanity of the Animal People." *Harper's*, Aug., 60–67.

Wilson, Edward. 1986. *Biophilia*. Cambridge: Harvard Univ. Press.

Wise, Stephen. 2001. *Rattling the Cage: Toward Legal Rights for Animals*. New York: Perseus.

Wood, Frank, and Scott Daymond. 1988. *Reflections of Kansas: A Prairie Postcard Album, 1900–1930*. Wichita: Daywood Publishing.

Wood, Lisa, Billie Giles-Corti, and Max Bulsara. 2005. "The Pet Connection: Pets as a Conduit for Social Capital." *Social Science and Medicine* 61: 1159–73.

Wooden, Wayne, and Gavin Ehringer. 1996. *Rodeo in America: Wranglers, Roughstock, and Paydirt*. Lawrence: Univ. Press of Kansas.

Zmyj, Peter. 1996. "'A Fight to the Finish': The Extermination of the Gray Wolf in Wyoming, 1890–1930." *Montana: The Magazine of Western History* 46, no. 1: 14–25.

Index

ARNOLD ARLUKE is Professor of Sociology and Anthropology at Northeastern University and Senior Research Fellow at Tufts Center for Animals and Public Policy. His research examines conflicts and contradictions in human-animal relationships. He has published more than eighty articles and ten books, including *Between the Species: Readings in Human-Animal Relations* (with Clinton Sanders), *Inside Animal Hoarding: The Case of Barbara Erickson and Her 552 Dogs* (with Celeste Kileen), *Just a Dog: Animal Cruelty and Ourselves*, *Brute Force: Policing Animal Cruelty*, and *Regarding Animals* (with Clinton Sanders). He also edits the Animals, Culture, and Society series for Temple University Press (with Clinton Sanders).

ROBERT BOGDAN is Distinguished Professor Emeritus of Social Science and Education at Syracuse University. He was the director of the Interdisciplinary Social Science Doctoral Program in Syracuse's Maxwell School when he retired. This is his third book dealing with real photo postcards. His latest, *Real Photo Postcard Guide: The People's Photography* (with Todd Weseloh), has been described as the definitive text on the topic. In 2004 Bogdan was awarded an honorary doctorate from Stockholm University for his contribution to qualitative research and disability studies. He is the author of fifteen books and more than one hundred articles on a wide variety of topics. He lives in Orwell, Vermont, where he regularly observes the relationship between humans and animals.